Trash Talk

Trash Talk

ANTI-OBAMA LORE AND RACE IN THE TWENTY-FIRST CENTURY

Patricia A. Turner

UNIVERSITY OF CALIFORNIA PRESS

University of California Press
Oakland, California

© 2022 by Patricia Turner

Library of Congress Cataloging-in-Publication Data

Names: Turner, Patricia A. (Patricia Ann), 1955- author.
Title: Trash talk : anti-Obama lore and race in the twenty-first century /
    Patricia A. Turner.
Description: Oakland, California : University of California Press,
    [2022] | Includes bibliographical references and index.
Identifiers: LCCN 2022006310 (print) | LCCN 2022006311 (ebook) |
    ISBN 9780520389236 (cloth) | ISBN 9780520389243 (paperback) |
    ISBN 9780520389250 (epub)
Subjects: LCSH: Obama, Barack. | Rumor in mass media. | Fake news—
    United States. | Racism—Political aspects—United States—History—
    21st century. | Racism against Black people—United States—History—
    21st century.
Classification: LCC P96.R862 U6 2022 (print) | LCC P96.R862 (ebook) |
    DDC 302.2/4—dc23/eng/20220412
LC record available at https://lccn.loc.gov/2022006310
LC ebook record available at https://lccn.loc.gov/2022006311

Manufactured in the United States of America

31 30 29 28 27 26 25 24 23 22
10 9 8 7 6 5 4 3 2 1

To the best of women friends,

Peggy Canale, Victoria Frisch, Rhonda Gomes, and Carolyn Whitehurst

And to the indefatigable crew at Snopes

Contents

Introduction

The election of Donald J. Trump as the forty-fifth president of the United States came as a surprise. It stunned professional pollsters who deployed complicated algorithms to measure voter sentiment. It vexed savvy politicians who thought they understood their districts and all of the voting patterns relevant to the election. Seasoned journalists who followed the major and minor candidates even prior to the state primaries were nonplussed by the headlines they had to draft in the days after the ballots were tallied on November 8, 2016. Millions of women who wore pantsuits to the voting booth or mailed their absentee ballots were flabbergasted and horrified by Hillary Clinton's loss. Indeed, many Republicans and Trump devotees acknowledged they had prepared themselves for a Clinton win. Some in his inner circle claimed that even Trump himself was caught off-guard by his victory—though he never publicly admitted to any self-doubt.

Most of these groups later sheepishly acknowledged there were indeed numerous signs that, had they been recognized, would have lessened the shock of the election's outcome. For instance, the domestic political environment signaled a renewed willingness on the part of those aligned with right-wing causes to proudly proclaim their conservative beliefs. The ever-growing size of Donald Trump's rallies, had they been measured, might have been a significant bellwether. And although Hillary Clinton boasted an ardent and enthusiastic band of followers, both the candidate and her supporters were deplored, despised, and denigrated by many critics on both the right and the left.

Other ominous forecasts could be gleaned from pop culture. Sales of the Halloween mask representing Donald Trump's countenance outsold those capturing Clinton's visage. It is a truth universally acknowledged that whichever American presidential candidate sells the most Halloween masks takes an oath of office on the steps of the US Capitol.

The shifting international balance of power also offered telltale clues. America's closest allies were listing toward the right. Although Emmanuel Macron of the more liberal En March! Party won the French election in the early summer of 2016, his opponent Marine Le Pen attracted significant support. The June 2016 Brexit victory—in which the voters of Great Britain unexpectedly opted to leave the European Union—was a potent harbinger of widespread dissatisfaction with all things considered "global," "progressive," and "intellectual." These were traits easily associated with the Democrats and Hillary Rodham Clinton, but just as importantly they were antithetical to the "America First" platform espoused by Donald Trump.

Political watchdogs should have been more attentive to the druthers of America's adversaries. Russian President Vladimir Putin's ruthless ambitions for himself and his country were undercut by the foreign policy positions of Barack Obama, and, by extension, Hillary Rodham Clinton, who had served as his secretary of state. Of course, many Republican elected officials were just as apprehensive about Putin and the Russians as Democrats. But Trump was an outlier Republican (to put it mildly), who seemed to crave a bromance with Putin. In the run up to the election, the US national security community noted and reported the evidence they were finding that Putin was interfering with the American presidential election, aspiring to derail Clinton, elect Trump, and create as much chaos as possible.

Finally, in order to understand the prevailing political winds of 2016, the wide range of attitudes about the forty-fourth president should have been evaluated. In the prominent avenues of coverage he was referred to as President Barack Obama and the First Lady as Michelle Robinson Obama. But folkloric discourse—everyday expressions shared and circulated in informal channels—was replete with evidence that many American voters were motivated to embrace candidates who rejected all things about Barack and Michelle Obama and everything about the voters who twice put Obama in office. His full name seemed to prompt a never-ending list of possibilities. Those who wanted to suggest that he was gay used "Bathhouse Barry." His middle name in particular provided fodder for those accusing him of being a Muslim; conservative talk host Rush Limbaugh typically made sure he always said Barack Hussein Obama. *Obama* itself generated a number of variations: O'bumma, Obongo, Ebolo, and on and on. "Moochelle," the most common nickname for Michelle, was so well known that it made its way into the Urban Dictionary, where we learn that it was bestowed upon her "for her advocacy to get everybody to mooch off the government."[1] Other insulting names ascribed to her include "Queen Michelle," a way of associating her with the common welfare queen stereotypes and "Big Mike," used by those who want to convince others that she was born a man and is transgender.

The ubiquity and tenacity of anti-Obama lore confirms just how many voters held the forty-fourth president in utter contempt and would back the candidate most likely to obliterate his presidential accomplishments. To these voters, Barack Obama, his family, and the Americans who adored and endorsed the Obamas were loathsome. And that hate was grounded in Obama's identity as the well-educated, successful, and popular son of an African man and a white woman, and the husband of an accomplished and ambitious black woman. *Trash Talk: Anti-Obama Lore and Race in the Twenty-First Century* documents and analyzes the emergence, dissemination, and impact of a constant stream of anti-Obama rantings that have followed the former president from his pre-candidate days, throughout his time as a candidate, through two terms in office, and now into his post-presidency years. (See table 1.)

Troubling racially inflected rumors and conspiracy theories about individuals and events unconnected to the Obamas also circulated in the era I will be focusing on—roughly the first two decades of the twenty-first century—and *Trash Talk* will probe some of these narratives as well. Before, during, and after the two Obama administrations, speculation about the lives and motivations of Barack and Michelle Obama exemplifies the full range of themes in anti-black lore. As the 2016 election grew closer, the

Table 1   Obama Lore and Elections

Elections	Most Prominent Narratives	Modes of Circulation	Fact-Checking
2004 Kerry Nomination–2008 Election of Barack Obama	Muslim/unpatriotic/ early birther, socialist Michelle radical thesis, angry ugly black woman	Word of mouth Email/blogs/ newsletters Early adopters of FB, Twitter, and early social media sites (Reddit, 4Chan) YouTube	Snopes/Politifact/ FactCheck Fight the Smears Sporadic debunking articles
2008 Election–2010 Midterms	All of the above (AOA) Heavy birther Michelle as entitled welfare queen	AOA More specialized social media sites Increase in users on all platforms	Snopes/Politifact/ FactCheck Fight the Smears (archived) Sporadic debunking articles
2010–2012 Reelection of Barack Obama	AOA Heavy birther Muslim heritage influencing Middle East decision-making	AOA Increase in users on all platforms	AOA
2012–2014 Midterms	AOA Ebola genocide Sexual identity/ preference Michelle/Michael, responsible for Joan Rivers death	AOA 8Chan Increase in users on all platforms	AOA
2014 Midterms–2016 Election of Donald Trump	AOA Pizzagate Malia and Sasha texts emerge	AOA Increase in users on all platforms	AOA *Washington Post* FactChecker Increased but selective coverage of misinformation
2016–2018 Midterms	AOA Deep state/early QAnon	AOA Increase in users on all platforms	AOA Increased but still selective coverage of misinformation
2018–2021 Inauguration of Joe Biden	AOA COVID-19 conspiracy Heavy QAnon Voting machine tampering	AOA 8Kun Parler Increase in users on all platforms	AOA *USA Today* FactCheck Increased but still selective coverage of misinformation

voluminous number of Facebook likes and forwarded emails of fraudulent statements about the Obamas was a clearer sign that his former secretary of state would lose than the number of Trump/Pence bumper stickers.

LISTENING TO THE LORE

The term *anti-Obama lore*, which will be a frequent reference point throughout *Trash Talk*, requires some explication, and it makes sense to offer an overview to my approach. *Anti-Obama lore* is a bucket term for several genres of everyday discourse that have in common unsubstantiated and erroneous statements about Barack Obama. *Trash Talk*'s source materials are the various folklore genres that are used when an individual or community is inclined to share a snippet of knowledge that is believed to be true but that others would claim lacks an authentic standard of evidence. To better describe the various formats I will be examining, consider the one connected to the initial statement in Barack Obama's first major speech nominating John Kerry for the presidency, "My father was a foreign student." From this biographical assertion, speculations emerged saying, "I heard Barack Obama's not even an American." Since this is such a vague and incomplete statement, it belongs to the category of *rumor*. A speculation about what he isn't, this utterance lacks a real story, more than one character, or a place. After a while, many on the right who shared what became known as the birther beliefs articulated more fully rendered stories such as, "I heard his mother gave birth to him in Kenya and when she returned with him to Hawaii, she lied and claimed that he was born there." These recitations offer us the characters of baby Barack and his mother, actions like international travel and lying, and geographical settings such as Kenya and Hawaii. If this utterance was shared in a conversational setting, a listener might reasonably ask for proof of birth or travel. Folklorists refer to this as an *urban* or *contemporary legend* because it conveys an apocryphal story that is told as "true" without any verifiable evidence.[2]

The core belief reflected in this rumor and contemporary legend captured widespread attention in the format of a *conspiracy theory*.[3] Conspiracy theories allege that there's been an organized effort, usually including government officials, to cover up a transgression or to inflict harm. Obama's critics, including then reality TV star Donald Trump, accused the president and his team of conspiring with Hawaiian authorities to falsify birth records. This is a bit of an oversimplification of the birther cycle; a far more thorough explication of it comes in chapter 3. What is important at this juncture is an understanding of the modes of discourse through which these beliefs are uttered.

When I first started doing research on this discourse in the 1980s, it was enough for me to explain the subtle differences between rumor, contemporary legend, and conspiracy theory. As the circulation of these materials has grown on the internet (which was not a factor in the '80s), the nomenclature around these beliefs has expanded. Some people inclined to dismiss the birther beliefs might well refer to them as a *hoax*, a term used to describe an intentional deception. The perpetrator of a hoax creates a believable but largely false story to serve a desired end.

The term *fake news* has also gained momentum during the past several years.[4] Some definitions suggest that all of the categories I have already described can be lumped into the category of fake news; for example, an email telling me that Obama was covering up his gay lifestyle or a social media posting alleging that Michelle Obama was born a man constitute fake news because they constitute shared but false information. Former president Donald Trump levied the fake news label frequently and capriciously, using it to characterize any unflattering news story about him or his administration.

In my academic circles, labels matter and we go to great lengths to make sure our students and colleagues understand why we are labeling one utterance a rumor and a similar one a conspiracy theory. However, I have penned *Trash Talk* with a larger audience in mind, one that might well be impatient with the linguistic nuances that intrigue academics. While I intend to be as specific as possible, there will be many instances when I use "anti-Obama lore" to refer to stories about Barack Obama and his family that are inaccurate but are shared and disseminated as though they are the truth. In deference to a wider readership as well, I have endeavored to tell a series of stories, to the extent possible, minimizing the more esoteric language of the academy and using references to related materials sparingly.

Folklorists start by collecting and then follow up with analysis. Collectors—whether they procure quilts, handmade musical instruments, or the genres of folklore—usually are the beneficiaries of copious contributions and leads from their personal and professional networks. My interest in compiling rumors, legends, and conspiracy theories predates the internet. In those days, church services, plane rides, backyard barbecues, and similar informal settings provided me with the introduction to many new materials. My students were valuable sources of lore. Before long, I had a reputation for being eager to hear anything suspicious gaining currency on the grapevine. I am still considered the pal or professor who actually wants you to forward her the ugly meme that your former classmate sent to you depicting Barack Obama with a crack pipe in the White House. Thus many of the texts I will be scrutinizing were just sent to me.

But I have pursued them as well. As the internet communities increased, I have endeavored to keep up with the most popular ones, the ones that will be familiar to rank and file voters, and occasionally I visit other darker places on the web, the sites no one wants in their browser history. In other words, I spend a lot of time on Facebook, not so much on 8Kun, although I know how to get there. Often the dialogue that surfaces following a posting is at least as rich, if not richer, than the initial post. The back-and-forth of online conversations offers valuable glimpses into what people want to be known for believing and what they think of the beliefs of others. The comments below an online news articles generate fruitful discussions.[5]

KATRINA AND OBAMA

I started documenting the condemnations of Barack Obama in the weeks and months following his searing nomination speech for Senator John Kerry at the Democratic Convention in Boston in 2004. Much to the audience's delight, Obama shared his personal story of post–civil rights movement opportunity and tethered it to Kerry's vision of a progressive and enlightened twenty-first century America. Arguably outshining the actual presidential nominee, the then third-term state senator from Illinois was widely praised for his inspirational speech. It wasn't long before Obama was being touted as a possible presidential contender in 2008, particularly after Kerry's 2004 bid for the White House failed.

As a left-leaning, well-educated African American woman, I was personally impressed by Obama, though I wasn't as smitten as many of my friends and colleagues, for whom it was love at first speech. By nature, I am not predisposed to fandom. But as a scholar trained to analyze folklore by and about African Americans, I was very intrigued by him as a subject of study. Based on a couple of decades of conducting analyses of folk belief—both as a student myself and then as a professor—I recognized that the sudden emergence of this particular black man and his fetching young family would be a lightning rod sparking both extremely positive responses in some spheres and extraordinarily negative ones in other conversation channels.

Like many other black Americans, I was initially quite pessimistic about his chances in 2008. My low expectations were fueled by the vagaries of racism that I had witnessed in my personal life as well as the research I had been conducting for more than twenty-five years. By that time, I had authored three books that were grounded in the vernacular expressions of racial biases. In the first, *I Heard It Through the Grapevine: Rumor in African American Culture*, published by the University of California Press in 1993, I traced the history of rumors and race in the United States, and documented and analyzed beliefs in the black community regarding everything from fast-food fried chicken to the proliferation of illegal drugs in black inner-city communities.

In the second, *Ceramic Uncles and Celluloid Mammies: Black Images and Their Influence on Culture*, images of African Americans in folk and popular culture served as my primary sources. Here, I examined items such as postcards, sheet music, movies, television shows, cookie jars, and other artifacts of popular culture. My work demonstrated that the purveyors of popular culture impose a limited range of possibilities for black characters. The unrelenting derogatory and degrading representations of blacks in popular culture often shaped the ways in which many majority consumers perceived "real" black people. These perceptions, in turn, influenced the ways in which whites conducted themselves as individuals and communities in their interactions with blacks.

Several years later, in 2001, after working with sociologist and fellow folklorist Gary Alan Fine, I coauthored *Whispers on the Color Line: Rumor and Race in America*. In addition to tracking texts that had surfaced since the publication of *Grapevine*, we looked more broadly at everyday discourse and the ways it reflected how blacks and whites thought about one another, as well as how they responded to unanticipated cultural and commercial developments.

A year after I started to track lore about the Obamas, and as Hurricane Katrina struck in August of 2005, I turned my attention to the Gulf Coast. The now notorious storm exposed a pernicious aspect of twenty-first-century racial politics. Most of the media attention focused on New Orleans, a city with a majority black population. Thus, the visuals that came out of New Orleans before, during, and after the storm were largely of black people enduring the oppressive humidity and other onerous climate conditions. Much of the mainstream media attention was seemingly sympathetic to those who were weathering the storm. But stereotypical biases quickly surfaced. After the first night, during which evacuees were sheltered in the Superdome, numerous media outlets reported that widespread sexual violence had erupted in the overcrowded arena. These were essentially unfounded rumors, as post-hurricane investigations found little evidence to support these stories. When white evacuees salvaged goods from abandoned stores, they were described as "taking" supplies, while blacks shown on-screen with salvaged goods were described as "looters." These themes were much more strongly discernible in legends and conspiracy theories that were widely scanned and emailed. As evacuees made their way to Texas and other locales, numerous chain emails used the conventional anti-black stereotypes to describe the men as brutes and thugs, and the women as welfare queens and whores.

I suspect many readers old enough to remember Hurricane Katrina may not recall seeing these reports and, in fact, may recall instead that celebrities and organizations quickly rallied to offer support to the region. If you logged on to Amazon.com, you saw an appeal to support storm survivors. Musicians and other performers gave benefit concerts or redirected the profits from already scheduled events to New Orleans. Brad Pitt, along with numerous philanthropic individuals and groups, committed to the task of building safer and more environmentally sound housing.

Nonetheless, legends claiming that the (white) do-gooders were misplacing their efforts and that the (black) evacuees were undeserving were widely disseminated on the internet, still a relatively novel mode of communication at the time. The pattern in these narratives became quite predictable. Evacuees (implicitly or explicitly black) were out of their designated space (inner city New Orleans "hoods") and were abusing the naive and well-intentioned white good Samaritans. One of the more frequently forwarded texts, four pages in length, starts by describing what the community has done to prepare for the evacuees: "I went upstairs to the third floor to find a **HUGE cafeteria created in under 24 hours! Rows of tables, chairs and food everywhere—enough to feed an army! I am not talking crap food either. They had Jason's Deli food, apples oranges, coke, diet coke, lemonade, orange juice, cookies, all types of chips and sandwiches. All the beverages by way was put on ice and chilled.** In a matter of about 24 hours or less an entire mini-city was erected by volunteers for the poor evacuees." For several paragraphs, the narrator bemoans how rude, sloppy, and unappreciative the evacuees were. As he winds up, race conspicuously enters the story:

> I used the restroom, washed my hands and saw this man throw his razor towards the trash can . . . he missed . . . he walked out leaving his disgusting razor on the floor for some other **"cracker" to pick up. Even the little kids were demanding. I saw only ONE white family and only TWO Hispanic families. The rest were blacks. . . . The majority of which are thugs and lifetime lazy ass welfare recipients. We are inviting the lowest of the low to Houston. And like idiots were are serving the people who soon steal our cars, rape, murder, and destroy our city while stealing from our pockets on a daily basis through the welfare checks they take. We will fund our own destruction.**

The lessons learned from Hurricane Katrina were clear and informed my projections about which racial dynamics would ensue in the following years. To be sure, there were white Americans predisposed to come to the aid of black Americans with generosity and care. Celebrities and companies were willing and even eager to engage in relief efforts. All of this goodwill would unfold with great fanfare in the public realm, on television, in mainstream print publications, and on the most frequented sites on the internet. But the positive attention would also trigger a backlash in the right-wing media and in the then fledgling social media outlets attuned to conservative voices. The anti-black stereotypes imposed in the nineteenth and twentieth centuries had not disappeared. There were still significant segments of the population unable to see blacks as "fellow

Americans," who used the emergent technologies of the twenty-first century to find and connect with each other. Just as they shared their distress over the support being given to the "undeserving," evacuees from Hurricane Katrina, so too would they share their unhappiness over the enthusiasm being voiced for the Obamas.

WHAT DO BARACK OBAMA AND SNAPPLE ICED TEA HAVE IN COMMON?

Participating in one of the academic world's most entrenched rituals, in 2008, I delivered a twenty-minute conference paper titled "What Do Barack Obama and Snapple Iced Tea Have in Common?" at the annual meeting of the American Folklore Society (AFS). I walked my audience through the primary rumors and legends attached to then senator Obama. At that time, allegations that he wouldn't salute the flag or sing the national anthem and narratives claiming that he was a Muslim or that he wasn't a natural born citizen were prevalent. As my folklore colleagues were well aware, some fairly predictable characteristics will trigger rumor mongering; I made the case that Barack Obama embodied these traits, much like Snapple Iced Tea had a decade earlier.

Following its early 1990s introduction to the marketplace, Snapple Iced Tea was the subject of a pair of contemporary legend cycles. Within some quarters of the African American community a contemporary legend circulated claiming that the Ku Klux Klan (KKK) owned the company and was funding its white supremacist agenda with Snapple profits. And within some sections of the white community, there were claims that the company was owned by anti-abortion activists who were using the profits to support Operation Rescue, a militant group willing to forcibly interfere with women seeking abortions and to attack health professionals serving them. Of course, both narratives are bogus. Comparing a consumer food product with a human being may seem like radical false equivalency, but understanding why Snapple (and other products and situations) invited legend cycles does illuminate the anti-Obama lore.

What *do* Barack Obama and Snapple Iced Tea have in common? There are certain characteristics and practices discernible in companies (and politicians) that trigger rumors and contemporary legends. Unusual names, unconventional promotional strategies, instant and unprecedented brand appeal of the variety associated with rock stars, perceptions that the status quo has been unfairly disrupted, can all add up to a consumer or voter backlash that manifests itself in the spread of unsubstantiated hearsay.

Snapple is an unusual name for a drink and many voters never expected to attach the label "serious presidential candidate" to someone with the name Barack Hussein Obama. Before Snapple, the non-alcoholic beverage world was defined by colas. Yet, after its launch, the early 1990s sales of Snapple Iced Tea seriously cut into the soft drink market. Likewise, before his electrifying speech at the 2004 Democratic convention, few political insiders would have predicted that a Hawaii-born, Harvard-educated half Kansan–half Kenyan with an Afrocentric name could attract so many supporters. Snapple distinguished itself as a different kind of beverage choice, and Obama depicted himself as a different kind of politician.

Today, one would be hard pressed to identify a difference in the way Snapple advertises from its competitors. But in the early days, Snapple executives (and the company has switched hands several times) initiated an unorthodox but very successful marketing campaign, using extensively and almost exclusively, radio air time on Rush Limbaugh and Howard Stern's morning talk radio programs. Known for his archly conservative political views, Limbaugh was an extraordinarily popular radio host with millions of listeners always eager to hear his bombastic denunciations of liberal politics and politicians. Also comfortable with a large and loyal audience, Stern's claim to fame was his "shock jock" persona. Thus, both radio personalities were associated with extreme points of view and boasted dedicated followings. By advertising on these programs, Snapple's owners were associating their product with radio personalities well known for their volatile, outlandish statements.

In the earliest days of his presidential campaign, Obama also tapped a source that was as untested in the world of presidential campaigns as niche radio programs were for beverage companies. At a time when political wisdom discredited such an approach to fundraising, Obama pursued donors who could afford to give relatively modest amounts to his campaign. Obama effectively used his internet homepage so that his campaign would not have to spend large sums of money to attract these small contributions.

Today, this fundraising strategy is business-as-usual, but in the early 2000s, a well-wrought campaign website was not yet considered essential. Jaded political pundits—clearly underestimating the impact the internet would have—dismissed Obama's approach. Just as Snapple's strategy effectively introduced consumers to the product, so too did Obama's campaign yield millions of online donors.

Both Snapple and Obama represented costly choices for their targeted audiences. Snapple broke the barrier for individual drinks; in other words, if you ordered a Snapple with your meal, it set you back at least a dollar at a time when Coke and Pepsi could be had for as little as thirty-five cents. Similarly, six packs of Snapple were more expensive than six packs of other non-alcoholic beverages. Analyzing corporate rumors in *Grapevine*, I hypothesized that many consumers internalize a formula that triggers ambivalence about new products that come with a high cost but limited actual utility.

Price + Risk > Utility = Rumor[6]

In the minds of some consumers, Snapple's high price and the unknowns of the fancy iced tea exceeded its benefits and, as a result of this conundrum, rumors were generated.

Obama's campaign was literally expensive for his followers in at least two ways. He made it clear that if he was going to be successful, he'd need lots and lots of donors contributing to his campaign, and many voters who had never put political contributions in their household budgets did so on Obama's behalf. Obama's own rhetoric also suggests that his candidacy was costlier in other ways as well. Many of his campaign positions warned the electorate that the nation's more tenacious problems would require sacrifices be made. After citing disappointing statistics about educational outcomes, he warned: "I don't believe government alone can turn these statistics around. Parents have the primary responsibility for instilling an ethic of hard work and educational achievement in their children."[7]

Thus, in voting for Obama, a citizen is supporting a candidate who expects Americans to be active and engaged participants in the arenas for which they want change.

Indeed, for many voters this "we all have to be a part of the change" philosophy struck a chord. Long before the Iowa caucuses, thousands of volunteers, particularly earnest college-aged men and women, went to work for the Obama campaign. Online communities of Obama supporters began to develop. Many individuals developed an allegiance to their candidate of choice much stronger than is usually seen in the political world. Obama was treated like a rock star, complete with sold-out venues and fainting fans. Consider, for example, the popularity of the Obama girl whose 2007 "I've got a crush on Obama" registered over one thousand hits in the first five hours of its posting. (In 2007, a thousand hits in an hour was a very high number.)[8] By the end of the campaign, YouTube offered hundreds of low-tech videos in which Obama's supporters did everything from sing his praises to choreograph a dance—the Obama hustle—in honor of their hero. By then, lots of people had a crush on Obama.

Clearly, Obama possesses charisma, but it proved to be a contagious and controversial charisma. The very characteristics that inspired some voters to sing and dance his praises deeply troubled others. His profile irked, frightened, and offended some voters. There are voters who preferred other candidates to Obama on the grounds that they considered him unseasoned and/or grounds related to their political priorities, preferring a candidate with different platforms on foreign and/or domestic policy. But some voters found the very features that resonated with "Obamaniacs" deeply troubling. In the early twenty-first century, however, they didn't think they could say publicly that *blackness* or *Harvard-ness* or *eloquence* were alarming and off-putting. As we shall see when we move through the Obama lore, these were the characteristics that were interpreted as problematic.

Snapple too had contagious and controversial charisma. The Obama girl had a sister from the 1990s, the Snapple lady. Wendy Kaufman, who has had her share of YouTube hits, was originally employed as a receptionist by the Snapple corporation. When she realized that the company was receiving iced tea fan mail and that the correspondence was going unanswered, she started to respond to the Snapple groupies. When the public relations firm representing the company discovered that the sincere receptionist was corresponding with Snapple fans, they launched a series of very popular Snapple advertisements featuring Wendy reading and responding to mail.

While there were fans whose affection for Snapple drove them to old-fashioned letter writing, there were other consumers who were quietly and profoundly suspicious of this new product. When I was documenting the Snapple rumors, I found myself in situations where I was asking individuals if they had heard anything that struck them as odd about a soft drink. Sometimes I'd end up mentioning Snapple by name. Interviewees who had never heard the rumors would really perk up at the mention of Snapple, "What's going on there? There's something weird about that stuff. I never heard of it a year ago and now it's everywhere. . . . There's got to be something screwy going on with them." In other words, some people were really primed to hear and even accept something outlandish about Snapple. The very attributes of the iced tea that seduced other consumers offended them. And, to add insult to injury, liking and being able to afford Snapple was cool. To reject Snapple because you couldn't afford it or didn't like it might compromise a consumer's hipness. Similarly, fawning over Barack Obama's potential as a president was becoming commonplace, so those who were underwhelmed by him felt compelled to offer socially acceptable reasons for their disdain.

Snapple was one of many consumer products that stimulated the transmission of contemporary legends. Other beverages (Tropical Fantasy, forty-ounce cans of malt liquor), virtually every fast food fried chicken franchise (Church's, Popeye's, KFC), many clothing designers (Troop, Tommy Hilfiger, Liz Claiborne), and idiosyncratic products such as Crown car air fresheners and menthol-flavored cigarettes spawned narratives about white supremacists profiting off of black consumers. Gary Alan Fine and I researched these legends extensively and unearthed no evidence that the KKK or any similar white nationalists had created a successful company and used it to finance an anti-black agenda.[9] Neither did militant pro-lifers find their way into board rooms to generate a revenue stream for the anti-abortion movement. Instead, we did determine that the way that corporations create, name, advertise, and sell their products does signal an indifference to their customers' well-being. But not all customers reacted the same way. Whites predisposed to extreme pro-life positions mapped their politics onto Snapple. African Americans inclined to distrust what they perceived as white institutions were hostile to Snapple.

This brings us to a final and an extremely significant attribute common to Snapple and Barack Obama. Both entities were perceived by some consumers as having moved into a sphere where they didn't belong, thereby displacing something or someone more deserving of that space.

By putting Snapple on their store shelves, grocers were guilty of sidelining colas. By supporting and financing a run by Barack Obama for the presidency, some Americans were enabling a black man to move into spaces where he didn't belong, thereby displacing a (white) candidate more entitled to that position.

What does it mean that Barack Obama (like Snapple Iced Tea) had a name that some consumers found vexing, burst on the scene way too fast and developed a large and ardent fan base in record time, channeled his "buy me" messages in unconventional formats, sold himself at a higher price than his competitors, and claimed space that had previously belonged to other brands? For one thing, it meant that Barack Obama was going to be a human political rumor magnet of the highest order. The intensity of his pull would be further compounded by his identity as an oddly named black man born to an African father and white mother. All of this would be further exacerbated by the public's growing fascination with what they could learn from like-minded people on the internet and the extraordinary amplification effects that resulted from those connections. This is the period of time when print, television, and radio news began to seriously cede ground to blogs and websites. The 2008 election season featured a perfect storm, comingling an ethnically charged candidate hardwired to trigger rumors with the emergence of history's most powerful and accessible information tool.

At the American Folklore Society meeting I acknowledged that Barack Obama was not the first candidate for the presidency to be subjected to blatantly false rumors and legends. In fact, his opponent, Republican John McCain, was himself plagued by false allegations that he had fathered a black child. Several potent conspiracy theories emerged during Bill Clinton's tenure at the White House, including one that he had authorized a series of murders to silence witnesses who could attest to his purported illegal activity. After only a few short years in the national spotlight Barack Obama had already acquired a suite of rumors and legends—almost all of which had strong racial underpinnings. He may not have been the first and only, but his challenges were of a different order of magnitude.

At the conclusion of my conference presentation I teased the audience by saying that in ten days the world would know the potency of the anti-Obama lore. If McCain/Palin prevailed (as I suspected they would), one of the reasons might well be that these forces had played a role in casting doubt about destroying Obama's chances. But, on November 4 the votes were counted and the Obamas were moving into the White House after all. My inbox swelled with examples of far more emphatic postings claiming that gullible American voters had been seduced by an unscrupulous charlatan who should be stopped from assuming the mantle of the presidency. All of the themes—which will be scrutinized in subsequent chapters—boiled down to a conviction that careless and naive white Americans were going to too far by allowing Barack Obama and his family to take up residence in the White House, and, by implication, that too many blacks were being granted access to the reins of power.

CENTURIES BEFORE THE OBAMA YEARS

The anti-Obama folks were certainly not the first whites to fret about where blacks did and didn't belong. Unauthorized or unanticipated black movement has always spawned the most rumor mongering. Since their forced enslavement to the present day, blacks have been expected to "stay in their place." To state the obvious, the perpetuation of American slavery was dependent upon the enslaved Africans having physical mobility only in so far as it served the labor needs of the master. A black male needed to be able to swing a machete to cut a sugar cane stalk but not to assault an overseer. One of the worst crimes a slave could commit was to run away. The master class went to great lengths to literally and figuratively shackle blacks in ways that prohibited them from unwarranted movement.

Restrictions on physical movement were partnered with prohibitions on intellectual and spiritual movement. In most slaveholding states, it was a crime to teach enslaved blacks to read, and the pros and cons of allowing the enslaved to convert to Christianity were widely debated. But some intrepid captives did manage to accrue some reading and writing skills. Using the well-known Underground Railroad, a small number of men and women found their way to Canada and to the North where they shared their stories of abuse with anyone willing to listen. My doctoral dissertation analyzed slave narratives, a potent body of published accounts of an enslaved person's firsthand experiences that painted ugly pictures of black bondage in the South. These books did move many readers who took up the cause of abolition. Alarmed by the prospect of northern interference in the perpetuation of slavery, southern pro-slavery activists embarked on what we would now call disinformation campaigns aimed at discrediting the black narrators and debunking their stories of the cruelty they and their brethren faced. According to the pro-slavery speeches, letters, and tracts, northerners should assume that blacks were inherently lazy and thoroughly dishonest and deceitful.

Pro-slavery forces warned abolitionists that ending the peculiar institution—a favorite euphemism for the brand of chattel slavery common to the American South—would release blacks into *their* world. The vision of black men and women at liberty to traverse the streets of the northern states did unsettle even those individuals who were otherwise committed to emancipation. Anti-slavery advocates, including Abraham Lincoln himself, seriously investigated the efficacy of moving emancipated blacks from the American landscape altogether by colonizing them in Liberia and elsewhere beyond the borders of the United States. The logistics of removing more than four million men, women, and children from the country proved too onerous, so the end of the Civil War upended the ability of whites to completely restrict the comings and goings of blacks.

In the early years of Reconstruction—roughly the first few years immediately following the end of the Civil War—some southern blacks were on the move in ways that whites found threatening. In addition to the physical movement that enabled them to leave their plantations or factories, they were also empowered—briefly—to vote and to enjoy political access to elected positions in southern state legislatures and Congress. They could develop businesses and establish residential footholds in previously all-white dominions. While this level of equality was endorsed by the most fair-minded of the former abolitionists, many Americans, even those who had been on board with ending slavery, were opposed to seeing blacks in positions of authority. Eager to short-circuit this black progress, apologists for slavery added new tropes to their mantras for discouraging other white Americans from affording blacks too much freedom. It is in this era that the specter of the black male brute surfaces, with depictions of aggressive and oversexed men singularly focused on raping white women.

By 1877, the political forces unnerved by post–Civil War black mobility had successfully recalibrated the opportunities that emancipated blacks could pursue. Laws and policies—commonly referred to as Jim Crow laws—that prohibited African Americans from gaining access to educational, economic, and social equality had been codified. Vigilante organizations such as the Ku Klux Klan (KKK) had been established to punish blacks who dared to exercise any untoward freedom of movement, such as being on the roads at night, applying for an aspirational kind of job, attempting to vote, attending a white school, and pursuing interracial relationships. Leveraging the viral rumors alleging black male attacks on white women, the KKK and similar vigilante groups pursued black men relentlessly and cruelly. In the rare cases where there were after-the-fact investigations, it was usually determined that no white female had been victimized. The black man's real offense was the gall to start a business or attempt to negotiate a competitive price for his crop. White supremacist organizations also inflicted their wrath on whites and white institutions that disagreed with their philosophy of black subjugation.

DECADES BEFORE THE OBAMA YEARS

The Jim Crow era continued well into the twentieth century with World War I and its aftermath proving to be an illuminating moment in American racial history. In need of enlisted men willing to fight and die for the United States, draft boards and elected officials veered from normal practice and encouraged blacks to don uniforms, to train and serve under a predominantly white command force, and to fight America's enemies. For many black soldiers, military training and service provided their first forays beyond their home counties, for some who served overseas it acquainted them with more freedom of movement than they had ever been allowed in the United States. Appreciative of the caliber of their military service, Europeans embraced and welcomed African American soldiers. Black men who survived the war's bloody battles returned to their home stomping grounds only to find that their white neighbors who were so pleased to have them march off to war envisioned them returning to an unchanged social order in which they would remain at the bottom.

White agitators made their point by deploying an early twentieth-century version of fake news and following it up with violence. The stereotypes of blacks as innately violent and lascivious undergirded rumors falsely alleging that the retailer Sears and Roebuck "was deluged with orders from Negroes for guns, pistols, shot and the like," and that black men had approached white soldiers in their communities making comments such as, "Don't worry about your wife, (daughter, sister, mother) we'll take care of her needs in your absence."[10] Black veterans were routinely assaulted at their home train stations where their white "neighbors" would force them to strip off their military uniforms before allowing them to complete their long journeys back to their homes.

Nonetheless, there were entrepreneurial blacks, many of them veterans, who embarked on successful and lucrative business ventures after the war. The story of Oklahoma's black business community is much more known now than when I wrote my earlier books. In the Greenwood district of Tulsa, Oklahoma, also known as Black Wall Street, white rioters looted and destroyed an entire thirty-five-square-block district that blacks had shaped into a business center where they could pursue transactions with one another unencumbered by the restrictions of Jim Crow. The alleged trigger for what is often considered the deadliest riot in US history was a rumor about a black man assaulting a white woman.[11]

The history of the civil rights movement can be read as an episodic narrative about increasing the potential for black mobility and access. The *Brown v. Board of Education* Supreme Court victory was about admitting blacks into the white public schools. The Montgomery Bus Boycott was about enabling blacks to access all of the seats on public transportation. Most depictions of the movement are illustrated by photographs of blacks placing themselves in public spaces that were considered off-limits to them: marching across the Pettus Bridge in Selma; parading into Washington, D.C., to the Lincoln Memorial; strolling into the front doors of Woolworth's and refusing to leave the whites-only lunch counter. The Civil Rights Acts of the 1960s were intended to codify African American access to the voting booth, end segregation in public places, and ban employment discrimination. Each of these steps forward was met with opposition from a powerful subset of whites who reverted to disinformation and violence. The most commonly disseminated conspiracy theories alleged that southern blacks were not really dissatisfied with the status quo, but that evil Communists had infiltrated their ranks, turning them against their white brethren. It should be noted that the advent of television news meant that violence didn't serve them as well as it once had. The brutality of the attacks, now broadcast into their living rooms, alarmed other whites in a new and destabilizing way.

By the mid-1960s the most ardent of anti-Communist zealots had fallen from favor, thereby diluting the scare factor in these conspiracy theories. As the decade came to an end, the focused work of black activists had at least partially paid off, as equal opportunity in housing, employment, and education, along with voting rights, had been established, essentially eliminating Jim Crow laws. Many optimistic Americans believed that the hard work of dismantling racism and sidelining racist institutions had been achieved. But the fact that blacks could apply to universities didn't mean that they thrived when they enrolled. The fact that blacks could apply for corporate jobs and bid on public contracts did not markedly increase their representation in board rooms or on government-funded job sites.

In order to accelerate minority access to once restricted domains, a cluster of policies that came to be known as affirmative action took hold. Affirmative action policies required institutions and municipalities to be proactive in their steps to ensure that minority aspirants fared well. For example, some municipalities set aside a percentage of contracts that had to be given to minority-owned businesses. Some colleges and universities developed alternative criteria for assessing and supporting minority applicants in their programs. To advocates for inclusion and equity, affirmative action practices were considered a reasonable remedy that could be expected to further level the playing field between whites and minorities. But there were numerous critics of affirmative action, individuals who bemoaned the acceptance of "unqualified" applicants and who regarded any and all affirmative action policies as reverse discrimination. While there may have been missteps in the application of these policies, the rumor mill was rife with unfounded examples of grossly underqualified candidates installed in schools and jobs at the expense of purportedly more qualified white applicants. As we shall see, Barack and Michelle Obama came of age during the affirmative action era and many of the accusations against them—and other blacks of their generation—alleged that they were unworthy of the schools they attended and the jobs they received. Indeed, I know of very few blacks attending college or seeking professional positions in the affirmative action years who didn't encounter doubters who presumed we (and I do mean we) were academically under prepared.

During the last few decades of the twentieth century some individual blacks, as well as some select black-owned businesses, were able to cross over into previously white domains. For the most part, public figures, corporations, and media outlets went to great lengths to avoid any signs of overt racist sentiment. The entertainment industry incorporated blacks into their storylines, usually in conspicuously asexual roles. Lots of doctors in shapeless scrubs and robed black judges—male and female—could be found in hospital and courtroom scenes. Love scenes in boudoirs were few and far between. Physically talented African American athletes commanded high salaries and enjoyed widespread acclaim. It cannot be denied that some African Americans had a greater presence in environs from which they had once been excluded. In the spirit of the lyrics of the popular theme song from the hit situation comedy, *The Jeffersons*, we were *moving* on up.

Even so, African American upward mobility was far from ubiquitous. Whereas Jim Crow schools in the South had stifled opportunity for blacks coming of age in the early twentieth century, underfunded urban schools had short-changed black children as the century came to an end. Anti-affirmative action forces successfully constrained black access to schools, jobs, and public contracts. For blacks whose conduct was deemed even marginally criminal, an expensive, intractable prison-industrial complex arose to stall African American mobility in no uncertain terms. One of the most telling contemporary legends of the 1990s was known as "Lights Out."[12] Circulated largely by photocopies (email was still a nascent mode of communication), it warned recipients that the coming weekend was earmarked for a gang initiation during which initiates would leave their hoods to infiltrate white suburban neighborhoods after dark. They would drive with their car lights off, waiting for a good Samaritan to blink their headlights. Gang membership then required the initiate to follow the good Samaritan and rape and/or murder them. Just as it had been true for the prior three hundred years, whites were using misinformation to perpetuate anti-black stereotypes and to discourage whites from enabling black mobility.

AND THEN CAME THE OBAMA YEARS

Barack Obama's arresting 2004 nomination speech for John Kerry—the speech that thrust him into the limelight—ignores this history. It makes no mention of anything that can be construed as ugly in past relations between blacks and whites. As his later campaign mantras would reinforce, he sought to define himself as the embodiment of all things good and promising about America. Any presidential pundit will point to that eloquent and relentlessly upbeat speech as the force that seduced the American voters for the next two election cycles.

In spite of Obama's intentions, it provided a political punch list for those who were predisposed to mistrust a nonwhite candidate. He notes that, "My father was a foreign student, born and raised in a small village in Kenya."[13] This aspect of his identity was fodder for the listeners who would become known as the birthers. Explaining his name, he says, "They [parents] would give me an African name, Barack, or "blessed," believing that in a tolerant America your name is no barrier to your success." Later on, while making the case that Americans embrace a diversity of belief, he says, "If there's an Arab-American family being rounded up without the benefit of an attorney or due process, that threatens my freedom." Applauded by many listeners, these sentiments underlying his worldview annoyed those disinclined to consider anyone "African" or "Muslim" as a fellow Americans. Naturally, the first cycle of rumors to really take off alleged that he was not a Christian. At the climax of the speech, the talented political orator exclaimed, "I believe we can provide jobs to the jobless, homes to the homeless, and reclaim young people in cities across America from violence and despair." This comment was music to the ears in the immediate audience, to others it smacked of socialism suggesting that this ethnic upstart was going to redistribute American assets.

The speech also contained what would become a phrase that Obama claimed to be transforming—the audacity of hope. Although he didn't offer a citation that evening, it was the title of one of his books, where he connected it to Michelle Robinson Obama's home church—the Chicago-based place of worship he joined during their courtship. His association with Trinity United Church of Christ's pastor, the Reverend Jeremiah Wright was a connection that would entangle him in rumors, legends, and conspiracy theories for years to come. Thus, the same speech that laid the groundwork for what was ultimately a successful run for the White House—and it is important to remember that he was elected—contained almost all of the remarks that would trigger the negative rumors, legends, and conspiracy theories about him and his family.

Trash Talk: Anti-Obama Lore and Race in the Twenty-First Century examines and deconstructs just how this dynamic was operationalized. It reveals how the three-hundred-year-old pattern of "black mobility pursued" followed by "white mitigation implemented," would be enacted in the twenty-first century. In the post–Civil War era, emancipated blacks who worked their way into property ownership, and even the halls of legislatures, were soon displaced by white supremacists armed with the physical weapons of vigilante justice and the cultural tools of flagrant disinformation. In the beginning of the twentieth century, black veterans and other blacks who had secured some measure of education and success were thwarted by the next generation of white supremacists who continued to deploy both strategies of violence and cultural mayhem in order to mark the territory they believed should remain segregated. The civil rights movement was intended to demolish any remaining restrictions on black access. Once again, whites unconvinced of African American worth deployed rumors and legends to curtail black success.

Barack Obama and his supporters may have assumed that the warmth and commitment so many white Americans had for him and his story would neutralize any lingering anti-black sentiment that might pose an obstacle to his aspirations. It was a new century, after all. Wasn't America beyond all that? But as the chapters ahead will demonstrate, the impulse to mitigate the success of blacks in America is a potent, pernicious, and persistent force.

TRASH TALK

Like many African Americans of my generation, I was raised in a household in which my parents were eager for me to be an exemplar of good behavior. The Turners didn't problematize the expectation that blacks would have to work twice as hard as white counterparts to get access to a good life, they just encouraged me to follow their lead and work twice as hard. My mother went to great lengths to make sure I was always punctual and that my clothes never had a single wrinkle or ripped hem. And it was certainly important that I never "talk trash" about anyone. To them, and I think this is true for other blacks who were born in the first couple of decades of the twentieth century, to "trash talk" was to indulge in the transmission of unflattering and inaccurate and potentially hurtful commentary about another person. To be sure, there were in-group settings and occasions when someone might interject "we're talking *trash* now," and everyone would have a good laugh. But I was discouraged from ever really aligning myself with habitual trash talkers, not just because the accusations were likely exaggerated or unfounded, but also because to be the kind of person who focused on the negative, who vocalized bad things about other people, was an inferior kind of person to be. My parents did not want to raise a trash talker; they wanted to raise a daughter who would be characterized by a strong moral foundation, preferably rooted in Christianity, hardworking, generous, and selfless.

Little did they know then that they were raising a daughter who would come to spend thousands of hours studying, analyzing, and writing about trash talk. Given their aspirations for my character, they would have been proud that when Hurricane Katrina hit I sent a check to my sister's church in Houston to enable her congregation to help evacuees they had adopted. But Mom and Dad would have lamented the time I spent tracking down the false stories of black men raping white women in the evacuation shelters, although that time investment would have met their "hardworking" criteria.

When Obama's 2008 election victory was announced and when his inauguration occurred two months later, I remember wishing my parents were alive to witness the movement of a black family into the White House. The fact that he was twice elected demonstrates that in some circles, he and his family were very much treasured. But in other domains, every aspect of his persona was being trashed. For the most part, the trash talk was dismissed or ignored, with little concern for the chickens that would soon come home to roost.

The relationship between whites and blacks in the twenty-first century is going to be both different from earlier centuries and much the same.

Mainstream news and conventional nonfiction discourse will focus on what is different and purportedly improved. There was a large enough segment of the white population willing to invest in and vote for a black president. Twice. But the trash talk highlights what forces have not changed. Longstanding anti-black hostility still characterizes the attitudes of a significant segment of the electorate. The tenacious articulations of these toxic old attitudes would gain power from a decidedly twenty-first-century phenomenon: the internet and social media—and the savvy opportunists who knew how to enrich themselves by fanning the flames of racism. Yes, American voters—black and white—enabled the election and reelection of Barack Obama. But with each election cycle, an escalating hate for Obama and other blacks intensified, paving the path for a radically different outcome in 2016.

1 Flagged Down

In *A Promised Land*, Barack Obama reflects on one of the first rumor-based controversies to plague his 2008 campaign for the presidency: "As I saw my colleagues wearing flag pins in the Senate blithely vote for budget cuts for funding to veteran's programs—I put my own flag pin aside. It was less an act of protest and more a reminder to myself that the substance of patriotism mattered far more than the symbol. Nobody seemed to notice, especially since most of my fellow senators—including former Navy POW John McCain—regularly sported flag-pin-less lapels."[1] Obama quickly learned that once he set his sights beyond the chambers of the US Senate and on to the corridors of the White House, some segments of the public and the press were going to notice and judge him by a different set of rules than those used for McCain, who would become his opponent in the 2008 race. To those who didn't want to see him as commander in chief, the symbols of patriotism far outweighed any high-minded ideals he may have held regarding the "substance" of patriotism. When his white opponents traversed the campaign trail without flag pins on their lapels, it was not fodder for the rumor mill. When Barack Obama left his pin at home, he was seen to be a flag-hating, unpatriotic opportunist.

Among the inventory of presidential attributes perceived as lacking in Barack Obama, patriotism was one of the first and highest on the list. All of the classic symbols of American patriotism were turned into a never-ending series of litmus tests for him—as candidate, president, and eventually former president. This chapter will examine rumors that surfaced before he was elected, falsely claiming that for ideological reasons he wouldn't wear a flag pin, salute the American flag, or sing "The Star-Spangled Banner." Once the White House was his home, other texts surfaced that accused him of insulting the Boy Scouts of America and members of the United States Armed Forces and committing a seemingly never-ending stream of slights against the American flag. This chapter will also offer some fundamental definitions and rubrics that will be used to illuminate the texts discussed throughout the book.

9/11 AND PATRIOTISM IN THE TWENTY-FIRST CENTURY

The far right's preoccupation with fundamentalist expressions of patriotism was fueled by the events and aftermath of September 11, 2001. The national trauma of witnessing hijackers kill almost three thousand people in a few short hours provoked a groundswell of nationalist activity—some of it healthy, some of it extreme—as distraught Americans endeavored to reconcile the day's unprecedented events. Conspicuous displays of patriotism largely defined the reactions of President Bush and members of Congress, forecasting the comfort these displays would produce for some Americans in the decades ahead.

Pursuing a typical day in the life of a president, George Bush was visiting an elementary school in Florida when his aides briefed him on the attack. Those secret service agents charged with keeping the commander in chief safe were obliged to extricate Bush from a first-grade classroom reading circle and secure him in the safest possible environment. Given that no one knew what was going to happen next, it was hard for them to be confident that any setting was impenetrable. After all, following the initial attacks on the World Trade Center, American Airlines Flight no. 77 soon crashed into the Pentagon, and shortly after that, the courageous passengers on United Flight no. 93 wrested control of their plane's cockpit when it became clear that its hijackers had charted a course for a Washington, D.C., landmark. The president's security detail couldn't be certain that other assailants were not queued up for more attacks.

Consequently, for much of that fateful day President Bush was airborne in Air Force One or at an undisclosed remote location, able to keep completely current on unfolding events but unable to address the American people. Finding that one-way communications bubble intolerable, President Bush insisted on returning to Washington. President Bush's temporary absence during this unprecedented crisis was noted, and in some quarters there was a fair amount of discontent about his lack of visibility. Many observers claim that he was finally able to reverse that dissatisfaction when he visited the ruins of the World Trade Center. Standing at the epicenter of the attack that killed thousands of people and demolished one of the world's most potent architectural icons, President Bush, wearing clothes more suited to a disaster zone than his usual business suit, initially approached the audience of first responders with soberness and care. After saying, "I want you to know that America today, America today is on bended knee in prayer for the people whose lives were lost here, for the workers who work here, for the families who mourn." A chance exchange with one of the men at the far reaches of the crowd created a memorable sound bite. When the first responder shouted, "George, we can't hear you" for a second time, President Bush responded with great intensity, "I can hear you. I can hear you and the rest of the world hears you, and the people who knocked these buildings down will hear all of us soon."[2] Amid the rubble, the assembled crowd cheered defiantly. Many pundits identified that exchange as a turning point during which the president, boldly promising retribution, regained the leadership footing temporarily lost during the morning of September 11.

Just as President Bush made himself visible and viable to the world, so too did the leaders of the American Congress recognize that they should make a noticeable public stand. With a contested November election on the horizon, the leadership of both the Republican and Democratic parties understood that they needed to convey unimpeachable solidarity and a sense of purpose unencumbered by the usual partisan bickering. The steps of the Capitol building in Washington, D.C., were selected as the appropriate backdrop for the party leaders of both the Senate and the House of Representatives, and their members, to unequivocally signal their unity. In front of dozens, if not hundreds, of cameras, they took their turns conveying their condolences to victims' families and expressing their outrage at the enemy. After the formal remarks concluded, a spontaneous singing of "God Bless America" sealed the solemn moment.[3] Footage of this impromptu concert became one of the most commonly re-televised snapshots from a day replete with memorable images.

It was clear from the positive response to both the Congressional gathering and President Bush's defiant moment at what was soon to be called "Ground Zero," that many constituents and journalists preferred a hefty dose of patriotic fervor to more measured expressions of condolences. Although there are literally thousands of images from Ground Zero, one of the most frequently used depicts a 2001 rendition of the iconic Iwo Jima photograph of three marines positioning the stars and stripes in the smoldering ruins. This World War II throwback was the image the Postal Service selected for its 2001 commemorative "Heroes" stamp. In the weeks and months following the attacks, American flags and red, white, and blue memorabilia were everywhere. To wear a flag pin or display a flag in front of one's house or business became a shorthand message that communicated remembrance and support. The preferred icons of mourning and defiance became those that embodied the American flag. Many observers made the case that this was the time to put country first, and visibly tethering one's self to a flag was often all one had to do to proclaim allegiance.

The events of September 11 dominated the American cultural landscape for many years, and, notably, the next several election cycles. Committed to delivering on his promise that the "people who knocked down these buildings will hear from us," President Bush, with support from international allies, announced a "war on terror." The object was to destroy al-Qaeda, the extremist organization responsible for the September 11 attacks. Not only in retribution, but also because the group was believed to be poised to orchestrate even more heinous assaults. To be sure, almost all Americans were outraged and unsettled by the human and environmental toll the attacks had taken. And when military forces were readied, support for the men and women in uniform was widespread. But the decision to authorize military tactics in the first place was contested, with many observers unconvinced that the best response to September 11 was armed combat.

While analyzing the complexity of the official response is beyond the scope of this book, it can be said that some in the corridors of power believed it appropriate to invade Iraq, while others in authoritative positions did not think the connection between the Iraqi government and the September 11 attacks was strong enough to justify military aggression.

Barack Obama, in a 2002 speech when he was still an Illinois state senator, voiced his opposition to the Bush administration's recent announcement of an investment in a war against Iraq. Hillary Rodham Clinton, a sitting Democratic senator at the time, supported the Republican president. By the time Obama and Clinton were vying for the Democratic nomination for the presidency in 2008, the monumental toll of the war was better understood. Many members of the Democratic party were convinced that the war in Iraq had cost too much—in lives and money—and ultimately had failed to make the world any safer from terrorism. Voters on the right were more likely to support the actions of a Republican president as appropriate, and Obama's record as an opponent of the war was not a plus for them. His status as the son of an African father and holder of a contested middle name, "Hussein," which, while translated as "handsome one," for many evoked associations with Saddam Hussein, an arch enemy of the United States. As a dark-skinned man who shared a name with an American enemy, who had also opposed a war intended as payback for the 9/11 attacks, Barack Hussein Obama was automatically unpatriotic in the minds of many on the right.

A RED FLAG

On the campaign trail, Barack Obama sometimes wore a flag pin and sometimes didn't. The other male front runners of both parties were just as inconsistent. John McCain, Mitt Romney, and Newt Gingrich all campaigned both with and without flag pins on their lapels. As many journalists came to observe, Rudy Giuliani, who was mayor of New York City during the 9/11 attacks, was the only candidate of either party to boast a perfect pin record.[4]

The absence of a flag pin on Obama's suit jacket antagonized some observers, prompting a naked lapel to be noted and critiqued. Any day

Obama was pin-less was a bad day. Before-and-after photograph pairings showing his suit jackets with and without flag pins were circulated via email and posted on blogs, often accompanied by blistering complaints about his pin moratorium. Rumors circulated that his lack of a flag pin was not a mere fashion faux pas but a byproduct of an aversion he had for Old Glory, and, by extension, America itself.

In an October 2007 campaign stop, a Cedar Rapids reporter for a local television station asked him why he wasn't wearing a pin that day. He responded, "My attitude is that I'm less concerned about what you're wearing on your lapel than what's in your heart. You show your patriotism by how you treat your fellow Americans, especially those who serve. You show your patriotism by being true to our values and ideals. That's what we have to lead with is our values and our ideals."[5] Assuming they even heard it, Obama's critics were not satisfied, and the accusation that his lack of a pin telegraphed a lack of patriotism persisted.

In the early months of 2008, the race for the Democratic nomination was tightening and the general election itself was just months away. What I call "Pin Watch" was becoming a serious pastime on social media. While many journalists dismissed the story as trivial, the relentless online folk musings occasionally propelled the accusation to the mainstream news world. In February 2008, Representative Jack Kingston (R-Ga) appeared on MSNBC to challenge Obama's pin choices, claiming, "Barack Obama says he won't wear one." The show's host, Dan Abrams, astutely pointed out that Congressman Kingston's own lapel was bare as he was denigrating a fellow member of Congress, Senator Obama, for a naked lapel. Undeterred by this apparent hypocrisy and willfully dismissive of photographic evidence to the contrary, Kingston defended himself saying that he "would" wear one and Barack Obama "won't."[6]

During one of the early Democratic debates on April 16, 2008, moderator Charlie Gibson of ABC News posed questions related to domestic and foreign policy. After noting that the internet was filled with commentary about Senator Obama's flag pin choices, the veteran journalist unearthed the topic of "electability" to justify asking the candidate to respond to a question submitted by a viewer, purportedly representative of so many other citizens disinclined to vote for him for this reason, asking Senator Obama why he didn't wear a flag pin. In response, Senator Obama started by stating, "I revere the American flag," and he continued to acknowledge that he believed America to be the only country in which someone with his background could experience the mobility that would result in his being a serious contender for the White House. Toward the end of his response, he noted that he had worn one given to him by a veteran the previous day and said, "I have never said that I don't wear flag pins."[7]

Although many journalists cited the flag pin question in a domestic policy segment as an example of what made this debate a poorly orchestrated one overall, this very public airing of his position did not stem the rumormongering. The belief that sinister ideological reasons kept Obama's lapel bare continued. Several weeks later, a May 2008 *Time* magazine article began, "In case you missed it, Barack Obama's American flag lapel pin is back. How long it will stay on is anyone's guess." The reporter, Jay Newton-Small, provided an inventory of recent Obama appearances and noted whether or not the trusty pin was in place.[8] Whereas other candidates' pin choices were not the subject of scrutiny, this became an issue that Barack Obama could not escape. Barack Obama was not going to be afforded the luxury of choosing to pin or not to pin on a daily basis.

Barack Obama was alleged to have disregarded other symbols of patriotism as well. The editors of the Snopes website, one of the oldest and most respected clearinghouses for urban legend evaluation, noted that in October of 2007, the same month that his pin was an issue, they received numerous queries regarding his alleged refusal to sing the national anthem or put his hand over his heart while it was being performed. The submissions they received usually contained "a picture capturing Democratic presidential hopeful Barack Obama standing in front of a US flag (at an Iowa political event) with his hands clasped in front of him during the playing of the national anthem (while other persons on the platform with him stood with their hands placed over their hearts)."[9]

The prospect of a president disinclined to honor the national anthem generated extensive criticism. It has been verified that the oft-circulated photo does depict an actual event at which the anthem was performed, and Barack Obama was the only person on the stage not to put his hand over his heart. Many of the blog posts and emails on this matter point out that according to the flag code, when the flag is present and the national anthem is performed, the proper conduct is to stand and put one's right hand over one's heart; it does state that "all other persons present should stand at attention with their right hand over their heart."[10] So, yes, it is true that Barack Obama did assume this posture on that warm Iowa day. However, this protocol may not be widely known, as many individuals are taught merely to stand and cease other activities when the anthem is being played. For those of us who most frequently hear the anthem at sporting events, it is quite common for attendees to stand during the anthem and not put their hands over their hearts.

This early manifestation of anti-Obama leanings reveals that some Americans were going to be unforgiving of any missteps on his part. Any momentary lapse—a day or two without a flag pin, an anthem performance without his hand on his heart—was going to be interpreted as evidence that he lacked the patriotism needed to be a president. That evidence would be shared through social media channels. In some of the most widely circulated emails regarding Obama's alleged disdain for all things American, his attitude is described in much more hostile terms. "Barack Hussein Obama will NOT recite the Pledge of Allegiance nor will he show any reverence for our flag. While others put their hands over their hearts, Obama turns his back on the flag and slouches."[11]

The use of Obama's middle name in this and many other contemporary legends speaks to the rhetorical goals of the sender and reinforces the power names have in rumor formation as outlined in the introduction. Those forwarding this message from 2007 wanted to remind the recipients that this aspiring president shared a name with Saddam Hussein, president of Iraq and aggressor in the Gulf War. By linking him to Muslim men and culture, tellers were assuming a guilt by association would undermine his credibility as a proud American.

Many of the legends about President Obama are "verified" through the use of actual photographs that are either mislabeled or lack key contextual information. In addition to the ones that show him wearing pin-less jackets or with his hands by his sides during the national anthem, there is a subset that shows his campaign plane complete with his campaign slogan "Change You Can Believe In" and the red, white, and blue circular logo. Those who forward these pictures claim that candidate Obama insisted that the flag images that were on the plane—it was apparently a used plane—be painted over because of his distaste for the American flag.

LABELS AND SOURCES

The accusations that Barack Obama would not salute the flag or wear a flag pin, and had obliterated a flag image from his plane fall into the category of rumors. One of the original scholarly definitions of *rumor* continues to be applicable, assuming we can augment its scope by allowing that in the twenty-first century the internet is functionally the same as "word of mouth." Sociologists Gordon W. Allport and Leo Postman defined a rumor as "a specific proposition for belief, passed along from person to person, usually by word of mouth, without secure standards of evidence being present."[12] A key word in this definition is "belief," and it fits well because the kind of rumors folklorists document are those that inspire belief at a level akin to belief in a religion. The narratives that support most major religions don't lend themselves to standards of evidence, but adherents of those faith systems accept them if they subscribe to a mutually agreed upon set of tenets. Similarly, the presence of a pin on Barack Obama's lapel one day when it has been missing on others will not convince some people that he is properly patriotic if their core belief assigns him as un-American.

In order to substantiate the rumors included in this book, I have made several references to the Snopes website. Snopes and several other fact-checking websites such as FactCheck.org and Politifact will be referenced frequently throughout. It is true that the validity of Snopes, as well as the others, has been challenged. And those challenges have been counter-challenged. In the interest of full transparency, I am noting that while I don't think they are infallible, by the same token, they are invaluable, and I find the journalists who defend them more convincing than those who condemn them. My own initial research into rumors and legends in the 1980s and 1990s predated those online resources. The process of tracking down the validity of rumors and legends was onerous, time-consuming, and expensive for an individual scholar, particularly in the days when phone calls, surface mail, and in-person library research was required. From my perspective, the professional staff—trained volunteers and trained students who do this work—would only be compromising their own reputations if their assessments were persistently illegitimate. For the purposes of clarity and transparency, I will always clearly attribute content from these sources.

FROM CHATTER TO LEGEND: "I'D LIKE
TO TEACH THE WORLD TO SING"

Given that there were early days when Barack Obama was pin-less, a case could be made that some of the rumors about him were not completely false. But before long there were fully fleshed out contemporary legends circulating that were wholly inaccurate. "I'd Like to Teach the World to Sing" reflects many of the anti-flag themes and vests them in a narrative form with a beginning, middle, and end. It has a frame story and dialogue from the implicated parties. It contains many of the markers of texts in which an interesting celebrity who boasts a significant following makes a damaging revelation on a popular television program. In the pre-internet days, these included the legends that while doing a segment on "The Oprah Winfrey Show," fashion designer Liz Claiborne casually confessed to making her pants and skirts too narrow for black women to wear because she didn't like the look of black women in her clothes.[13] Those texts tended to circulate verbally through webs of families and friends. While "I'd Like to Teach the World to Sing" may have some verbal versions, it is in a much more fixed form, with those inclined to find it plausible emailing it to like-minded associates or posting it on social media.

The individual who narrates or forwards the text does so to warn others that said celebrity's true colors have been acknowledged for all the world to see. Those who received or read it often received this version that is now available on Snopes:

> Yes, he told us in advance what he planned to do. Few were listening. The following is a narrative taken from a 2008 Sunday morning televised "*Meet The Press.*"
>
> From Sunday's 07 Sept. 2008 11:48:04 EST, Televised "Meet the Press" the THEN Senator Obama was asked about his stance on the American Flag. General Bill Gann' USAF (ret.) asked Obama to explain WHY he doesn't follow protocol when the National Anthem is played.
>
> The General stated to Obama that according to the United States Code, Title 36, Chapter 10, Sec. 171 . . .
>
> During rendition of the national anthem, when the flag is displayed, all present (except those in uniform) are expected to stand at attention facing the flag with the right hand over the heart. Or, at the very least, "Stand and Face It."

Senator Obama replied:

"As I've said about the flag pin, I don't want to be perceived as taking sides." "There are a lot of people in the world to whom the American flag is a symbol of oppression." "The anthem itself conveys a war-like message. You know, the bombs bursting in air and all that sort of thing." Obama continued: "The National Anthem should be 'swapped' for something less parochial and less bellicose. I like the song 'I'd Like To Teach the World To Sing.' If that were our anthem, then, I might salute it. In my opinion, we should consider reinventing our National Anthem as well as 'redesign' our Flag to better offer our enemies hope and love. It's my intention, if elected, to disarm America to the level of acceptance to our Middle East Brethren. If we, as a Nation of warring people, conduct ourselves like the nations of Islam, where peace prevails—perhaps a state or period of mutual accord could exist between our governments. . . ."

When I become President, I will seek a pact of agreement to end hostilities between those who have been at war or in a state of enmity, and a freedom from disquieting oppressive thoughts. We as a Nation, have placed upon the nations of Islam, an unfair injustice which is WHY my wife disrespects the Flag and she and I have attended several flag burning ceremonies in the past."

"Of course now, I have found myself about to become the President of the United States and I have put my hatred aside. I will use my power to bring CHANGE to this Nation, and offer the people a new path. My wife and I look forward to becoming our Country's First black Family. Indeed, CHANGE is about to overwhelm the United States of America."

Yes, you read it right.

I, for one, am speechless!!!

Dale Lindsborg, *Washington Post*[14]

Since "I'd Like to Teach the World to Sing" is the first of many of the more structured contemporary legends to be documented in this and subsequent chapters, I would like to offer a list of the attributes that characterize these texts and then pinpoint those that are evident here. As additional texts are treated elsewhere in this book, this master list can serve as a reference point. Although these attributes are particularly evident in narratives circulated through the internet, they will be familiar to those who recall the format of verbally circulated contemporary legends. It should also be noted that some of them are contradictory. The list that follows is indebted to a number of rumor and legend scholars whose work has informed my own.[15]

CONTEMPORARY LEGEND ATTRIBUTES

Authorial Dispassion—The author's tone is dispassionate, with a clear attempt to project an ethos of even-handedness and reasonable judgment.

Authorial Indignation—In contrast, the author can barely contain his/her dismay regarding the story being narrated. In many cases the initial voice is dispassionate but the indignation rises as the text proceeds.

Embedded Details—The narrative contains very precise details regarding times, dates, and specific codes that all lend an air of authenticity.

Kernel of Truth—A verifiable piece of information is included in the story but that truth is subjected to extensive and erroneous speculation.

FOAF—The narrator authenticates his/her story by attributing it to a "friend of a friend" or FOAF.

Direct Incriminating Quotes—The text contains quotations attributed to the person under scrutiny so that the person under scrutiny seems to hang himself.

Media Paradox—On the one hand, the alleged revelation is said to have occurred on a respected media outlet and the embedded details above often substantiate the time and date of the broadcast or publication. On the other hand, the media is said to be covering up the confession of outrageous behavior or beliefs.

Rhetorical Questions—The narrator challenges his audience directly with questions that aren't really answerable, given the format. Usually these are personalized with the word "you."

Celebrity Substantiators—High profile individuals are said to have conducted the interview or discovered the revelation being disclosed in the story.

Grammatical and Spelling Inconsistencies—It is often easy to identify numerous errors in the prose.

Random Capitalization—Usually indicating a desire to convey intensity, these texts often rely on randomly capitalized words.

Final Punch—The story ends with a narrative shift articulating a more damning accusation, usually framed by utter disgust or dismay.

Many of these attributes can be discerned in "I'd Like to Teach the World to Sing." First of all, it grounds its truth claim in not one but two respected media outlets, in this case, the venerable *Meet the Press*, the longest running program on television and the *Washington Post*, a revered newspaper. In the 1980s, many alleged exposés of perilous consumer products were said to have taken place on *The Phil Donahue Show*, once the most popular daytime talk show, while political malfeasance was often said to have been revealed on *60 Minutes*. In my earlier work on rumors and race, the revelation of a conspiracy was often alleged to have happened on *The Oprah Winfrey Show*, which, during its heyday in the 1980s and 1990s, was a ratings winner and also featured segments devoted to topics on race. Thus it seems completely plausible that a candidate such as Barack Obama would appear on *Meet the Press*. But, whereas in those earlier contemporary legends the teller claimed to have seen the startling segment only on the television program, this one further authenticates its claim by saying that the revelation also was reported in the *Washington Post*, complete with a byline from the alleged author.

General Bill Gann USAF (ret.) serves in this legend as the celebrity substantiator. While his is not a household name, he is portrayed as a very senior military officer, purportedly retired, who would likely gain the reader's trust. He's the Pentagon's version of Oprah Winfrey or Phil Donahue or Mike Wallace. Embedded details appear throughout. The tale contains very specific references such as 11:24:04 EST and United States Code, Title 36, Chapter 10, Sec 171.

The alleged quote from "THEN Senator Obama," is the bulk of the narrative. Within it, the presidential hopeful seems to offer substantiation for several of the prevailing accusations about his perspective. It sounds measured, articulate, and intelligent. The grammar and vocabulary are befitting of an Ivy League–educated lawyer with phrases such as "less parochial and less bellicose" and "disquieting oppressive thoughts." The direct incriminating quotes then unfold.

He documents his flag ambivalence by confirming his reluctance to wear a pin by

- acknowledging his aversion to the pins on the grounds that other nations might take offence;
- suggesting that after realigning foreign policy he might endorse a redesigned flag; and
- noting his attendance at flag burnings.

Like many contemporary legends of this ilk, this one has a motif that many listeners will find particularly outrageous. The candidate initially critiques the national anthem using the same arguments that have been raised by others who find the song inappropriate. The "bombs bursting in air" refrain *has* antagonized some, who argue that its militaristic overtones are disturbing. Many of these critics make the case that other recognized patriotic songs would be more suitable anthems, with "America the Beautiful" often garnering the most approval. But Barack Obama does not favor a song already on the playlist for the 4th of July and Memorial Day; instead, he advocates for a 1970s commercial jingle first used to advertise Coca-Cola. "I'd Like to Teach the World to Sing" inspires a utopian longing for a thoroughly tranquil vision of a universe free from tensions, jealousies, and heartache. Although it is performed by a wholesome looking group—The New Seekers—on a hilltop, it contains no references to anything American, further making it a poor choice for a national anthem. With references to "snow white turtle doves," "apple trees," and "honey bees," it's the kind of wish one might expect from a particularly vacuous Miss America contestant, not from a serious and learned candidate for the presidency. Had Barack Obama actually said this, he would have been lambasted on the show itself (though he never appeared with General Gann on *Meet the Press*) and other media outlets would have had a field day with the suggestion.

In this alleged extended quote, Obama self-indicts on much more than flag beliefs. But he serves up Michelle Obama as possibly even more anti-American than himself by reflecting on their flag burning dates, never suggesting that she has any regrets, while implying that his candidacy has caused him to rethink his own participation. The next chapter will chronicle the evolution of the beliefs about his faith, but here we certainly see a pronounced sympathy for Islamic nations. The last paragraph of the quotation includes the random capitalization of the word "CHANGE." During Obama's candidacy, change was one of the key tropes his campaign used, intending to signal that his presidency would mark a departure from conventional party politics. The narrator is suggesting that the "CHANGE" Obama will advocate for is one that turns the country to the mindset of Islam. This constitutes the final punch, essentially telling the reader that the real problem with an Obama presidency is not having a commercial jingle as the national anthem; rather, what is to be truly feared is his desire to engineer a major shift in the nation's religious identity.

This "interview" never took place, and in no setting has Barack Obama urged substituting a soft drink jingle for the national anthem, nor has he advocated for changing the religious leanings of the nation. Political columnist John Semmens, crafting a satirical column from the flag pin/ national anthem emails for the *Arizona Conservative*, invented the story.[16] The article was cut and pasted and circulated widely as though it was an accurate report. Some individuals readily accepted the notion that a serious presidential candidate could express disdain for the national anthem on a highly rated television program and the only "news" about that moment would come through email and not widespread reporting in every major news outlet. The existence of fact-checking websites affirming that Obama wore pins, sang the anthem, didn't repaint his plane, and that a satirically inclined journalist invented the Coke-jingle-as-anthem story were likely convincing to some recipients of the texts who took the time to consult the fact-checkers. But to some critics inclined to believe the worst about the presidential candidate, satirical clues were opaque.

The disdain and distrust developing about Barack Obama also provided a business opportunity for individuals with a track record of capitalizing on misinformation about Democrats. Jerome R. Corsi, author of *Unfit for Command: Swift Boat Veterans Speak Out against John Kerry* (2004) a highly contested but ultimately best-selling book on 2004 Democratic presidential nominee John Kerry, turned his sights on Obama, where they stayed for more than a decade. In *The Obama Nation: Leftist Politics and the Cult of Personality*, Corsi concluded, "Obama and his supporters may think it is not important to wear a flag lapel pin or to hold his right hand over his heart while the national anthem is played, but try explaining that to veterans and thousands of American families who have lost loved ones in this country's foreign wars, as well as those currently serving in the military and their families."[17] In subsequent books Corsi's critiques and accusations would intensify.

PROJECTING PATRIOTISM

That so many voters would uncritically accept such extreme accusations about "THEN" Senator Obama posted a problem for those who were tasked by his campaign to get him elected. Barack Obama recalls his concerns:

Soon enough, conservative talking heads were hammering on the purported meaning of my bare lapel. Obama hates the flag, Obama disrespects our troops. Months later they were still making an issue of it, which began to piss me off. Just why was it, I wanted to ask, that only my pin habits, and not those of any previous presidential candidates had suddenly attracted so much attention? Not surprisingly [Robert] Gibbs discouraged me from any public venting.

"Why give them the satisfaction?" he counseled. "You're winning."[18]

With no end in sight to the rumors and legends, Gibbs and Obama's other campaign staff did finally concede that it was not good for the candidate to allow blatantly false rumors to circulate. They titled a section of Obama's website "Fight the Smears" and offered clarifications or rebuttals of those texts that came to their attention. This effort will be scrutinized more in chapter 4 but at this juncture it should be noted that this was a reactionary step on the part of the campaign, and it neglected the reality that a person would only take this proactive step if they were already harboring skepticism about an account. The voter already convinced that Barack Obama wouldn't wear a flag pin would be unlikely to go to his campaign website for the answers. Clearly anti-Obama critics had their minds made up.

In spite of all of these accusations, Barack Obama was elected to the presidency on November 4, 2008. To his supporters, it was a great day. To his critics, it was a profound political and even cultural setback. President-elect Obama and his staff understood that his election in and of itself would not obliterate the notion that he was not a patriot. They knew that he would be watched with far more suspicion than prior presidents.

Even after all of the votes were counted, and his election was confirmed once and for all, their work was not over. They embarked on a second campaign, this one designed to reinforce his "Americanness" and to convey the image of a leader whose love for America was indisputable.

One of the more obvious steps they took was to ensure that there would be no future opportunities for him to be seen without a pin, mute during the anthem, or not pledging allegiance. They also developed a strategy that can be classified as the "contradict with expressions of respect" approach. A clear example of this strategy can be seen when you scrutinize the choices made for Obama's first inauguration.

Even before January 20, 2009, the choreography of the first black president's inauguration received a great deal of visibility.[19] On December 17,
2008, the Joint Congressional Committee on Inaugural Ceremonies announced that Pastor Rick Warren of the Saddleback Church in Orange
County, California, would deliver the invocation. Obama's more liberal supporters decried Warren's anti–gay marriage statements and his association
with conservative evangelicals. Petition drives to demand that Obama re-
scind the invitation were initiated. Many people who had given time and
money to the Obama campaign saw the selection of Warren as a betrayal.
I believe that Warren's selection reflected the campaign's desire to mitigate
the number of people who would embrace the Obama-as-Muslim beliefs.
If the pro-life Warren could be persuaded to participate in the inauguration, to literally give it a Christian blessing, then maybe the message that
Obama is Muslim would have less traction.

About six days after the announcement of Warren as invocation speaker,
the committee announced that Michelle Obama would hold Abraham
Lincoln's Bible as her husband took the oath of office. Virtually every
major media outlet from the networks to the cable news shows, to the
blogosphere, reported on the fact that the Library of Congress was hon-
oring Obama's request to use the same Bible used by Lincoln. Although
George H. W. Bush did as several other presidents have done and used
the Bible used by George Washington, most other presidents such as
George W. Bush, Bill Clinton, and Jimmy Carter, used a Bible with sen-
timental meaning to their own families. The use of such personally significant Bibles was not normally considered newsworthy. However, given
the lingering association of Obama with the Muslim faith, had he "just"
used a family Bible, those members of the public who associate him with
his father's heritage would have had fodder to condemn him. The persistent attention to Lincoln's Bible deflected speculations that the volume he
swore upon was a copy of the Koran.

As is always the case with first ladies, Michelle Obama's inauguration
wardrobe received extensive media attention, and the president's apparel
was little more than a sidebar. But it is worth noting that President Obama
wore flag pins both on his overcoat as seen in the inauguration ceremony
and on his suit jacket as seen on inaugural luncheon photos. He wore one
on his tuxedo at the inauguration balls as well.

Celebrating party over country, John McCain did not wear a flag pin, he wore a pin associated with the Republican party on his overcoat. The inauguration ended with another hard-core Christian hero, albeit a man much more associated with liberal Christian teachings, the civil rights movement hero Joseph Lowery. When the national anthem was performed at the end of the ceremony, President Obama and First Lady Michelle Obama were clearly moving their mouths when the United States Navy Band "Sea Chanters" sang the anthem. In virtually all of the ceremonial—and some might argue superficial—components (decorations, wardrobe, music, the Bible choices, prayers) of the inauguration, the message that Barack Obama was a patriotic Christian was persistently reinforced. While modern presidential inaugurations are replete with signs of all things American, the Obama inaugurations were saturated with material and symbolic totems of patriotism.

FROM THE OVAL OFFICE AND AIR FORCE ONE: UNIFORM DISTASTE

With the pomp and circumstance of the inauguration behind him, Barack Obama commenced the real and honorific work of being president of the United States on January 21, 2009. All of the trappings of the presidency were bestowed upon him. His address was 1600 Pennsylvania Avenue. His desk was in the Oval Office. He traveled in "the Beast," accompanied by a presidential motorcade, Air Force One or Marine One. When he was in attendance at ceremonial events, "Hail to the Chief" was played. Members of the armed forces saluted him. Between January of 2009 and January of 2017, the labels "leader of the free world" and "commander in chief" could only refer to Barack Obama. Any list of presidents of the United States identifies his name as the forty-fourth president and, although Donald Trump violated custom by refusing to hang his official portrait in the White House, that insult has been rectified.

But the allegations that President Obama was insufficiently patriotic persisted through both of his terms in office and beyond. Some new texts surfaced and some of the classics were updated to better fit his prerogatives as a sitting president. The underlying assumption of many of these recycled texts is that President Obama is a cunning trickster who can make it appear as though he's genuinely patriotic but is always able to signal his true anti-American sentiments to insiders who know the signals. Much of the folk speculation focused on his alleged indifference, or even hostility, to the ceremonial duties of the role of "commander in chief." According to the rumors and legends in this category, President Obama has complete disdain for the whole lifecycle of Americans in uniform. There are narratives that show him to be contemptuous of scouts (youth), active military members (middle age), veterans (elderly), and even deceased veterans.

Not long after his election, texts began to circulate claiming that he was rejecting the duties, embraced by other presidents, connected with assuming symbolic leadership of the Boy Scouts of America (BSA). Folklorist Jay Mechling, author of *On My Honor: Boy Scouts and the Making of American Youth*, began to see the posts reiterating this allegation on a troop list. The one Mechling shared with me, which differs slightly from the one version chronicled on the Snopes website, is complete with a title:

Obama Snubs Boy Scouts of America

This guy is such a scumbag. It is with tremendous sadness that I send this to my friends, unfortunately this information goes a long, long way to confirm the worst possible motives behind the man who fooled so many gullible Americans into voting for him.

The story you heard yesterday about President Obama refusing to sign Eagle Scout Awards is true.

He won't sign life saving awards either.

Every President since 1912 has been the honorary President of the Boy Scouts of America.

President Obama refused that honor.

I heard Beauregard on the radio this AM. I don't think the CEO of the Boy Scouts would lie.

Did you hear anything about the Boy Scouts 100th Anniversary? Why did the press ignore it? Let's see, they promote honor, integrity, putting others first, love of country and of course they believe in God.

Not much press coverage of this story, the first president in 100 years to insult his finest citizens, Eagle Scouts.

John Beaurguard, CEO of the South Texas Council of the Boy Scouts of America joins us just after 7 am. David Haynie has two sons who have achieved the rank of Eagle Scout. Dave Hiser's son is working on his Eagle Scout award now.

This is the E-mail Linda Thacker, sent to Glen Beck and I forwarded it to Glenn's producer Adam.

Dear Mr. Beck,

On March 24, 2009 I had the honor of attending my Grandson, David Osborne's Eagle Scout Court of Honor. I imagine you have attended these wonderful ceremonies. I am confident that you are very knowledgeable about what it means to have earned the status of Eagle Scout. Our entire family is so very excited and at the Court of Honor we were all just beaming as our wonderful young man was honored for his achievements. After the court was closed David's leaders pulled him aside and explained to him that they regretted t[o] have to explain it to him, as sad as it is, that his certificate was different from others they had presented because his certificate did not have the signature of the President of the United States. They explained that Obama does not support the Boy Scouts of America and therefor does not respect and serve on their Eagle Certificates. To my knowledge Congress chartered BSA in 1916 part of which the President of the United States is the Honorary President of The Boy Scouts of America and President Obama is the first sitting president to personally refuse to sign these certificates. I belief if the country were to be educated on national television of what the Boy Scouts of America stands for they would join those of us who already know, and would be as outraged as we are!

Also your good friend Jim Lago [w]as also in attendance at this Eagle Court of Honor. I had the privilege of speaking with him this morning on his radio talk show here in Corpus Christie and shared with him this same information. He was equally alarmed to say the least.

This information should ignite in every parent the urgency to instill the great values held by the Boy Scouts of America in their young men for the cause of maintaining this great nation. We must stand united. With appreciation, Linda[20]

An Eagle Scout himself and a lifelong supporter of scouting, Mechling recognized the multitude of contemporary legend attributes, everything from authorial indignation to celebrity substantiation as well as several others, and referred his fellow scouting enthusiasts to the Snopes website where they could read the rather innocent explanation for the absence of Obama's signature on some certificates. In 2010, the BSA had run out of certificates carrying George W. Bush's signature before ones carrying Barack Obama's name could be generated. Therefore some young men who had advanced to the rank of Eagle during that part of 2010 received unsigned certificates. Once the Obama-signed certificates were available, those in possession of an unsigned one could exchange it. Thus, there is a kernel of truth to the story: some Scouts did receive unsigned certificates. However as the lengthy missive received by Mechling indicates, some members of the scouting community did not assume that this was a transition issue. Instead, the kernel of truth—unsigned certificates—was embellished with a tale of an anti-scouting president.[21]

Following the "contradict with expressions of respect" strategy established during the campaign and implemented during the inauguration day events, President Obama took great care to periodically welcome scouts into the White House and bestow congratulatory letters as the organization hit significant milestones such as celebrating its one-hundredth birthday. Once the Obama-signed certificates were available and routinely distributed to freshly minted Eagle Scouts, the legend did begin to subside. It did resurface from time to time through Obama's first term in office, but by his second term, when his signature was routinely affixed to the certificates, fewer members of the scouting community were familiar with the legend.

As president and commander in chief, Barack Obama was often in the presence of current members of the armed forces. According to the updated version of "The missing flag pin," he had a low tolerance for young Americans in uniform. One narrative that received quite a bit of play starting in 2012 demonstrates how someone truly motivated can *look* patriotic while truly harboring anti-American sentiments. In the Snopes version:

> A few weeks ago a young female Marine Staff Sergeant (one of very few chosen for this post) was serving with HMX-1, the Presidential Helicopter Squadron. She had just finished her tour as a Drill Instructor and is/was obviously a squared away Marine that was on a fast track and who planned on making the Marine Corps her career. I am assuming that she excelled on the Drill Field which landed her the "choice" assignment with HMX-1.
>
> A few weeks ago she was assigned to the flight crew and after giving our illustrious President her best "Main Gater" hand salute, she respectfully advised the President that the American flag pin on his lapel was upside down, you got to remember that this young lady has been around for a while and had just finished her tour as a Drill Instructor, I have no doubt that she advised him in the proper way. . . . do you?? Anyway, President Obama relieved her on the spot. Apparently he doesn't like being told that he doing something wrong, especially by lowly military personnel. . . . WTF That asshole

just ruined a young lady's career when all she was trying to do was prevent him from being embarrassed. . . . what a gem. This information comes from a very, very reliable source who has the "inside" scoop on the Marine Detatchment at HMX-1. Is he really the best man for "Commander-in Chief"????? What a joke. I am sure other Marines will be "lining up" for that assignment now.

Note: He was put to task for noting having an American flag on his lapel so now he displays it upside down to show his Muslim Brotherhood and Muslim friends that he is anti-American.[22]

The authenticity websites agree that no such incident occurred. The text contains several familiar attributes of a contemporary legend. The narrator cites a FOAF or friend of a friend in the form of a "very, very reliable source." It is characterized by extensive authorial indignation. President Obama is thoroughly demonized as he sacks the young female marine who is clearly on a fast track for military honors. Since the narrator is putting his complete faith in the reliable source, he concludes that the unnamed marine approaches the president in an un-antagonistic or "proper" way, and then he inserts the rhetorical "do you?" wanting his audience to concede this point as well. The narrator puts himself in a privileged position; he is smart enough to see what the president is attempting to hide from all. The unnamed fired female marine joins slighted young Eagle Scout David Osborne as an American committed to the American way, but felled by the unpatriotic president.

Just as was the case in "I'd Like to Teach the World to Sing," there's a final punch in which it is clear that the firing of the marine provides the narrator with a rationale to draw attention to the president's allegiance to Muslim beliefs. To make the narrative sound more erudite, he frames this accusation as a "Note," which serves as an informal scholarly citation of sorts.

President Obama's attendance or absence from certain ceremonial events was the subject of much scrutiny and speculation. Often these texts possess a kernel of truth, but omit key historical data, usually related to the practices of past presidents. In 2010, a rumor circulated alleging that President Obama was the first president to forgo laying a wreath at Arlington National Ceremony on Memorial Day. For many who heard this text, it was further evidence of his disdain for men and women in uniform, and was particularly troubling in its purported disregard for those who died serving the country. It is true that the president opted to go to his home in Chicago for that Memorial Day, but while there, he participated in a ceremony at a military cemetery. More importantly, the motif in the rumor that alleges that no other president had stayed away from Arlington was not true. Indeed, as the careful research on the Snopes website indicates, Bill Clinton is the only president to have attended Arlington every year of his presidency.[23] Throughout Obama's two terms in office, there were always those who found fault with where he was or wasn't. In the last year of his presidency, he was criticized for not attending the funerals of Supreme Court Justice Antonin Scalia and former First Lady Nancy Reagan. But as was the case with the laying of the wreath at Arlington, he was held to a standard not imposed upon his predecessors. Sitting presidents do not routinely attend the funerals of either Supreme Court justices or former First Ladies.

Given the number of ceremonial occasions in the life of a president, it would be very difficult for someone to avoid singing the national anthem or pledging allegiance to the flag. But the efforts to condemn him on these grounds didn't evaporate after his election. Instead of maintaining that he refused outright, the new accusations are that he found a way to distort the pledge, or that he just didn't know the proper pledge protocol. FactCheck.org, an arm of the Annenberg Public Policy Center, was the recipient of numerous emails requesting confirmation of the president's behavior. Well after Obama's first term was underway, reporter Jess Henig noted, "The rumor that President Barack Obama refuses or doesn't know how to say the pledge of allegiance just won't die. Since early in his presidential candidacy we have been getting emails with photos that purport to show Obama failing to properly salute the flag during the pledge of allegiance or the national anthem. The photos have been reliably real, but taken out of context. The most recent example, for instance, included a genuine photo of Obama standing with hands folded while everyone else saluted or put their hands over their hearts—but that was because "Hail to the Chief" was playing.[24]

Henig continues to document a much-forwarded digitally altered picture of the president and the First Lady with their hands over their hearts. The problem, according to critics, is that they have their left hands, not their right hands over their hearts, as would be appropriate for the pledge. The evidence is that their wedding rings are conspicuous on their left hands. FactCheck.org includes the accompanying email, which complains: "Really! A U.S. President and his wife who do not even know how to stand for the Pledge of Allegiance. This is embarrassing! Don't bother to see if the photo is printed backwards. Just look at the suit buttons and their ring fingers. Perhaps when you never recite the Pledge of Allegiance, you don't know what to do."[25]

Whereas it might have been expected that the accusations that Barack Obama wouldn't fly in an airplane containing an image of an American flag would have died after he was elected and given access to Air Force One, that wasn't the case. Given that Air Force One is a military airplane, it would follow that there's not much an individual president could do to alter its external façade. Nonetheless, as his campaign for reelection in 2012 began to get off the ground, rumors began to circulate that he had found a way to remove the American flag from Air Force One in favor of his preferred campaign logo:

HOW DOES ANYONE GET AWAY WITH THIS? SAD.

Obama removes American Flag from his Plane
   He has turned Air Force One into a campaign slogan carrier . . . not only the Obama Campaign logo on the tail, it bears his Campaign slogan. I do believe in most States there are laws against something so blatantly an abuse of power, using public funds for campaigning. Atop this personalization of Air Force One," Obama has logged more miles than any previous President. We have a triple A president Audacity, Abuse and Arrogance. . . . He should pay for the cost of repainting/restoring the craft. . . . this guy has to go.[26]

The de-flagging of Air Force One texts circulated at the same time that President Obama was running for his second term in office. During the 2012 election cycle, he was both a sitting president and a candidate for the presidency. His critics are making the case that he abused presidential privileges by converting, at the taxpayer's expense, the look of the presidential aircraft, probably one of the most recognizable airplanes in the world. The picture circulated with these texts was of his 2008 campaign plane, not Air Force One.

Reelected in 2012, Obama had Air Force One at his disposal for another four years. The patriotism rumors did not subside. Even though he was always pinned, always sang the anthem, and invested time in interactions with Boy Scouts as well as members of the armed forces, he was still tinged as un-American in the minds of many on the far right. In 2015, a new rumor emerged alleging that while he had ordered flags to be flown at half-mast for pop singer Whitney Houston, he had not done so for decorated Navy SEAL Chris Kyle. As articulated in a tweet, "If you fly flags at half mast for a crack smoking drug addict (Whitney Houston) but not an American hero (Chris Kyle)."[27] Two years later the same rumor surfaced alleging that he had not ordered the flags to be flown at half-mast following the death of former First Lady Nancy Reagan, in spite of having done so for Houston. According to a tweet, "So our president lowers the U.S. flag for Whitney Houston but not Nancy Reagan? Drug Overdose vs First Lady."[28] As the fact-checking sites quickly determined, Republican New Jersey governor Chris Christie ordered the flags lowered in that state alone (Houston's home state) and there was no national recognition of her death ordered by Obama.

The picture that accompanied many of these rumors contrasts Houston, who struggled with substance abuse for much of her adult life, at one of her worst moments with a picture of Chris Kyle and a summary of his commendable military accomplishments. This summary does not contain Kyle's discredited claim that following Hurricane Katrina he traveled to New Orleans and found a good position from which he could use his skills as a sniper to shoot looters. He claimed to have killed thirty people, but no evidence was ever uncovered.[29] To those who shared the rumors and the picture, Barack Obama was perceived as inappropriately loyal to another drug-abusing black person (other rumors allege Obama never abandoned his indulgence in illicit drugs) and disdainful of a white male, who, as a trained and capable sharp-shooter, had killed for America.

FLAGGED DOWN

If Barack Obama's problems with the official flag of the United States weren't bad enough, he was eventually confronted by problems generated by his very real comments on the Confederate flag. He stayed away from the controversies over the Dixie flag for most of his presidency. Only after the horrific murder of nine African Americans in a South Carolina church by an avowed white supremacist—an incident that will be discussed later in this book—did he come down on the side of those who wanted the flag retired once and for all. Although his comments at a funeral for a victim of the shooting were met with applause, he was greeted by a band of Confederate flag–waving protestors when he traveled to Oklahoma the following month. Asked about their protest, the president opined that the Confederate flag belonged in a museum. In the months and years ahead, the Confederate flag would become even more prominent, as it was waved by those who claimed themselves to be American patriots.

Barack Obama and the voters who put him in office were operating with one set of assumptions about what can be construed as "patriotic" behavior, but by now it should be clear that an alternative one was taking hold with a growing segment of the population. In fact, even before September 11, 2001, thinkers on the far right had begun to use "patriot" as a label for citizens dismayed by what they perceived as outsized governmental services and unconstitutional interventions into their everyday lives. Usually passionate about Second Amendment rights, pro-life positions, and efforts to minimize taxation obligations, those folks connected these tenets with core American values. Almost exclusively Christian—often the most fundamentalists swaths of the Christian church—they often express anti-Muslim and anti-Semitic sentiments. The symbols of patriotism were very much in evidence as they moved forward. Following Obama's 2008 election the TEA (Taxed Enough Already) Party formed with a mission centered on cutting taxes. An affiliated organization, Tea Party *Patriots* set its sights on health care, in particular on undermining the Affordable Care Act, which they derisively called Obamacare. In *Prophets and Patriots, Faith in Democracy across the Political Divide*, Ruth Braunstein traces their mobilization to, "the wake of President Barack Obama's election and debates about 'Obamacare,' a policy they felt represented everything wrong with American politics today."[30] John McCain's running mate, Sarah Palin dedicated her 2009 best-selling memoir to "all *Patriots* (emphasis added) who share my love of the United States of America and particularly to our women and men in uniform, past and present, God bless the fight for freedom."[31] President Donald Trump used the word *patriot* to describe those he encouraged to come to Washington on January 6, 2021, and as they stormed the Capitol, they could be heard shouting, "We need more patriots in here." In discussions about whether or not Trump and his supporters should leave the Republican Party and form a third party, the label "Patriot" is often identified as the likely name for the new political party.

It seems reasonable to think of the initial "he won't wear a flag pin" crowd as the eventual cohort of voters who responded favorably to Trump's Make America Great Again mantra. Barack Obama's strategy of contradicting with expressions of respect may have worked with some middle-of-the-road voters, but for those who viewed Chris Kyle (someone who boasted about illegally shooting "looters") as the manifestation of an American patriot, the steps taken by Obama would never suffice. An erudite, dark-complected man with a Muslim-sounding name who had opposed the war in Iraq could never be considered a patriot and didn't belong in the White House. From the earliest days of his campaign to his last days in office, Barack Obama was forced to wage an identity war that had not been required of any previous president. And as the following chapters will confirm, whether or not he would wear a flag pin was the least of it.

2 Articles of Faith

According to *The Audacity of Hope*, Barack Obama and his advisors knew from the earliest days of his political career that voters' misapprehensions about his ethnic identity and religion could be a significant distraction and an impediment as he pursued higher offices. In the very first pages, he describes a late September 2001 lunch meeting with a media consultant who used a front-page newspaper article on Osama bin Laden to confront the proverbial elephant in the restaurant—one that would loom over any campaign in which the name Barack Obama would be on the ballot. Obama recalls the consultant saying, "Really bad luck. You can't change your name, of course. Voters are suspicious of that kind of thing." Summarizing his response, Obama noted, "I suspected he was right, and the realization ate away at me."[1]

Nonetheless, the ambitious young man decided to move forward and ran for reelection to the Illinois state legislature. Even though he had been pummeled in a 2000 run for the US House of Representatives, he opted to pursue a Senate seat in 2004. Thanks to an unlikely cluster of problems for his opponents and his own good fortune with the Democratic National Convention speech, he triumphed in that election. As a Senator from Illinois, he was in a much better position to contemplate a much-speculated-about White House run. In order to inject some financial resources into his household and further establish his identity, he penned his second book, *The Audacity of Hope: Thoughts on Reclaiming the American Dream*. Describing his motives, he said, "I am new enough on the national political scene that I serve as a blank screen on which people of vastly different political stripes project their own views."[2] Obama's heartfelt and best-selling book succeeded in making a new narrative of resilience and hope indelible in the minds of readers, permanently inking over the blank screen in a way that could blot out others' preconceived notions. Clearly he wanted to craft a story that would offset the concerns some voters might have about checking the box next to the name Barack Obama.

Although he engages religious topics elsewhere in *Audacity*, he titles the fifth chapter "Faith," and he has much to accomplish in these thirty-odd pages. Given how significant the rumors about his faith would become, it is worth exploring his own words in depth. He starts by showcasing encounters he has already had with the religious right—in particular, pro-life activists—and makes sure the reader knows that he respects those activists' point of view in spite of his holding a different one. When protestors show up at a campaign rally, he eschews his campaign director's advice to avoid a confrontation by entering through the back door. Instead, he approaches the men and women carrying "handmade signs or banners held before them like shields" and tries to convince them to come inside.[3] He also modifies his campaign website's language about his pro-choice position after agreeing with a pro-life doctor's assessment that he has not shown himself to be "fair-minded."

From here, he delves into his own spiritual background with the focus on his white mother, Ann Dunham, and her side of the family. Living with his maternal grandparents in Hawaii for much of his childhood, he notes that "religious faith never took root in their hearts."[4] Their headstrong daughter was similarly disinclined, although her anthropological disposition was evident in her attitude:

> For my mother, organized religion too often dressed up closed-mindedness in the garb of piety, cruelty and oppression in the cloak of righteousness. This isn't to say that she provided me with no religious instruction. In her mind, a working knowledge of the world's great religions was a necessary

part of any well-rounded education. In our household the Bible, the Koran, and the Bhagavad Gita sat on the shelf alongside books of Greek and Norse and African mythology. On Easter or Christmas Day my mother might drag me to church, just as she dragged me to the Buddhist temple, the Chinese New Year celebration, the Shinto Shrine, and ancient Hawaiian burial sites.[5]

Perhaps because he had spent more time talking about his father and stepfather in his first book, *Dreams from My Father*, he devotes little ink to them in *Audacity*. Barack Obama Sr., from whom his mother divorced when he was two, gets exactly one sentence, in which Obama Jr. acknowledges: "Although my father had been raised a Muslim, by the time he met my mother he was a confirmed atheist, thinking religion to be so much mumbo-jumbo of witch doctors that he had witnessed in the Kenyan villages of his youth."[6]

His stepfather, with whom he had a five-year relationship, rates about a paragraph. Like the Dunhams and Obama Sr., Lolo Soetoro was purportedly dismissive of organized religion. He was "a man who had grown up in a country that easily blended its Islamic faith with remnants of Hinduism, Buddhism, and ancient animist traditions. During the five years I would live with my stepfather in Indonesia, I was sent first to a neighborhood Catholic school and then to a predominantly Muslim school; in both cases, my mother was less concerned with me learning the catechism or puzzling out the meaning of the muezzin's evening call to prayer than she was with whether I was properly learning my multiplication tables."[7]

The inconvenient fathers dispatched in less than half a page, Obama returns to his benevolent but skeptical mother and takes pains to depict her as an admirable anchor of old-fashioned Christian values: "For all her professed secularism, my mother was in many ways the most spiritually awakened person that I've ever known. She had an unswerving instinct for kindness, charity and love, and spent much of her life acting on that instinct, sometimes to her detriment. Without the help of religious texts or outside authorities, she worked mightily to instill in me the values that many Americans learn in Sunday school: honesty, empathy, discipline, delayed gratification, and hard work."[8] Obama followed his maternal family's minimalist religious philosophy through his educational years and into young adulthood.

But, as he documented in *Dreams*, his attraction to Michelle Robinson and affection for her much more traditional African American Chicago family led him to the sanctuary of Trinity United Church of Christ. His conversion story is much more cerebral than has become commonplace in narratives about stray black men finding their way into the black church. Barack Obama is not mesmerized by a soulful, stomping gospel choir or struck by the lightning metaphors of a charismatic colorfully robed preacher. Sounding like a religious studies scholar with just a hint of a black pastoral cadence, Obama proclaims:

> In the black community the lines between sinner and saved were more fluid; the sins of those who came to church were not so different from the sins of those who didn't, and so were as likely to be talked about with humor as with condemnation. You needed to come to church precisely because you were of this world, not apart from it; rich, poor, sinner, saved, you needed to embrace Christ precisely because you had sins to wash away—because you were human and needed an ally in your difficult journey, to make the peaks and valleys smooth and to render all those crooked paths straight.[9]

Obama's professorial stance continues as he leads his readers through a cogent and informed Constitutional history lesson on the separation of church and state. He moves nonchalantly through the tensions between Benjamin Franklin and Thomas Jefferson, who were on the side of religious freedoms, versus Patrick Henry and John Adams, who were more willing to privilege Christianity in the founding documents. He also speaks with casual authority about the different positions established by the "dominant Anglican Church in the South and the Congregationalist orders of the North."[10] Not only does he establish a command of political history, he shows he knows his Bible as well by raising the contradictions inherent in comparisons of the messages embedded in Leviticus, Deuteronomy, and the Sermon on the Mount.[11] Discussing this section of the autobiography in *Yes We Can: Barack Obama's Proverbial Rhetoric*, one of the first full-length folkloristic analyses of the words and life of Barack Obama, proverb scholar Wolfgang Mieder notes, "There is no doubt that Obama is well-versed in religious rhetoric. . . . Is this mere mentioning of the 'Sermon on the Mount' (Matthew, chapters 5–7) enough information to understand what Obama is striving at? Simple allusions are not always effective, and Obama must be careful that he will not be one of those politicians, who in his own chastising words, 'sprinkles in a few biblical phrases to spice up a dry policy speech.'"[12] To be sure, these are the kinds of studied insights that would sway his more cerebral readers, although more fundamentalist Christians might find it off-putting and unnecessarily pedantic.

As the chapter winds down, Obama shifts from the voice of a professor to the perspective of a son and father. He places himself in church, but not the Trinity United Church of Christ; rather, it is the iconic Sixteenth Street Baptist Church, site of a horrific Sunday School bombing in 1963. His visit includes a moment in which "the pastor, the deacons, and I said a prayer in the sanctuary."[13] When he returns to his Chicago home after his emotional day in Birmingham, he finds himself thinking of his late mother's last days: "Although she fought valiantly, endured the pain and chemotherapy with grace and good humor to the very end, more than once I saw fear flash across her eyes."[14] Still preoccupied by thoughts of the parents of the four girls in Birmingham, he concludes the chapter with its most wistful words: "I knew what I hoped for—that my mother was together in some way with the four little girls, capable in some fashion of embracing them, of finding joy in their spirits. I know that in tucking in my daughters that night, I grasped a little bit of heaven."[15]

Barack Obama was not the first, and will be far from the last, presidential contender to publish an autobiographical book toward the beginning of his campaign in order to woo voters. But few such books have been more successful than *The Audacity of Hope*. Obviously, the book in some sense *worked*. Just as the book sold extremely well, so too did candidate Obama, who enjoyed several state party primary wins in the same weeks and months when his book was outselling a new release by perennial favorite John Grisham. And, after all, Obama did get elected to the presidency.

HE'S AN ARAB, 2008

However, Obama and his unnamed political advisor from 2001 were right to be worried about the ability of many American voters to accept his assertions of Christianity. By scrutinizing several aspects of the media coverage of the death of Obama's 2008 Republican opponent, this point can be clearly made.

During the days following the death of Senator John McCain on August 25, 2018, most television networks, online news sites, and print news outlets relied upon a relatively limited range of images and anecdotes as they eulogized the six-term Republican senator from Arizona. As McCain's health had long been deteriorating, the press had ample opportunity to prepare journalistic obituaries for a protracted period of public mourning. Given his status as a long-term and often contrarian senator—he embraced the title "maverick"—his party's nominee for the White House, and arguably the most well-known prisoner of war of the Vietnam era, there was no shortage of angles that could be covered. With few exceptions, stories were illustrated by grainy images of the young and gaunt prisoner of war along with formal pictures of the young McCain in his crisp, white, Navy uniform, and the more mature McCain in a tidy conservative suit befitting his status as a career politician. If a woman was in the picture, it was one of four women: his wife, Cindy; his celebrity daughter, Meghan; his 2008 running mate and former Alaska governor, Sarah Palin; or Gayle Quinnell. Although they are known to have only met one time, John McCain's encounter on October 10, 2008, with seventy-five-year-old Gayle Quinnell at a Minnesota campaign rally has come to symbolize McCain's political values, and, more significantly to this book, it stands as a signature moment in any time line documenting the rumors and legends about Barack Obama's faith.

In an exchange that lasted just over a minute, Quinnell uttered one of the most significant articulations of the many rumors that belong to what I call the "he's not the Christian he says he is" category. Certainly, other individuals had been penning similar remarks for years. But with cameras rolling, Quinnell passionately shared her convictions with the man who had the most to gain from a public distaste for Obama. Wearing a bright red McCain/Palin T-shirt, the blond-haired Quinnell told McCain that she could not "trust Obama," that she "had read about him" and that "he was an Arab."[16] Initially, Senator McCain seems to be in agreement with her as he nods his head while she is verbalizing her profound mistrust. But when she links her aversion to a mistaken understanding of his ethnic and religious identity, McCain swiftly takes the microphone from her and says, "No, ma'am. [Mr. Obama is] a decent family man, citizen, that I just happen to have disagreements with on fundamental issues."[17]

When reporters caught up to Quinnell—who volunteered at the McCain Headquarters in Burnsville, Minnesota—she continued to insist that the local library had a cache of materials that confirmed that Obama was an Arab and that she would willingly share this documentation with the reporters. It becomes clear during the exchange that Quinnell lacked an understanding of basic ethnic, religious, and geographic identity markers. She refers to Obama as an "Arab," but almost certainly means that she thinks he's a practicing Muslim, particularly when a reporter attempted to clarify the distinction between the two. To Quinnell, Barack Obama Sr.'s identity as a Muslim was sufficient grounds to dismiss his son's professions of Christianity. He's "got Muslim in him," she assured the reporters.[18]

As a multitude of social media posts note, Quinnell's assertion that "he's an Arab," and the later self-correction in which she acknowledged that she probably meant to say "he's Muslim," neither of those identities, even if they were accurate, would bar him from the presidency of the United States. None of America's foundational documents, nor subsequent court cases, call for the disqualification of members of any faith or ethnicity from standing for election to any office in the United States. Although some Democrats and Republicans alike praised McCain for interrupting and contradicting Quinnell, other commentators have drawn attention to an anti-Arab slight in his correction. After she says he's an Arab, McCain takes the microphone and says "No, he's a good family man." This response can be interpreted as meaning that the categories of "Arab" and "good family man" are mutually exclusive, making McCain guilty of Arab bashing. Having reviewed the video multiple times and considered it within the larger context of McCain's parlance, I do not think we can conclude that John McCain didn't respect Arab men as loving fathers. Clearly flummoxed by Quinnell and needing to think on his feet, McCain reached for language that might soften Quinnell's stance without jeopardizing the loyalty she and other Republican supporters were offering to him.

The post-confrontation question-and-answer exchange is also valuable because it offers a glimpse into the dissemination patterns of rumors, legends, and conspiracy theories. The rumors alleging that Obama was not a Christian had been swirling in the background for a couple of years at this point. In the days following this incident they were at least temporarily in the foreground. In the exchange with reporters, Quinnell was asked for evidence that Obama was not a Christian. Quinnell refers to books, brochures, letters, and conversations with other McCain volunteers. She provides no actual titles or written documentation to the reporters, implying that she had already distributed all of her copies. She certainly makes no reference to having read any books actually written by Barack Obama himself. She states that she has sent four hundred letters to potential voters sharing information regarding Obama's real identity.

Neither McCain's denial nor the skepticism of the journalists sways her from her anti-Obama convictions. For Quinnell and likeminded voters, John McCain's refusal to embrace the rumor actually diminished esteem for the Republican candidate. Responding to a reporter's questions regarding why McCain, who was willing to criticize Senator Obama on any number of counts, would disavow this particular claim, a clearly frustrated Quinnell offered: "I don't think he wanted to cut him down so he just kind of brushed me off. Maybe they don't want to bring up that, I don't know why."[19] Thus, Quinnell placed more faith in the authors of the anti-Obama documents—whom she couldn't even name—than she did in the well-known and respected candidate for whom she had been volunteering. The Quinnell/McCain exchange is a striking example of the power of a rumor that reinforces a person's or community's worldview.

There are other examples of this in the realm of rumormongering that reinforce this feature of rumor dissemination. My personal favorite concerns a once-popular contemporary legend about the fashion designer Liz Claiborne. According to the story, Claiborne acknowledged during an episode of the *Oprah Winfrey Show* that she didn't like to see black women wearing her clothes, particularly her pants and skirts. When I was collecting versions of this contemporary legend in the early 1990s, I explained to someone absolutely convinced of its veracity that Oprah herself had confirmed to the press that not only had Liz Claiborne never said that on her show, Liz Claiborne had never even *been on* the *Oprah Winfrey Show*. My friend shook her head and said with dismay, "Well, I guess they got to Oprah; I just wish I could find my tape."[20] Just as McCain's aura was tarnished for his defense of Obama, so too did fans of Oprah dial back their affection for her rather than question their own assumptions.

David Benjamin, a blogger who later tried to determine what actual documents Quinnell had seen, theorizes that it was the well-circulated musings of Kenneth E. Lamb that must have come to her attention.[21] Cited by conservative pundits such as Rush Limbaugh, Monica Crowley, and Laura Ingraham, Lamb's blog entry on February 16, 2008 reads:

Mr. Obama is 50% Caucasian, that from his mother. What those who want Mr. Obama to write history by becoming "America's first African-American president" ignore is that his father was ethnically Arabic, with only 1 relative ethnically African Negro—a maternal great-grandparent (Sen. Obama's great-great grandparent, thus the 6.25 ethnic contribution to the senator's ethnic composition.).

That means that Mr. Obama is 50% Caucasian from his mother's side. He is 43.75% Arabic, and 6.25% African Negro from his father's side.[22]

As Benjamin points out, Lamb merely asserts this genealogically incoherent statement without offering any substantiation. To those predisposed to doubt any and all things Obama, the seemingly scientific references to "6.25 ethnic contribution," is the kind of embedded detail that sounds persuasive, leading to an uncritical acceptance of it.

Benjamin seems convinced that Quinnell's statements are tied solely to either direct exposure to Lamb's blog or to one or more of the conservative political pundits who cited it as evidence of Obama's duplicity. But to me it seems more likely that Quinnell, clearly distraught by the prospect of Obama moving into the White House, could have also been familiar with the many other contemporary rumors in circulation about his identity.

A September 2008 interview on ABC's *This Week* with George Stephanopoulos—one month before the campaign rally confrontation—seemed to forecast the McCain/Quinnell exchange. Stephanopoulos asked then senator Obama about his recent accusations that the McCain campaign was exploiting beliefs connecting him to the Muslim faith. At the end of the interview Obama says that "he [Senator McCain] hasn't suggested that I'm a Muslim, and I think that his campaign upper echelons haven't either. What I think is fair to say is that coming out of the Republican camp, there have been efforts to suggest that I'm not who I say I am when it comes to my faith, something which I find deeply offensive, and that has been going on for a pretty long time."[23]

Quinnell fits the profile of the rank-and-file members of the McCain "camp" who were sharing stories about Obama with one another. Given that one month later Quinnell would confirm to reporters that "all the people (McCain volunteers in Burnsville, Minnesota) agree with what I'm saying to you about Obama," it is easy to understand candidate Obama's frustration with his opponent's unwillingness to have more forcefully denounced those spreading the stories in the earliest days of the campaign.[24] At the relatively late date of October 10, 2008, Senator McCain and his campaign leadership had no reason to be surprised by Quinnell's declarations, Senator McCain himself was no stranger to the havoc that can be caused when unfounded rumors surface during a political campaign. In his 2000 bid for the Republican presidential nomination, his campaign had to grapple with rumors that his wife, Cindy, was a drug addict and that he had actually fathered their adopted daughter Bridget, whose mother was purportedly African American.[25]

Whereas the McCain/Quinnell exchange stands as a prominent and public verbal acknowledgment of the rumors about Obama's faith, the pre-election months of 2008 were also marked by an equally controversial visual articulation of the claims. On July 21, 2008, the tony *New Yorker* magazine's cover encapsulated several of the then-current rumors and legends about both Barack and Michelle Obama. Barack is depicted in sartorial splendor in full Muslim garb from the sandals on his feet to the Muslim prayer cap on his head. Michelle sports an Angela Davis style Afro and wears stylish fatigues, complete with an AK-47 strapped around her bodice. There's a picture of a Muslim cleric over the Oval Office fireplace and an American flag burning within it. Barack and Michelle are locked eye to eye and are making a fist-bump, which some viewers interpreted as part of an internal terrorist code. Titled "The Politics of Fear," cartoonist Barry Blitt artistically rendered the rumors that Barack was a Muslim, that Michelle was a militant black radical who had attended flag burnings, and that their ultimate joint aspiration was to radically reshape the United States.

A controversy over the cover began even before the magazine hit the newsstands. Editor David Remnick—who would go on to write one of the most compelling books about Barack Obama—explained why he gave a green-light to a cover that might well fuel anti-Obama sentiment.

> What I think it does is hold a mirror up to the prejudice and dark imaginings about Barack Obama's—both Obamas'—past, and their politics. . . . It combines a number of images that have been propagated, not by everyone on the right but by some, about Obama's supposed "lack of patriotism" or his "being soft on terrorism" or the idiotic notion that somehow Michelle Obama is the second coming of the Weathermen or most violent [of] Black

Panthers. That somehow all of this is going to come to the Oval Office. . . .
The fact is, it's *not* a satire about Obama—it's a satire about the distortions
and misconceptions and prejudices *about* Obama.[26]

Remnick's cerebral editorial explanation did not appease all of the critics who fretted that the *New Yorker* may have been over-endowing the
American reading public with more sensitivity to satire than it possessed.
After all, as outlined in the last chapter, there were voters who thought
Obama wanted to convert "I'd Like to Teach the World to Sing," into the
national anthem. To those voters who had been disseminating the rumors
about the first family, the cover of a highly respected magazine might well
serve as the ultimate confirmation of the derogatory blogposts, emails,
and newsletters they had been receiving. As journalist Paul Lewis pon-
dered: "By ridiculing these ideas about Obama, is the *New Yorker* helping
to peel away layers of conspiratorial mud? Or, in the subconscious minds
of the masses, will the image simply reinforce lingering fears about the
Democratic candidate?"[27]

HE'S NOT THE CHRISTIAN HE SAYS HE IS, 2004–2007

Just when did the "conspiratorial mud" start to form? The earliest known
comments date back to the weeks following Obama's speech at the Democratic Convention in 2004. Andy Martin, a conservative journalist with
questionable credentials, issued a press release claiming that Obama had
"misrepresent[ed] his own heritage" and announced that Obama was a
Muslim. When Barack Obama was "just" an Illinois-based politician, the
fledgling rumors received little attention beyond a group that might be
considered the fringe of the right-wing fringe.

But by January 2007, his name was on the list of possible candidates for
the 2008 Democratic ticket. Political junkies began to recognize the presence of American voters, even regular run-of-the-mill white American
voters, who would support the presidency of a man with the birth name of
Barack Hussein Obama. Conservative outlets realized they needed to find
fault with Obama. *Insight Magazine*, owned by the same company that
then owned News World Communications and the *Washington Times*,

indulged in standard dog whistle politics by asking, "Are the American people ready for an elected president who was educated in a Madrassa as a young boy and who has not been forthcoming about his Muslim heritage?"[28]

Shortly after the appearance of this article, emails began to circulate offering more, albeit erroneous, narrative cohesion to the allegations. The most frequently forwarded one starts with and repeats the query "Who is Barack Obama?" After falsely claiming that the Snopes website has verified the content, it goes on to take core elements of Obama's biography— no doubt extrapolated from *Dreams* and *Audacity*—and recasts them in ways many will consider negative. Statements related to his faith include:

> Barack Hussein Obama was born in Honolulu, Hawaii, to Barack Hussein Obama, Sr., a black MUSLIM from Nyangoma-Kogel, Kenya and Ann Dunham, a white ATHEIST from Wichita, Kansas.
>
> His mother then married Lolo Soetoro a RADICAL Muslim from Indonesia. He also spent two years in a Catholic school.
>
> Obama takes great care to conceal the fact that he is a Muslim.
>
> Lolo Soetoro, the second husband of Obama's mother, Ann Dunham introduced his stepson to Islam. Obama was enrolled in a Wahabi school in Jakarta.
>
> Wahabism is the RADICAL teaching that is followed by Muslim terrorists who are now waging Jihad against the western world. Since it is politically expedient to be a CHRISTIAN when seeking major public office in the United States, Barack Hussein Obama has joined the United Church of Christ in an attempt to downplay his Muslim background.
>
> ALSO, keep in mind that when he was sworn into office he DID NOT use the Holy Bible, but instead the Koran.
>
> Let us all remain alert concerning Obama's expected presidential candidacy. The Muslims have said they plan on destroying the US from the inside out, what better way to start than at the highest level—through the President of the United States, one of their own!!!![29]

"Who Is Barack Obama?" exhibits several of the characteristics of a rumor-saturated email. Although the overall tone is not conspicuously emotional, dog whistle words such as "MUSLIM," "ATHEIST," and "RADICAL" are capitalized and nonstandard punctuation occurs throughout.[30] Identifying him as a black Muslim with a Kenyan father, the speaker is indicating that he embodies all of the worst kind of blackness imaginable in a man. The final punch is an unambiguous warning that, should he be elected, Obama will be an instrument of a pernicious Muslim agenda to destroy the American way of life.

As the email gained traction, several mainstream news organizations fact-checked it; indeed it was one of the first of the anti-Obama rumors to be taken this seriously. Just as the author of "Who Is Barack Obama?" consulted the Obama autobiographies for his/her inventory of accusations, so too did the fact-checkers. They used his books, as well as other legitimate sources, for their research. "Who Is Barack Obama?" does contain some factual information. It starts out by claiming that he was "born in Honolulu, Hawaii." The fact that one of the first hefty anti-Obama missives acknowledges his Hawaiian birth is a reminder that the eventually notorious "birther" beliefs to be discussed in chapter 3 were not among the first to plague him. The email also says his legal name is Barack Hussein Obama. The Hussein middle name is repeated twice in the first sentence, indicating that he and the unnamed political consultant discussed in the introduction to *Audacity* were right to think that having names reminiscent of Middle Eastern enemies would be exploited.

Rather than analyze each individual erroneous element, I will focus on just one. The fourth item alleges that Lolo Soetoro, the second husband of Obama's mother Ann Dunham, introduced his stepson to Islam. Those familiar with *Dreams* or *Audacity* know that Obama acknowledged his mother's second marriage to Soetoro and that her second husband was born a Muslim. In *Dreams*, Obama describes his stepfather's faith: "Like many Indonesians, Lolo followed a brand of Islam that could make room for the remnants of more ancient animist and Hindu faiths. He explained that a man took on the powers of whatever he ate: One day soon, he promised, he would bring home a piece of tiger meat for us to share."[31] Obama goes on to describe having gone to an Indonesian school, but certainly never referring to it as a Wahabi (usually spelled Wahhabi) one.

CNN did the most extensive fact-checking on that element of "Who is Barack Obama?" by sending a reporter to Indonesia to track down the school the candidate had attended many decades before. Upon arriving at the school, senior CNN correspondent John Vause observed, "boys and girls dressed in neat school uniforms playing outside the school while the teachers were dressed in western style clothes." Well-versed in the ways of that part of the world, Vause further noted, "I came here to Barack Obama's elementary school in Jakarta looking for what some are calling an Islamic madrassa . . . like the ones that teach hate and violence in Pakistan and Afghanistan. . . . I've been to those madrassas in Pakistan. This school was nothing like that."[32] After reviewing the claims in the email and comparing notes with other journalists, FactCheck.org summarized their findings by confirming, "Subsequent news stories in *The Washington Post*, *The Los Angeles Times* and *The Chicago Tribune* found no merit in the madrassa claim."

Reporting by CNN and analyses by fact-checking organizations did not result in widespread public condemnation for this text, or, for that matter, any other texts about Obama. For one thing, other news outlets—some with clear political agendas such as Insight or Fox News—continued to insinuate a Muslim identity. Nonetheless, long before "fake news" was in the vernacular, verifiable information about a presidential candidate was being subjected to relentless and irresponsible scrutiny in the name of a political cause.

HE'S A RADICAL CHRISTIAN, 2007–2008

Rather than call attention to the rumors and attempt to debunk them, Obama continued to conduct himself in ways that subtly discredited the stories. Just as he had countered non-patriotic noise by presenting himself in patriotic settings, he initially reinforced his membership and loyalty to the Black Christian church and its pastor. By titling his book, *The Audacity of Hope*, he set himself up to have to explain repeatedly that his affection for the concept stemmed from one of his pastor's most moving sermons. Thus neither he nor his campaign issued statements disparaging journalist Andy Martin's claims that he was a Muslim in hiding, but rather made sure his allegiance to the Christian faith was always in evidence.

Obama's critics soon directed their attention to his church home, however, and incorporated it into the "he's not the Christian he says he is" category. In December of 2007, Snopes analyzed an email inquiry in which his Chicago church—Trinity Church of Christ—is identified as a racist institution. After claiming to have studied the church's website, the anonymous author takes a snippet from the website and offers his own interpretation of the church's politics and philosophy: "This congregation has a non-negotiable commitment to Africa. Nowhere is AMERICA even mentioned. Notice too, what color you will need to be if you should want to join Obama's church. . . . B-L-A-C-K!! Doesn't look like his choice of religion has improved much over his (former?) Muslim upbringing."[33]

Using a reference to Trinity's commitment to Africa, the author paints a threatening picture that suggests that no church or individual could be simultaneously supportive of both Africa and America and that white members would be rejected. And, of course, the Muslim reference is incorporated in a manner that suggests that Barack Obama had been a member of the Muslim faith but converted, or perhaps gave lip-service to converting in order to improve his electability. Once again, Obama is defined as a racial triple threat, a man who is black, African, and Muslim. The fact that his mother was white and he was often under the care of his white grandparents is ignored. The email ends with what for December 2007 would have been read as an ominous twist, "To think that Obama has even the slightest chance in the run for the presidency, is really scary."[34]

Although this rumor did not get quite as much traction as "Who Is Barack Obama?" it did signal the attention that Obama's chosen place of worship would receive. Several months after this email began to circulate, scrutiny of Trinity United Church of Christ intensified when news outlets reviewed sermons delivered by the charismatic Reverend Jeremiah Wright, the then spiritual leader of Trinity. Reverend Wright had befriended Obama during the latter's community organizing days and even officiated at his wedding to Michelle. The anonymous author of "Holy Trinity" makes much of the fact that "America" was not mentioned on the Trinity webpages; other critics might note that in his account of his faith, Obama never describes himself as "born again," a phrase that might well have resonated with many readers wanting to confirm that this presidential candidate was serious about the religion he came to as an adult.

As his candidacy became more and more of a certainty, journalists and Obama-doubters dug into his own statements about his faith and probed any available connections that could be made between him and religious practice. The Reverend Jeremiah Wright's oeuvre provided ample evidence that could be quoted or misquoted in ways that would damage Barack and Michelle Obama.

Reverend Wright's sermons do include comments such as, "America's chickens are coming home to roost," and "God damn America—that's in the Bible—for killing innocent people." In speeches and interviews following the initial reports on his sermons, Reverend Wright did make disparaging remarks about "them Jews." Obama critics needed only to excise the Reverend's most troubling comments and make the case that this young, black presidential hopeful had shown his true colors by aligning himself with a radical, unpatriotic pastor and a militant congregation.

Those observers whose first exposure to the discourse of many African American congregations were the sermons of Reverend Wright were quite dismayed by what they found. Black church leaders have long considered historic and current political affairs to be appropriate, and even necessary, topics for commentary from the pulpit. In his compelling *The Black Presidency: Barack Obama and the Politics of Race in America*, Michael Eric Dyson meticulously compares the sermons and speeches of Jeremiah Wright with those of Martin Luther King Jr. concluding: "Had You-Tube been in play when King walked the earth, he might well have been slammed as an anti-American racist who allowed politics to get the best of his religion, the same way many view Wright today."[35]

Initially, Obama defended Wright, but as more and more of his pastor's words became public, he was forced to disentangle himself and his family from the church where he and his wife had been married and where his daughters had been baptized. The Trinity incident served to further buttress the anti-Obama accusations being lobbed by those who didn't want him to get elected. The Obamas continued to stress their family's commitment to Christianity, but the Reverend Wright/Trinity incident proved a difficult one from which to recover.

The seeds of doubt regarding Obama's religious leanings persisted throughout the 2008 political primary season. Some cable television pundits and other critics of Hillary Clinton suggested that her campaign actually started and actively fueled the rumors. Evidence supporting her campaign as the actual architect or as knowingly weaponizing the Muslim lore is paper thin, although two of her relatively low-level campaign workers during the Iowa primary season did resign after they forwarded the "Who Is Barack Obama?" emails.

The Obama campaign was quiet on the subject, but the Obama headquarters in Iowa did keep a letter on file signed by five clergymen attesting to Obama's Christian faith. The rumor escalated during the period leading up to the South Carolina Democratic primary, one of the most charged contests of the entire primary season. The mainstream media picked it up and more and more polls included questions regarding Obama's faith. The numbers held steady: approximately 12 percent of those polled by Pew responded that they believed Obama to be a Muslim. The remaining voters did not assume that he was a Christian; a sizeable percentage (25%) indicated that they "didn't know."[36]

HE'S NOT CHRISTIAN, FIRST TERM, 2008–2012

Surrounded by multiple symbols of Christianity and taking the oath of office on Abraham Lincoln's Bible—his critics had claimed that he used the Koran when he took the oath for senator from Illinois—Barack Obama was inaugurated in January 2009. To his most strident opponents, the only thing worse than having Obama as the forty-fourth president in 2008 was the prospect of him being reelected in 2012. Presidential campaigns commence on inauguration day, and many of Obama's opponents were eager to make sure someone else's hands were on the Bible in January of 2013. As chapter 3 will point out, the birther texts began to outpace the Muslim ones following Obama's election. But the "Obama is not Christian" ones did maintain a consistent stride throughout his first term in office.

Five months in, rumors began to circulate that he had canceled the National Day of Prayer. According to FactCheck.org and Snopes, they were asked to establish the veracity of these claims for every year of Obama's two terms in office. A 2009 one read in part: "President Obama has decided that there will no longer be a National Day of Prayer held in May. He doesn't want to offend anyone. Where was his concern about offending Christians last January when he allowed the Muslims to hold a day of prayer on the Capitol Grounds. As an American Christian, I am offended. If you agree, copy and paste no matter what religion you are. This country was built on freedom. If he get's re-elected, 'it's all over but the crying.'"[37] As the fact-checkers took pains to establish, President Obama signed the proclamation declaring a national day of prayer for every year of his two terms in office. Unlike President George W. Bush, he did not host an annual public celebration in the White House, but Bush's protocol was different from that of earlier presidents.

It is of course puzzling to some observers that those who disseminated this statement anticipate agreement from readers "no matter what religion you are," and that after falsely accusing the president of canceling an observation that isn't even an officially recognized holiday, he proclaims that "this country was built on freedom." The persistence and popularity of this text is a reminder that individuals predisposed to believe the worst of President Obama could simultaneously accept without evidence that he had canceled prayer day, that it was an offense worth voting him out of office for, and that all of this reinforced the premise that America is a free country.

Several of the "not Christian" texts adhere to the hiding-in-plain-sight pattern common to many contemporary legends. The popular "Muslim prayer curtain in the Oval Office," which found its way to the fact-checkers by mid-2010 (and continued to be submitted through 2018) is accompanied by several pictures and reads: "For a long time, I have noticed that the décor at the White House has changed since BHO moved in. The Oval Office is now stripped of the traditional, red, white, and blue and replaced with middle eastern chairs, drapes, etc. And the thing that has bothered me the most is the bright yellow drape behind him every time he speaks from the white house. It's a Muslim prayer curtain with Arabic symbols on it and it has been there from the beginning."[38]

The picture is usually followed by images of other presidents, all standing in front of American flags. And just as pictures could easily be found that show other presidents in front of American flags, pictures can be found of them making official remarks without flags. And there are photos of recent presidents in front of these gold drapes, which predate the Obama presidency. As Snopes points out, there's really no such thing as a "Muslim prayer curtain," nor are there any "Arabic symbols" in view.

"Arabic symbols" and the ability to discern them is also evident in the accusations that Barack Obama's wedding band was inscribed with the phrase, "There is no God but Allah." The original source for this is World News Daily, a website that proudly proclaims its specialty is satire and doesn't disguise the illegitimacy of its content.[39] But just as some observers assumed the *New Yorker* was outing the Obamas as Muslims, so too did others conclude that the wedding band story was accurate. It quickly circulated, and as it was posted to social media outlets and emailed, it seemed to further evidence that a Muslim had been elected to the presidency.

But those who reveled in stirring up trouble about Barack Obama—be they satirists, alt-right conservatives, fundamentalists, or Russian bots— crafted more sinister images than those of a curtain or a wedding band. Again, using various software programs of the Photoshop ilk, much more could be done with actual images of Obama himself. A picture of him wearing traditional Kenyan garb from a 2006 visit to his ancestors was circulated as evidence of the "real" Muslim Barack Obama. His visage was also juxtaposed with those of men who were alleged to be his compatriots in the Muslim Brotherhood.

In April 2011, Mitt Romney announced his candidacy for the Republican nomination for the presidency. Although there were other Republicans vying for the chance to run against Obama, the extremely wealthy businessman and politician was largely the front runner until it became official at his party's convention in August of 2012—the former governor of Massachusetts would be the Grand Old Party's nominee. Although the campaign that followed did its share of criticizing Obama's first term, it stayed away from attacks on the incumbent's identity and his faith. Romney, like McCain before him, was a member of a generation that considered it counterproductive for a candidate or his first line surrogates to stoop to the realm of dirty politics. Or perhaps Romney and McCain authentically believed that exploiting the rumors about Obama's faith would have been scurrilous and at odds with their own moral compasses. Maybe these were guys who wanted to win a fair fight.

To be sure, more so than other Republican candidates, Romney—as the first nominee from the Church of Jesus Christ of Latter-day Saints— had a vested interest in keeping matters of faith in the background of the presidential race. The topic of Romney's faith was of sufficient interest that the Pew Research Center polled on it. Their results suggested that "the vast majority of those who are aware of Romney's faith say it doesn't concern them. Fully eight in ten voters who know Romney is Mormon say that they are comfortable with his faith (60%) or that it doesn't matter to them (21%). . . . Republicans and white evangelicals overwhelmingly back Romney irrespective of their views of his faith, and Democrats and seculars overwhelmingly oppose him regardless of their impression."[40]

It is important to remember that Romney really *is* a member of the Church of Jesus Christ of Latter-day Saints and Obama was *not* a Muslim. However, throughout his first term the belief that he was continued to escalate. Around the time of the 2010 midterms, the Pew Research Center used the same wording to ask respondents if they believed Obama was a Muslim. Whereas the figure had been 12 percent in 2008, it reached 18 percent in 2010, dropping just a bit to 16 percent in 2012. This polling was done at the same time as the poll that found so many voters seemingly indifferent to Romney's faith: "45% of voters say they are comfortable with Obama's religion, while 19% are uncomfortable. . . . Among those who describe him as a Muslim, just 26% are comfortable with his beliefs."[41]

Mitt Romney did not conspicuously leverage the beliefs that Obama was a Muslim. No doubt there were voters who believed that Obama was a Muslim who cast their ballots for Romney. But he didn't actively solicit them and it seems fair to conclude that hard-core anti-Obama types were insufficiently inspired by the wealthy and polished politician and businessman to come to the polls. Romney lost the election. The next wealthy businessman to earn the Republican nomination did not ignore this constituency and the discourse that animated them. And he would go on to become the forty-fifth president of the United States.

HE'S NOT CHRISTIAN / HE'S MUSLIM, 2012–2016

It is easy to see how Obama's two-time electoral success might be interpreted as evidence that despite an increasing number of Americans expressing doubts about his religious beliefs, these doubters were in a small but loud political silo—not a force to be taken seriously. The Pew Research Group, which regularly polled voters on their beliefs about Obama's religious leanings from early 2008 (in time for primary and general election consideration) through his first term in office, issued its final question on religion in July of 2012, four months before election day for Obama's second term. Since US presidents are limited to two terms in office, the movers and shakers at Pew probably concluded that there was no good reason to poll on this question because, after all, Barack Obama's name would never be at the top of the ballot again. It didn't seem to occur to them that whether or not people believed mistruths about Barack

Obama might have an impact on a subsequent election in which he was not a candidate.

And the beliefs kept coming. Snopes, FactCheck.org, Politifact, and the others had no shortage of submissions. Within three months of Obama's 2013 inauguration, the following narrative gained traction: "Is this true? In a stunning attack on the speech rights and free religious exercise of U.S. soldiers, the Obama administration has released a statement confirming the unthinkable: any soldier who professes Christianity can now be court-martialed and may face imprisonment and a dishonorable discharge from the military, even if they are a military chaplain."[42] And the holdovers from his first administration remained in vogue. In 2016, when he was within months of the end of his second stint in the White House, the "Cancel National Day of Prayer," narratives resurfaced in April, just in time to create strife for the annual May commemoration.[43]

President Obama did not just face rumors in the United States that he was a Muslim. As his second administration progressed, he and his team were stymied by the proliferation of these beliefs in the Middle East itself.[44] When the president took a stance perceived to be at odds with the proclamations of Israeli president Benjamin Netanyahu, Netanyahu sympathizers proclaimed that it was due to the anti-Semitic proclivities of a Muslim American president. Even within the Muslim world—which has as diverse a range of orientations as the Christian one—policies endorsed by the president seeming to favor one Muslim group at the expense of another were chalked up to his innate loyalties. Most commonly, members of the Sunni Muslim community lamented that he was beholden to the Shiite sect, purportedly that of his Kenyan father, although most Kenyans did not follow the ways of Shiites.

As Obama's second term progressed, the campaign for 2016 commenced. Once again, Hillary Rodham Clinton seemed the likely candidate for the Democrats. The Republican field was quite crowded in the early days, with a mix of career politicians such as Jeb Bush and Chris Christie, female candidates such as Michelle Bachmann and Carley Fiorina, and candidates who proudly proclaimed their distance from the Washington political scene such as neurosurgeon Ben Carson and Donald Trump. To the surprise of many, Donald Trump blustered and bullied his way to the head of his party's pack. Throughout his political campaign for the

Republican nomination for the presidency, and into his campaign for the presidency itself, Trump confused seasoned political observers by ruthlessly criticizing Barack Obama. Conventional wisdom held that candidates ought to focus their attacks on their actual opponents, and not waste any energies on the sitting second-term president. To be sure, Trump had plenty to say about those running against him in the primaries—Little Marco Rubio, Lyin' Ted Cruz, Low-Energy Jeb Bush—and his eventual opponent—Crooked Hillary—but he also directed an enormous amount of venom at Barack Obama.

Trump also spent a fair amount of time criticizing Obama's 2008 opponent, then senator John McCain. These diatribes were even more puzzling than the anti-Obama ones. After all, McCain and Trump were both Republicans, and as a long-term prisoner of war the senator from Arizona was widely regarded (even by his critics) as an American hero owed some measure of respect for his sacrifice. Political pundits wondered what possible value Trump could gain by so fervently attacking McCain.

The answers are apparent in a campaign moment comparable to the one McCain experienced with Gayle Quinnell. In a November 2015 speech, after Trump had buoyed his loyal crowd by misrepresenting the Iran nuclear deal, thoroughly trashing President Obama for signing on to it, repeating, "Who would make such a deal?" one of the attendees yells out, "He's a Muslim." As McCain had done eight years before, Trump reacts. But he starts by asking the attendee to repeat his accusation, assuring everyone will hear it. He continues in a feigned and exaggerated voice, with which he proclaims, "I didn't say it. I didn't say it." The crowd erupts with raucous applause. Trump physically pivots to the direction of the press section and says in a voice dripping with sarcasm, "Oh, and I'm supposed to reprimand you." After finding the guilty audience member, he turns to him and says very quickly and disingenuously, "How dare you." Then back to the press he says smugly, "I reprimanded him."[45]

The crowd applauds even more robustly. They take delight in a candidate who unabashedly reinforces what they have read on social media, received in emails, and perused on websites. They didn't want to vote for a Republican candidate who called a man named Barack Obama a "good family man." They wanted a leader who was at least as anti-Obama as they were. They were telling the world they would organize, campaign, and vote for a candidate who abhorred Barack Obama, even though Barack Obama could no longer be elected president. Trump's campaign antics and ignominious tweets had captivated and emboldened the cohort of American voters now known as Trump's base. His modus operandi became predictable. *He* didn't say Obama was a Muslim, he provoked others into doing it. Thrilled to have a candidate truly willing to trash Obama, they hoped that Trump would undo all of the damage done by the black Muslim from an African father, so they put him in the White House and they fought like hell to keep him there.

3 Born to Run

When white presidential hopefuls pursue the presidency, their campaign checklist does not include convincing voters already enamored with them to support their candidacy. But Barack Obama had to do just that. My own experience with reluctant Obama fans is mirrored in that of William Jelani Cobb who noted: "Time and again I encountered people who believed they were doing Obama a favor by not supporting him. 'He has small children,' they would point out. 'He needs to be around to see them grow up.' Or, 'I want to support him, I just don't know what might happen . . .' and the sentence would trail off, leading bad echoes of the past to fill in the blanks."[1] Those echoes of the past were the assassinations of black leaders, a historical reality that is engrained in the African American psyche.

In my earlier books, I discuss a category of rumors, legends, and conspiracy theories in the black community that is commonly referred to as "the Plan." Those who believe in "the Plan," assume that an organized and well-resourced network of white conspirators are hell bent on restraining African Americans who have gotten out of place. This network of collaborators includes vigilantes—the Ku Klux Klan and White Citizen's Councils—as well as ostensibly legitimate law enforcement officials, governmental authorities, and business magnates. Sometimes the Plan's architects demobilize a successful black man—and it's almost always a man—by arranging for him to be disgraced. Early examples include New York State's first African American congressman, Adam Clayton Powell Jr. Elected from Harlem, he was expelled from his House of Representatives seat in the 1960s for using federal money to travel outside the United States with his mistress. And thirty years later, Washington, D.C., mayor Marion Barry was cast as a Plan victim when he was arrested in an FBI sting operation for smoking crack cocaine. Even though credible evidence suggests that both Barry and Powell were guilty of the charges against them, the assumption that they were unfairly set up, or treated differently than white men engaged in similar misconduct, persisted in the minds of many of their black supporters. Barry was even reelected to the mayorship of Washington after his release from prison.[2]

The Plan's leadership was alleged to have orchestrated far more sinister assaults. The assassinations of Martin Luther King Jr. and Malcolm X were said to have been carried out by the Plan's operatives. Similarly, they were said to be behind the death of Ron Brown, the first black politician to head the Democratic National Committee and the eventual Secretary of Commerce in the Clinton administration. Traveling on sensitive state business, Brown died in 1996 when his plane crashed in Croatia.

The official explanation for Brown's death seemed so implausible that it actually spawned more than one contemporary legend. Largely popular in the black community was the belief that Ron Brown was a traditional victim of the Plan. As a black man with a seat in the president's cabinet, he was deemed too close for comfort to the oval office. But many anti-Clinton whites laid the blame at the first couple themselves, alleging that Brown, like Vince Foster, another Clinton administration appointee whose official cause of death—suicide—seemed unlikely, was taken out by operatives bent on protecting the then president and First Lady from scandalous accusations about their past illegitimate conduct.[3]

Even African Americans and others who *didn't* subscribe to the Plan as an ongoing conspiracy fretted about the possibility that Barack Obama would be assassinated. In other words, folks of all races who accepted the official explanation for Martin Luther King Jr.'s assassination as the work of a rogue racist murderer acting alone *and* those who believed that the civil rights leader was killed by a more organized sinister conspiracy were worried on behalf of Obama and his family. In my own informal and quantitatively weak survey of my family, friends, and colleagues, I could not find anyone old enough to have remembered the assassinations of the 1960s who did not recall thinking Obama would be more of a target than any white candidate.

The Obamas were well aware of both the perception and the reality of these beliefs. Responding to an African American fundraiser who had polled both white and black Democrats about their likeliness to give money to an Obama presidential campaign run, Obama said, "Yeah, yeah, I know. The white folks want me to run. And the black folks think I'm going to get killed."[4] As his campaign progressed, he did, in fact, receive more credible threats than other candidates. Michelle Obama recalled, "It was the earliest a presidential candidate had been given a protective detail ever, a full year and a half before he could become president elect, which said something about the nature and seriousness of the threats against him."[5] Both Obamas refused to show any public concern about their safety. Michelle was sanguine and often responded to concerned voters by reminding them that as a black male "he could get shot just going to the gas station." Barack, as well, "would make jokes about "getting shot" in order to put friends and relatives at ease. The Obama's responses to this concern reveals much about the lived experiences of upper-middle-class black life in the twenty-first-century in America. I think it is safe to say that only black candidates would assuage their family's fears about assassination by reminding them of their vulnerability to being shot in day-to-day life.

The Secret Service was available and up to the task of keeping Barack Obama safe from the physical harm that a conspiracy or lone assassin could inflict during his candidacy and presidency. But there was no functional equivalent to the Secret Service available to protect him from the shenanigans of those bent on discrediting him by manufacturing and perpetuating stories against him. Instead, I heard from many black Obama watchers who assumed that the rumors alleging he had misrepresented the place of his birth were the most recent work of those foot soldiers charged with implementing the Plan.

FRAMING THE BIRTHERS

In 2009, *birther* was a runner-up for new word of the year in the New Oxford English Dictionary. While *unfriend* took the honors that year, its place on the shortlist is one of the indicators of the pervasiveness of the rumors.[6] Oxford defines a *birther* as "a conspiracy theorist who challenges President Obama's birth certificate." No anti-Obama rumors have received more journalistic and academic scrutiny than the birther ones. In 2011, the fact-checking website PolitiFact revisited its earlier documentation efforts regarding Obama's birth story by updating and republishing its 2008 entry on the controversy and noting that the original story, as of that moment, was "the most widely read PolitiFact article in our history."[7] Birther beliefs were not the first blatantly false misstatements about Obama—as chapter 2 points out—the "Who Is Barack Obama" email chain, which even leads with "Barack Hussein Obama was born in Honolulu, Hawaii," holds that honor.[8] But once versions started to appear online, they piqued more attention than others, and when they were embraced by individuals accustomed to advancing conspiracy theories and high-profile celebrities committed to circulating them, profiting from them, or ridiculing them, they became a part of mainstream discourse, making their way into news stories, legal documents, dictionaries, and Wikipedia pages.

THE BIRTH OF THE BIRTHERS

Origin stories of the disputes over Obama's place of birth often refer to an alleged exchange in 2004. Asked to substantiate their belief that Obama himself acknowledged he wasn't born in Hawaii, some birthers reference a televised election debate that occurred between Obama and his Republican opponent, Alan Keyes, when the two African American politicians were competitors for the Illinois Senate seat. Anti-Obama conservatives allege that after Keyes pointed out that his opponent wasn't "born here," Obama replied, "Well, it doesn't matter if I wasn't born here, I'm running for—I'm not running for president."

There are several revealing clues about the accounts of this "exchange." References to "it" didn't actually surface until several years after the actual debate, when Obama was a sitting senator and a candidate for the Democratic nomination for president. In 2004, there was no morning-after rehashing of the debate in the news media focusing on this revelation. In fact, Keyes himself didn't jump on the birther bandwagon until 2008. In other words, it never happened. The transcript and tapes of the CSPAN-televised debate were scrutinized, and no such conversation is in the record. Instead of dismissing the rumor because of this lack of proof, believers tend to presume that all of the tapes (including ones sitting in sundry home VCR cabinets) and transcripts have been altered by Obama operatives, and the person who has told them or emailed them is remembering it accurately. Further, by the time fact finders located and probed the available evidence on the Keyes/Obama 2004 debate, the birther accusations had become rampant.

Those of us who study contemporary legends, rumors, and conspiracy theories are accustomed to this "trust the teller/not the investigator" phenomenon. At least as far back as the 1980s, there was a proliferation of legends that a Proctor and Gamble corporate executive acknowledged on Phil Donahue's popular television talk show that they were funneling their profits into Satanist activities. Decades later, those who are predisposed to believe it continue to do so. For the record, no Proctor and Gamble spokesperson ever appeared on Phil Donahue. In an attempt to diffuse the rapidly spreading accusations, the company dispatched corporate representatives and academics to other media outlets to curtail the legends. No doubt some listeners were convinced by professors who had investigated and discovered no Satanic proclivities on the part of Proctor and Gamble, but many people who had heard the denials reported that, in fact, their suspicions of the company had been amplified by the company's defense.[9]

Both in the days when the Proctor and Gamble cycle went viral—1980s style, by word of mouth—and in the 2000s when the birther beliefs took off, the power of a compelling story told by someone perceived as credible was clear. Noting the rhetorical impact of this dynamic, sociologist Tamotsu Shibutani emphasized that rumors were more than mere speech utterances, they were "*modes of activity* used to influence the conduct of others."[10] The son of a Kenyan father was actually getting close to the White House. Much to the dismay of the anti-Obama camp, other Americans, an increasing number of *white* Americans, did not see how wrong this was for the United States. Before long, the proverbial floodgates opened and rumors, legends, and conspiracy theories proliferated claiming that the US Constitution itself held the key to keeping him out of the office.

According to most sources, the first "in print" reference to issues related to Obama's place of birth came in the form of a question posted on Yahoo! Answers in 2007, "If Obama bin HUSSEIN al Barack was born in Kenya, how can he run for president in the US?[11] With comments that run the range from tame correction to vulgar denunciation, the majority of the forty-four individuals who responded at the time of the posting chastised the poster for confusing Barack's birthplace, Hawaii, with that of his father, Kenya. The responders tended to ignore the manipulation of Obama's name, although one added, "He's not a Muslim either." A few pointed out that even if he were born outside of the United States, his mother's American citizenship would enable him to run for president.

More incendiary stories, followed by more volatile comments and actions, soon proliferated. Some conceded that he was born in Hawaii but that he was still ineligible to be president. In one set of related chain emails, his mother's age was at issue. Some birthers argued that she had lied about her age and was actually sixteen when Barack Jr. was born. An even more convoluted line of reasoning claimed that she was, in fact, eighteen, but if only one parent is a US citizen at the time of birth, that citizen-parent must have resided in the United States for at least ten years, at least five of which had to be after the age of sixteen.

Other arguments spared his mother and homed in on either his father's, stepfather's, or faux father's identity as the impediment. One claim was that his father was a British subject at the time of his birth and no one whose parent who was a British subject can be president of the United States. *Wrotnowski v. Bysiewicz*, one of the many lawsuits filed in the fall of 2008 regarding the citizenship issue, used this line of reasoning. A related claim was that as holder of dual citizenship, he was ineligible for the presidency. The case of *Donofrio v. Wells* filed that fall was dependent upon the dual citizenship claims. To be fair, I should note that Leo Donofrio of New Jersey also considered John McCain ineligible because he was born when his father was stationed in the Panama Canal Zone.[12] Some birthers argued that Barack Obama senior had not been his birth father in the first place, that his stepfather (apparently inclined to name his son after his wife's first husband) was Barack's real father, and that he was born in Indonesia. Other claims were that Obama was born in Hawaii, but when his mother and stepfather relocated to Indonesia, he (as a minor child), renounced his US citizenship and never took an oath of citizenship upon his return to the United States. Often accompanied by carefully selected pictures of the two men, there are also claims that Barack's father was black activist Malcolm X. As far as I know there is no evidence that Malcolm X, né Malcom Little, was not a citizen of the United States.

According to some, the state of Hawaii and its history and policies were also at fault. These accusations conceded that he was born in Hawaii, but argued that he had misrepresented his date of birth and that it actually predated Hawaii's statehood (August 1959). The legitimacy of Hawaii's very statehood was questioned, implying that not only Barack Obama, but anyone born in Hawaii, wasn't really eligible to be president. There was also a set of arguments that espoused the view that an understanding of "natural born citizenship" was dependent upon accepting the legitimacy of the Fourteenth Amendment and that this amendment is illegal.

The core birther belief, the one that stuck, alleged Ann Dunham Obama gave birth to her son in Kenya and that the candidate and his team had covered it up. Soon, there were demands on the internet and eventually on billboards calling on the state of Hawaii and/or Barack Obama to release his birth certificate.

The more Obama supporters endeavored to point out the flaws in the accounts, the more the birthers held fast to their claims. Initially, attorney Loren Collins, one of the most steadfast challengers of the accounts, assumed that analytical critical thinking skills, research acumen, and fact-finding prowess could be persuasive: "It was about this time, in November 2008, that I began encountering Birther claims on Internet forums, even nonpolitical ones. I adopted a posture of debunking the claims I saw, saying "this is the sort of easily disproven conspiratorialist hoohah that needs to be nipped in the bud now before it's allowed to fester for the next four years."[13] But Collins was soon barred from the major birther online forum, and his well-measured blog, which eventually was labeled *Bullspotting*, didn't squash birther beliefs.[14] Collins wasn't the only one to assume that access to the "real" information and the ability to read and comprehend the Constitution of the United States would diminish the rumormongering. When the Obama campaign finally responded to the proliferation of the rumors by augmenting his official campaign website with a section entitled "Fight the Smears," journalist Thomas Goetz applauded the move on the grounds:

By putting their own website out there front-and-center, and then getting everybody to link to it (starting with all the media covering the launch of the site), the result will be to drive fightthesmears.com towards the top of a Google search on, say, "Obama muslim or "michelle obama whitey." Ideally, if enough of the pro-Obama network links to fightthesmears.com, it'll drive the sites that peddle in the rumor-mongering, which are now the first results of said searched, off the top of the results list. Ideal long term result: any curious low-information voter who eventually bothers to google these pesky rumors will immediately be led to the debunking rather than the rumor.[15]

Journalist Ben Smith who also wrote about the launch of the website shared Goetz's mistaken assumptions about the sway of accuracy by commenting, "Did the Obama campaign create fightthesmears.com to game Google? If so, they're even more net-savvy than folks give them credit for."[16]

These and other journalists gave undue credit to the persuasiveness of fact-based explanations. Such statements didn't work in the pre-internet era and were even less likely to work after this technology behemoth democratized access to audiences and resources. While they could see how individuals such as themselves would use the internet, they didn't consider the advantages it gave to those with a different worldview. They assumed that users would Google dubious claims rather than just accept them. They didn't appreciate that smart conspiracy theorists were empowered, not weakened, in the computer age. Prior to the internet, those dedicated to exposing alleged conspiracies had limited resources. Skeptics who believed that NASA had faked the moon landing had to depend upon homemade newsletters and late-night AM radio programs to connect with likeminded individuals and spread the word. A conspiracy theorist with computer savvy is a very powerful individual.

Obama and his campaign staff were in a no-win position. They were well aware that his critics would dismiss any document he released as fake. But refusing to release anything opened them up to accusations that they had something to hide. Nonetheless the persistence of the birthers and the attention the mainstream media was giving them forced the issue. On June 12, 2008, one of the first documents posted to fightthesmears.com was a copy of Barack Obama's birth certificate.

As expected, its appearance did little to assuage the birthers, who immediately identified a catalog of flaws that they assured their followers proved its inauthenticity. Certificate scrutinizers didn't like the nomenclature used by Hawaii that labeled the document a "Certification of Live Birth," and insisted that the campaign had forged a document inferior to a genuine birth certificate. They quarreled with the designation of Obama senior's race as "African," claiming that in the 1960s, black children were routinely identified as Negro on Hawaiian birth certificates. Dubious skeptics claimed to see evidence of Adobe Photoshop document manipulation and worried about the lack of a raised seal. Hawaii, like many states, had recently undergone a process of digitizing its vital documents and birthers used that process to further delegitimize the birth certificate. Although hardcore anti-Obama critics remained unconvinced by the release of the document they had implored the campaign to issue, they were disappointed that their critiques weren't derailing Obama's run for the White House. While the far-right blogs and websites were giving them some attention, even conservative radio icon Rush Limbaugh was still a couple of years away from giving serious air time to their arguments.

Conspiracy theory research has been conducted since the 1960s, but the 2016 election saw a renewed interest in the subject. In *A Lot of People Are Saying: The New Conspiracism and the Assault on Democracy*, Nancy L. Rosenblum and Russell Muirhead discuss the birther movement and claim, "The conspiracy was born in 2008, the work of a California dentist, Orly Taitz."[17] But the birther movement beliefs were circulating well before Taitz's involvement with them. What distinguished Taitz and a few other individuals was their willingness to embark on an all-consuming campaign to discredit Barack Obama. In addition to being a dentist, Taitz, often tagged as the queen bee of the birther movement, was also an attorney with questionable credentials. Between 2008 and 2016, she filed at least eleven lawsuits and challenged the legitimacy of five state primaries and three state general election ballots. Although she didn't win any of these efforts, her personal visibility steadily increased. She is best known for releasing a document she claimed to be a Kenyan birth certificate ostensibly verifying that Senator Obama was born in Mombasa, Kenya. The poorly crafted document had more in common with 1960s Australian birth certificates and was immediately dismissed as a fraud. Nonetheless, she remained engaged in the birther world from its earliest days to the present.

Rosenblum and Muirhead singled her out because of her prominence. By this time, the birther sphere contained at least two recognizable levels of engagement. The majority of birthers read and forwarded the chain emails, posted questions in the comments sections after articles, vented to their affinity groups, and disdained those who expressed trust in Obama. But birtherism wasn't their *business*. I have come to think of them as the worker-bee birthers; these were the people that "Queen Bee" Taitz sought to do the grunt work of challenging Obama. For them, birtherism was just a cause, not a cause/business. Taitz wasn't the only boss birther, she was joined in a very loose coalition with several others who were devoted to both sabotaging Obama and promoting themselves in the process. Several of these individuals—I think of them as the boss birthers—had experience in promoting themselves through other conspiracy-oriented efforts.

In the early days, one of the most prominent "boss birthers," was Philip J. Berg, an attorney whose prior claims to fame included introducing a lawsuit against President George Bush claiming the forty-third president was complicit in the 9/11 attacks. He soon turned to filing litigation as a way of compromising Barack Obama's chances of being elected. Berg was both a 9/11 truther and a birther, and in August of 2008, he filed a complaint in federal district court alleging that Obama was born in Mombasa, Kenya. After that complaint was dismissed, he made several efforts to get his case in front of the Supreme Court.

Jerome Corsi, a Harvard-educated PhD, used his keyboard rather than the courts in his efforts to keep the Obama birth certificate controversy alive. Like Berg and Taitz, he came to the birther debate with a track record of capitalizing on other conspiracy theories. Corsi had even made it to the *New York Times* best seller list with his 2004 book *Unfit for Command: Swift Boat Veterans Speak Out against John Kerry*. His book *The Obama Nation: Leftist Politics and the Cult of Personality* published in the months before the election became a best seller—a dubious achievement that should have been a harbinger of the seriousness of what anti-Obama critics could achieve—but in that book he did not yet subscribe to birtherism, saying only that "Obama can trace his heritage back to his mother, who was born in the United States and was an American citizen when he was born, and to his father who was a Kenyan citizen when Obama was born." A birther debunker would point out that technically speaking, Kenya was still a part of the British Empire when Barack Jr. was born, making Barack Sr. a British subject. Corsi also served as senior staff reporter for World Net Daily (WND) where, under the editorship of Joseph Farah, he eventually led the newspaper's charge to support anything and everything birther.[18]

With experience fueling other conspiracies under their belts, these three and some select other boss birthers knew the system and were quick to adapt to the new tools the internet gave them to advance their cause. Unlike the staunchest advocates of pre-internet conspiracy theories, they had easy access to a multitude of public records, more available than ever, to be interpreted or misinterpreted. If radio or television talk show hosts were dismissive of their evidence, they could appeal to conservative You-Tube hosts or even create their own channels. Whereas mainstream print newspapers and magazines might have once ignored a poorly written and flimsily reasoned letter to the editor, most major papers had loosely monitored comments sections. Establishing a headquarters was just a matter of developing a website, and that website could feature a link where their readers could contribute to their cause. As of this writing, Orly Taitz still has such a button under her picture on the website with the message, "If you love your country, please help me fight this creeping tyranny and corruption, Donations no matter how small will help pay for airline and travel expenses."[19] The desire to prevent Barack Obama from assuming the presidency of the United States had become a part of their overall identities and provided an income stream for them.

The efforts of these boss birthers inspired the multitude of worker-bee birthers who sent query after query to Politifact, Snopes, FactCheck.org and other similar resources. The worker-bee birthers posted on blogs, tweeted, and sent chain emails. They even resurrected old-fashioned communication technologies. The *Honolulu Advertiser* reported on November 1, 2008, that "State Health Department employees continue to be barraged by requests from people demanding to see Barack Obama's birth certificate, including some who have called the departments registrar of vital statistics at home—in the middle of the night."[20]

By the time of Obama's election in 2008, the foundation for the birther industry had been established. Even though other accounts remained in the mix, the core accusation that he was born in Kenya dominated the discourse. Of course, staunch believers still attempted to defend contradicting narratives, saying that he was born in Kenya but even if he *was* born in Hawaii, he was still ineligible for the presidency. With a couple of notable exceptions, the basic cast of characters had been established, Corsi, Berg, and Taitz were front and center of the debate. By clever use of social media and legal avenues they were able to gain footing in the more mainstream press and with respected book publishers. They had put Obama and his supporters in a difficult defensive position. They understood that while there were voters who would read the Constitution and turn to respected fact-finding outlets, there were many others who would accept as gospel the implication that if a Kansas-born woman gave birth to a child in Kenya, that child was not a citizen of the United States. As Loren Collins has noted, they had shifted confirmation bias to their side. It was up to Obama to prove that he was born in the United States, just as it had been up to Proctor and Gamble to prove its trademark didn't signal a Satanist agenda, just as Snapple Iced Tea had to prove that it was neither owned by white supremacists nor radical pro-lifers.

OBAMA'S ELECTION: KEEPING THE BIRTHERS IN BUSINESS

The election of Barack Obama in 2008 was probably more disconcerting news to the worker-bee birthers than it was for the boss birthers. The former group's goal was to prevent his election. While Taitz, Berg, and Corsi ostensibly shared that goal, there was an upside for them—his election kept them in business; no need to hunt for a new conspiracy. An interesting comparison can be drawn with the firearms industry. The Republican Party is more supportive of the gun lobby, but gun manufacturers realize much higher profits when a Democrat is commander in chief. That situation enables them to use fear tactics—buy our product before our opponent abolishes your Second Amendment rights—to line their corporate bank accounts. The presence of the Obamas in the White House meant the boss birthers already had a legacy conspiracy theory blazing, now they simply needed to feed the fire.

As the election and inauguration grew closer, both the leadership ranks of the birthers and their followers expanded. Between June of 2008 and Obama's election in early November of that year, World Net Daily (WND), a far-right website established in the late 1990s, probably covered the birther debate more than any other media outlet. But its pre-election coverage was nothing compared to its post-election coverage, at which point its editorial mandate was almost exclusively focused on trashing Barack Obama and his family. Shortly after the election, editor in chief Joseph Farah wrote and disseminated a petition that his readers could sign to prevent Obama from being inaugurated:

> I hope you will now join me in this fight for truth, justice and the American way by signing the petition. Help me spread the word. Let's turn up the heat. Send this column and the petition far and wide. Share it with your neighbors. Honor the constitution. Save the country's most vital institutions and its honor. Seek the truth. Demand accountability. Time is running out. The Electoral College is due to convene December 15—less than a month. Barack Obama is to be sworn in as the next president Jan. 20—less than two months from now.[21]

Members of the electoral college did receive copies of this and other documents urging them not to ratify the election results. The appeal to electors captured the attention of some of the more respected media outlets who covered the birthers' attempts to stop Obama's ascendency to the oval office. *The Christian Science Monitor* tracked down a North Carolinian who had been persuaded by Philip Berg's postings to do something in her state:

> Melanie Stewart, a stay-at-home mom in Kernersville, N.C. says her lobbying efforts mark the first time she's been actively involved in the political process. The questions raised by lawyers like Mr. Berg, she says, are substantial enough to throw doubt on Obama's eligibility.
>
> "I'm not asking electors to overturn their vote, but really to, before we vote, to make absolutely sure," says Ms. Stewart who has contacted most of North Carolina's 15 electors. "This is not being a sore loser or racist. This is just about ensuring that our leader is being truthful about who he is.[22]

Discussing how this played out in Colorado, the *Denver Post* reported that electors did their homework and no electors took the bait. However, anyone who opened the WND article not only received the contents of the article but also became subjected to advertising that supports the website, Farah, and his staff. Advertisements run the gamut from WND-generated products such as Farah's own books to the more traditional commercial fodder of advertising-sponsored websites such as supposedly bargain mortgage companies and menswear. With Obama on his way to the White House, WND and its advertisers had a reliable readership for its multitude of daily stories demonizing him and, on a nearly daily basis, questioning his eligibility. Farah complemented his online assault on Obama by paying for a number of billboards throughout the nation with the query on them "Where's the Birth Certificate?"

Momentum accelerated in the summer of 2009 after President Obama had been in office for approximately six months. The birther leadership was able to add one of its biggest names yet to its roster. Anchorman Lou Dobbs, while at the desk for CNN, at that juncture widely considered a middle-of-the-road news outlet, became the first major media figure to offer coverage at all sympathetic to the birthers and tantalized his audience with appeals to Obama to release his long-form birth certificate. Dobbs, a long-term and highly respected anchor, straddled the debate itself. He voiced respect for the questions being asked by the birthers and suggested that their request for the purportedly more comprehensive certificate—the short-form one released in 2008 was rejected as incomplete—was an entirely reasonable one, but he countered those remarks by saying that he did believe Obama was a citizen. CNN distanced itself from Dobbs's views and the anchor soon left the network, more as a result of backlash from his anti-immigrant positions than his support for the birthers.

An enlightening glimpse of the birther worker bees in action can be seen in a YouTube video posted on July 10, 2009. Meeting with constituents in his home district in Maryland, Representative Mike Castle was confronted by an impassioned flag-waving constituent who, after detailing the contents of her own birth certificate, which she claimed to have with her, implored: "I want to go back to January 20. I want to know why you people are ignoring his birth certificate. He's not an American citizen. He's a citizen of Kenya. . . . *I want my country back* (emphasis added)."[23]

The crowd enthusiastically applauds her remarks and shouts of "He was born in Kenya" can be heard. A confused Castle quietly counters her by saying, "If you are referring to the president, he's a citizen of the United States. He's a citizen of the United States." When the congressman tries to change the subject by going to another questioner, the flag waving woman stands up and rouses most of the crowd (including Castle) into saying the pledge of allegiance with her. Referring to this episode in its coverage of the birther movement, NPR notes that within two weeks of the video's posting on YouTube, it had over a half a million views, a sizeable figure in 2009.[24]

In 2009, the month of July ended with a news release from the Department of Health in Hawai'i (often preferred spelling): "I, Dr. Chiyome Fukino, Director of the Hawai'i State Department of Health, have seen the original vital records maintained on file by the Hawai'i State Department of Health verifying Barack Hussein Obama was born in Hawai'i and is a natural-born American. I have nothing further to add to this statement or my original statement issued over eight months ago."[25]

It is possible that Fukino's unequivocal statement satisfied some doubters who were willing to accept the words of the person in authority best placed to offer a judgment. She was, however, criticized in WND for breaking the law by sharing private information about a citizen's public records. For the remainder of 2009 and well into 2010, the WND kept its billboards in place and continued to publish and promote any story that cast doubt on Obama's citizenship.

AND THEN CAME TRUMP

The midterm elections in 2010 marked a familiar litmus test for a president, who had enjoyed having his own party as a majority in both houses of Congress for his first two years in office. The midterms are the traditional point at which voters lodge their satisfaction or dissatisfaction with the sitting president and the party in power. A clear signal was sent that support was eroding for the direction the Democratic Party was taking. Republicans gained the majority in the House of Representatives and picked up seven seats in the Senate, although the Senate remained under the control of the Democrats. Nonetheless, it was the biggest congressional turnover in more than sixty years. These statistics did not bode well for a man who aspired to a second term in office. They did, however, give hope to potential opponents interested in turning the Democrats' losses into their advantage.

Within two days of the midterms, Donald Trump enlisted his then "fixer," Michael Cohen, to introduce his name into the conversations about Obama opponents for 2012. It's hard to tell whether or not the first queries were serious explorations into his chances for election or simply strategies to drive viewers to his popular reality television show, *The Celebrity Apprentice*. In any case, a twitter feed entitled "Should Trump Run?" was launched. The initial tweets were as much about *The Celebrity Apprentice* as they were about pursuing a slot on the presidential ballot. Neither Trump nor his followers registered anything smacking of birtherism on that feed, nor did it surface on his website of the same name. With such lackluster interest in his candidacy coming from the public, Trump turned to Joseph Farah and Jerome Corsi at WND. Andrew Marantz recounts the process:

> He was looking for a smoking-gun kind of sound bite that would resonate with people," Farah later told the *New York Times*. The sound bite Trump chose was the meme about Obama's forged birth certificate. Trump knew instinctively that the attention marketplace was oversaturated, that the usual things (an interview with Larry King, a visit with a prize-winning deerhound) were growing easier for the public to ignore. But an outrageous conspiracy theory about Obama's foreign birth—birtherism, as it became known—would incite a sharp spike of activating emotion, either positive or negative, in everyone who heard it.[26]

And so Donald Trump entered the birther community. There is no evidence that Farah or anyone else convinced him that Barack Obama was not a citizen. They convinced him that aligning himself with this issue would distinguish him from all other Republican contenders and would likely attract voters who might back a Trump presidential campaign. Because of his connections and notoriety, he was able to access highly visible media outlets unavailable to the likes of Taitz and Berg. I have come to think of him as the Big Boss Birther. But he was still called The Donald in those days, so he could (and did) spar with Whoopi Goldberg and Barbara Walters on the popular television show *The View*. Trump soon began to claim that he had sent a team of investigators to Hawaii and that "they cannot believe what they are finding." In March of 2011 he invited Ashleigh

Banfield, a correspondent from *Good Morning America* to interview him on his plush private 727 where he bemoaned the criticism birthers were subjected to, "they label them as an idiot," and tracked his own doubts about Obama's birth to a notion that "he grew up and nobody knew him . . . the whole thing is very strange."[27]

With Trump so invested in the birther debate, media outlets above and beyond WND, conservative radio show hosts, and far-right blogs were paying attention. Using Trump's status as their justification, the major network and cable television stations and respected print journalism outlets were all filing birther stories. In April of 2011, Obama made copies of what became known as the "long form" of his birth certificate available to the press. Trump immediately took credit for bringing closure to the issue by saying he was, "proud of myself because I've accomplished something nobody has been able to accomplish."[28]

Trump watchers weren't sure what to make of his actions in the days ahead. He continued to register pushing Obama to release the document as a "win," in his column. In the political arena he still wasn't getting the kind of support needed to make a serious run for the 2012 Republican nomination. Many of his public statements were more in service to *The Apprentice* than his candidacy.

According to polls, because by now the birther question had found its way on to opinion polls, the tide was beginning to turn. In May of 2011, a Gallup poll indicated that more Americans said that he was definitely born in the United States (47%) than did so before the long-form birth certificate's release (38%) and they are joined by 18% who say this is probably the case. Significantly fewer—but still 13%—said he was probably or definitely born in another country.[29] The timing of the polls suggests that the release of the birth certificate itself was convincing to the public. While that may be the case, my folklore colleagues and I would draw attention to another possible factor.

Reporters and politicians weren't the only ones paying attention to Trump and the birther debate. Professional comedians and talk show hosts were having a field day with jokes about Trump as birther in chief. Within a few weeks of the release of the long-form birth certificate the ideal forum for birther jokes came in the form of the annual Washington Correspondents' Association dinner. A high-profile televised soiree, the dinner is hosted by a first-tier comedian and celebrities from the worlds of journalism, politics, and the entertainment industry all take part. Most presidents have participated—Bush and Obama did, Trump didn't—and take the opportunity to both laugh at themselves and to unleash a few zingers of their own. In 2011, the birther debate gave those at the podium their best material. President Obama did not shy away from the topic saying: "'Now, I know he's taken some flak lately, but no one is happier, no one is prouder to put this birth certificate matter to rest than The Donald,' Obama said. 'And that's because he can finally get back to focusing on the issues that matter—like did we fake the moon landing? What really happened in Roswell? And where are Biggie and Tupac?'"[30]

Host Seth Meyers also zeroed in on Trump with a series of jokes so cutting that later some analysts claimed that Trump's ultimate decision to run in the 2016 race could be traced to that night.[31] If you were a fan of late-night television, you couldn't avoid the birther jokes, as Jimmy Kimmel, Seth Meyers, Jay Leno, Bill Maher, Jon Stewart, Jimmy Fallon, and Conan O'Brien didn't disappoint. But it wasn't just professional comedians who interjected humor into the birther arena; riddles, jokes, and humorous asides were commonly posted on social media forums, usually after a story on the birth certificate. For example: "Q: How do you drive a birther mad? A: Put him in the Oval Office and tell him the president's Kenyan Birth Certificate is hidden in the corner." or "Q: What's wrong with birther jokes? A: Birthers don't think they're funny and other people don't think they're jokes."

With the word "birther" increasingly being fodder in a joke, more and more people were reluctant to admit that they questioned Obama's eligibility for the White House. This dynamic has surfaced in other contemporary legends and conspiracy theories. As folklorist Bill Ellis reminds, "Humor has been recognized as an effective antidote to the anxieties that underlie legends."[32] Ridicule can do more than reason to deter folks from aligning themselves with conspiracy theories. Thus, the perception that the polls reflected less momentum for the birther beliefs because Obama released his long-form birth certificate may be only partially correct. It may be that by showing his own willingness to spoof the situation and make fun of birthers, he contributed to a downturn in birther believers in an altogether different way.

When Barack Obama ran for reelection in 2012, his campaign sold mugs and T-shirts that contained an image of the birth certificate on one side and photo of the president on the other side with the stamp "Made in the USA." On the grounds that he wasn't eligible, foes filed official legal challenges in thirteen out of fifty states. Nonetheless, in spite of the concerted efforts of the boss birthers and birther worker bees, in January 2013, Barack Obama put a flag pin on his overcoat lapel, his right hand on the Bible and took the oath of office, once again promising to "the best of my ability preserve, protect and defend the Constitution of the United States."

SECOND-TERM BIRTHERS

The pantheon of boss birthers shifts a bit following Obama's second inauguration. Taitz, Berg, Farah, and Corsi continue to aggressively promote their anti-Obama agenda. But Trump's engagement with the issue visibly ebbs, although he continues to claim victory for his role in "forcing" Obama to release the long-form birth certificate in the first place. Just before the election, however, a new sheriff arrived on the outskirts of town, one eager to take a place at the birther community town square, preferably with as many cameras on him as possible. Sheriff Joe Arpaio was to Maricopa County, Arizona, what Donald Trump was to New York City. A larger-than-life personality who believed any publicity was good publicity, he was known for writing his own law enforcement rules, mercilessly abusing immigrants and any marginalized population that annoyed him, and assembling around him a cadre of hyper-loyal far-right suppliants willing to do his bidding. His original national notoriety stemmed from his unapologetic defense of Maricopa County's substandard jail conditions, his unfiltered disdain for immigrants or anyone resembling an immigrant, and his penchant for disregarding the rights of the accused. A shameless namedropper and a man whose statements and actions suggested that he didn't feel obliged to adhere to conventional definitions of "truth" and "fiction," Arpaio ruled over Maricopa County, which according to its website is "the nation's fastest growing county, home to approximately four and a half million people," with an iron hand for twenty-four years.[33] Arpaio was reelected sheriff four times by the far-right voters who constitute the majority population in Maricopa.

The timing of Arpaio's entrée into the birther debate is almost as interesting as Trump's. Both men knew from their compatriots that for the far right, Obama's eligibility remained a hot-button issue. Trump wanted to get his name and face into the press; Arpaio wanted the same thing, but he also sought retribution against Obama for a Justice Department investigation that was released in December of 2011. Authorized during the Bush administration, but announced and concluded during Obama's, the findings document copious evidence of racial profiling and civil rights abuses. Following the release of the report, Homeland Security retracted Arpaio's power to incarcerate and deport undocumented immigrants. Arpaio was defiant, refusing to cooperate with the Justice Department's plan to place a federal monitor in the Sheriff's office. According to a revealing August 2012 interview in *Rolling Stone*, a publication Arpaio referred to as "that marijuana magazine," the unrepentant sheriff told an audience at an anti-immigration fundraiser, "After they went after me, we arrested 500 more just for spite."[34] In an approach also reminiscent of Donald Trump's modus operandi, Arpaio decided to go after President Obama, whom he blamed for his Justice Department woes.

If Arpaio was the boss birther, his worker-bee birthers were members of the Taxed Enough Already (Tea) party and also a group of volunteers whom he referred to as his Cold Case Posse. Shortly after the Justice Department issued its findings, Sheriff Arpaio announced that members of the Arizona Tea Party had asked him to determine if President Obama was entitled to serve as president, and in response to their petition, he had asked the Cold Case Posse to investigate. This "posse" was a volunteer group of unpaid former police officers and attorneys who had received some investigative training from current members of the Maricopa Sheriff's Department. Under the guidance of former police officer and Arpaio's volunteer aide-de-camp, Michael Zullo, they purportedly were on task for six months, scrutinizing the digital image of the long-form birth certificate. Assisted by a supposed expert in electronic documents, they concluded that there was probable cause for forgery and fraud. Their findings were announced with much fanfare in a lengthy press conference in March of 2012 where they summarized their doubts about the legitimacy of documents related to President Obama, and made a written report available to members of the media. In addition to misspellings and grammatical errors that most authors of a report would want to avoid, the very materials supplied by the Cold Case Posse themselves contained falsified documents.[35]

While Sheriff Arpaio didn't enjoy *quite* the access to the media that Trump commanded, the tough talker did find his way onto CNN, ABC News, CBS News, and into the major print newspapers, where he repeatedly asserted the definitiveness of his investigation and noted that no tax payer dollars had been spent on it. In yet another similarity to Trump, however, the financial facts as asserted by Arpaio didn't always resemble the realities. He was known to be capricious in his allocation of state monies; in 2011 an audit had determined that he had misspent at least $100 million. Throughout much of his tenure in office, and after, Maricopa County was forced to pay out tens of millions of dollars in settlements and expenses related to legal cases brought against him and his department. He had long ago learned how to capitalize on his image and reputation. The *Rolling Stone* article notes that he raised over $7 million for his own reelection bid, much of it coming from his out-of-state fan base, enamored of his anti-immigration practices and his relentless attacks on Barack Obama.[36]

Arpaio's financial stake in the perpetuation of the birther beliefs was raised in a contentious televised exchange with a reporter for the local CBS affiliate, KPHO. After Arpaio declared the Obama birth certificate a fraud from the podium, reporter Morgan Loew asked Arpaio to explain why the public should believe two investigators (Corsi and Zullo) who are profiting (through the sale of books) from the dissemination of the conspiracy theory and whether their collective financial well-being was the real motive for their efforts. Arpaio took umbrage at the comment and merely pronounced, "You don't get your stories straight when you do your hit pieces, CBS, you."[37]

The forty-one comments following the YouTube clip of the interview may be more interesting than the exchange itself. Coming from seven viewers, we can see in these remarks the categorical loyalty of members of the group I call the "worker-bee birthers," and their disdain for anyone criticizing the conclusions of the boss birthers. A commenter with the handle "beer," was one of several who took Arpaio's lead and shot the messenger, posting, "CBS you are PIMPS to the status quo—no wonder your ratings are low." Someone identified as Chris Cannizzaro made eight attempts to discredit the birther theories. He even acknowledges, "I didn't vote for him, I'm just trying to educate you about the bullshit you've been spewing about the birth certificates." In several of her nineteen comments on the story, Candy Smith (assuming female because most people named Candy are female) repeats the misquotes from the Constitution and repeats the misstatements about Kenya and Indonesia that the boss birthers have been advancing. Her wrath is as much directed at Cannizzaro, as seen in her statement, "Its people like you who ruining this country, because you refuse to wake up and see the puppet . . . romney is just as bad obama has broke all of the articles of the constitution and congress is doing nothing about it. i quoted from the constitution as well, i just simplified it for sheep like you to understand." In his last attempt to sway Smith and others, Cannizzaro writes, "I quoted the constitution correctly and I quoted the law that makes Obama a citizen regardless of his birth location." Smith then makes nine comments, going back and forth between declaring that if he wasn't born here, he isn't a natural born citizen, and pronouncements citing her views of why he is a bad president. She has the last word on the comments section with prose laden with misinformation:

> and you are what's wrong with the world, you refuse to wake up. we are in a recession, the unemployment rate is higher then ever. our rights are being taken away. we are in an endless war we cant afford . . . obama is spending money we dont have . . . he is signing bills that are unconstitutional, he gives weapons to our enemies . . . he raised the deficit. congress is useless. his wife is spending our money, he raised taxes by 200 percent . . . he shut down countless oil, coal and electric companies.[38]

This 2012 exchange is replete with deep red flags, signals of a segment of the voting public's growing allegiance to the far right's leaders. CBS, the media parent in this case, would have considered itself a neutral, nonpartisan outlet. A few years before the emergence of the "fake news" allegation, several of the commenters hurled vile invectives at the station and its reporter. With confidence in the veracity of their sources, the anti-Obama posters—by far the majority—reiterated the messages from WND and similar extremely conservative websites. At the time of this posting, the United States was not in a recession, the unemployment rate was low, and most of the other accusations are inaccurate.

Mitt Romney, the Republican candidate for the 2012 presidency, was not considered anti-Obama enough for this crowd, and they were also profoundly unhappy with Congress. There was really only one poster inclined to defend Obama's legitimacy as a candidate and he was treated with utter contempt by the anti-Obama crowd. There was never even the mildest suggestion that someone holding a different view of the president and his policies was deserving of respect. After much derision, Cannizzaro left the conversation. With his departure, all properly spelled and capitalized words embedded in grammatically sound sentences left the conversation as well. The final comments are characterized by misspellings and idiosyncratic punctuation.

The whole encounter could be considered a microcosm of the 2016 elections. Traditional media outlets were disregarded. The anti-Obama/anti-Romney/anti-Hillary members of the electorate put their trust in biased sources and eagerly condemned the communities they perceived as anti-American. Any more moderate individual willing to take them on—even a fellow Republican—was trashed. And on November 8, 2016, they had the last word.

Arpaio wasn't at all daunted by the reporter's accusations of his profiting from the perpetuation of the birther conspiracy theories. Although he wasn't alone as a second-term birther, Arpaio was the most persistent, and this press conference was far from his last. Throughout Obama's second term in office, and during his increasingly contentious fights with the Justice Department, Arpaio did not back down and never passed on an opportunity to tell anyone with a microphone or a tape recorder about the invalidity of Barack Obama's birth certificate.

Barack Obama's citizenship was an issue in three presidential elections. His own in 2008 and 2012, and the contest between Hillary Rodham Clinton and Donald J. Trump in 2016. When Republican Ted Cruz was asked in June 2015 if his birth in Canada might make him ineligible for the presidency, he explained that since his mother was an American citizen, he was eligible. He went on to say, "It's interesting, the whole birther thing was started by the Hillary Clinton campaign in 2008 against

Barack Obama."[39] Cruz wasn't the first to make that claim, but since he was a candidate for the presidency, his accusation put the issue back into the news. Cruz was one of the several Republican presidential hopefuls defeated by Donald Trump. Less than two months before the election, on September 16, 2016, Donald Trump stated, "President Barack Obama was born in the United States. Period." Questioned about his reversal, Trump referred to Hillary Clinton as one of the first birthers.[40] His implication was that by forcing Barack Obama into releasing his long-form birth certificate and proving himself, he should be considered the hero and Hillary Clinton the villain.

Fact-checkers and journalists set themselves to the task of determining if there was any merit to these allegations. As the beginning of this chapter documents, the first birther rumblings were from the devotees of the far right. As was the case with the Muslim beliefs, there were members of Hillary's team who received and forwarded some of the birther emails. The emails were so ubiquitous that it is not surprising that they reached the inboxes of some of her campaign workers. The evidence contradicts the assertion that she was "birther zero" as Breitbart News labeled her, or that her campaign leadership exploited birtherism.[41] Thus, Trump and his followers used the eligibility issue to seal his status as an Obama hater for as long as it was politically advantageous, and then when it was a distraction in the national race, he transferred the heat to his opponent.

Because of this deft sleight of hand, as the 2016 election approached, "birtherism," was an asset in Donald Trump's column and a deficit in Hillary Clinton's. For voters who considered John McCain and Mitt Romney too tame for their liking, the brash and belligerent man whose contempt for Obama rivaled their own, was extremely appealing.

BIRTHERS IN THE LIVES OF THE OBAMAS

The birther cluster of accusations proved to be the most tenacious of any that confronted Barack Obama during his presidency. By referencing, even incorrectly, the Constitution's prescription for a president's identity, they became the rumors with the most potential to actually evict Obama from the White House. That prospect attracted numerous far-right voters and inspired several individuals schooled in the ways of forging connections between their political preferences and their professional goals.

It is worth considering whether taken together the birthers might constitute a leadership team akin to the ones some African Americans described as architects of the Plan. There does not seem to be evidence of a coherent and organized roadmap for the attack dating back to Obama's ascendency in 2007 and 2008. But it is certainly the case that as these individuals realized that they could profit by promoting birtherism, they found and used each other. And among them they had a range of specializations that could be useful to the cause. Berg and Taitz, while not legal masterminds, could file lawsuits. Farah could build and sustain a high-traffic website. With his Harvard PhD, Corsi was the best writer in the bunch and could get his literary wares on the best-seller list. Years of television experience and a significant loyal audience were advantageous to Lou Dobbs. Trump and Arpaio were publicity magnets, able to get birtherism into the mainstream news, whereas most of the other anti-Obama rumors and legends had remained in the shadows. All of the boss birthers possessed the ability to serve as instigators for countless fans—worker bees—who adored anyone willing to get Barack Obama out of the White House.

On the one hand, the case could be made that if the birther episode represents an enactment of the "the Plan," it didn't work. Obama was elected two times and was never impeached or evicted. By the end of his second term, the fates of the boss birthers were decidedly mixed. Philip Berg's legal ineptness (in other cases) led to his being disbarred in Pennsylvania. At seventy-plus years old, he joined the gig economy, driving for Uber and Lyft. Orly Taitz still maintains a right-wing website. In between daily postings regarding the offenses of the left, the site is choked with advertisements for water resistant shoes, luggage, and the like. WorldNetDaily faced ongoing and severe financial challenges once Obama was out of the White House. For Trump's term in office, Lou Dobbs remained his advocate from an anchor seat on Fox News where he landed after his pro-birther stance contributed to his ejection from CNN. However, he was fired by Fox News, purportedly for putting the company in legal jeopardy by recklessly accusing the voting machine companies of fraud. Sheriff Joe Arpaio, who likely entered the birther fray as a result of his anger at the Department of Justice charges, was convicted of criminal contempt in

July of 2017. And Donald Trump, the big boss birther who always seems to outperform the members of any group to which he belongs, was elected president. Showing boss birther brother loyalty, he pardoned Arpaio the next month. There's no denying that the birthers scored some wins, personally and professionally.

There were no wins for the Obamas. The birthers may not have evicted him but they sullied him. Images of his marked-up birth certificate are widely available on the internet. Post-presidency polls indicate that many Americans continue to doubt his legitimacy; in 2017 more than 50 percent of Republicans voiced doubts, as did 14 percent of Democrats.[42] For the Obama family, the assassination concerns described at the beginning of this chapter intensified as a result of the heated anger evident in the words and actions of the birthers. According to Michelle Obama:

> The whole thing (birtherism) was crazy and mean-spirited, of course, its underlying bigotry and xenophobia hardly concealed, But it was also dangerous, deliberately meant to stir up the wingnuts and kooks. I feared the reaction. I was briefed from time to time by the Secret Service on the more serious threats that came in and understood there were people quite capable of being stirred. I tried not to worry, but sometimes I couldn't help it. What if someone with an unstable mind loaded a gun and drove to Washington? What if that person went looking for our girls? Donald Trump, with his loud and reckless innuendos, was putting my family's safety at risk. And for this, I'd never forgive him.[43]

The list of challenges Barack Obama faced as a result of his identity were not his alone to bear. Michelle Obama's words above demonstrate the impact that they had on his entire family. As the next chapter will illustrate, many on the right considered Michelle Obama out of place as First Lady of the United States. She was confronted with a long list of rumors, legends, and conspiracy theories more specifically targeted at her identity as a black woman. Or in the minds of some, as a black man.

4 Michelle Matters

In *The Audacity of Hope: Thoughts on Reclaiming the American Dream,* Barack Obama recalls his first impression of Michelle La Vaughn Robinson, the Harvard Law School graduate who was assigned to mentor him through a summer legal internship at the prestigious Chicago law firm where she served as a young associate: "She was tall—almost my height in heels—and lovely, with a friendly, professional manner that matched her tailored suit and blouse."[1] He was soon smitten, and although she famously resisted the initial romantic overtures of her lanky mentee, she eventually succumbed to his charms.

They were married in the fall of 1992, and by the time Barack Obama launched his presidential campaign over a decade later, the couple were the parents of two young daughters and had weathered many of the familiar challenges faced by modern professional couples. Long-term residents of Chicago, an ethnically complicated city rightly characterized as an exemplar of the seedier side of political machinations, both Michelle and her parents were ambivalent about Barack's increasingly concrete aspirations toward a political career. After concluding that he wanted to move beyond the offices aligned with his adopted Illinois home and make a run for the presidency in 2007, he wisely enlisted the persuasive help of her beloved older brother, Craig Robinson, in his efforts to coax his wife into agreement.

Michelle Obama had more than a superficial understanding of the disruptive impact pursuing the presidency would have on a black family. Santita Jackson, daughter of the Reverend Jesse Jackson, the prominent black civil rights activist and religious leader who twice ran for the Democratic Party's nomination for the presidency, was one of her closest childhood friends and maid of honor at her wedding. Yet even Michelle's proximity to the Jackson family only gave her a partial understanding of the scrutiny and shenanigans a black family would encounter in the twenty-first century. Although he received a lot of skeptical press attention during his run, Jackson had pursued the oval office in the 1980s and he received 1980s press attention, involving talk radio, television, and print journalism. Campaigns did not yet have to deal with social media, blogs, and viral memes.

Even so, he was fodder for anti-black vitriol at the time. The folklore about Jackson did stand as a harbinger for what the Obamas might face. In the late 1980s, I conducted an analysis of jokes about Jesse Jackson and found the humor in them inevitably played to familiar anti-black stereotypes:

PERSON A: Did you hear Jesse Jackson had to pull out of the race?
PERSON B: No. Why?
PERSON A: He found out his mother was a centerfold in *National Geographic.*[2]

The Jesse Jackson campaign did not have to concern itself with the circulation of such dehumanizing humor on social media or deal with the other vagaries of internet political gamesmanship. Since he didn't secure the actual democratic nomination, he and his family were spared exacting and inflammatory journalistic investigations into their personal histories. Only Jackson's most devoted followers would have even known the names of his wife and children.

But in the 2000s, an Obama run for the White House would have to confront many of the same race-based identity issues the Jackson one did, as well as a host of newly generated ones born of the digital age, including vast and varied interpretations and misinterpretations of the identities of the Obama family. The closer the Obama family got to the White House, the more the aspiring "mom-in-chief," as she sometimes was criticized for labeling herself, would find that just as every aspect of Barack's identity would be maligned by his harshest critics, so too would she be subjected to accusations that she was guilty of misrepresenting everything from her political loyalties to her gender identity and sexual orientation. Like Reverend Jackson's mother and generations of black women, she would find her looks compared to those of primates. Using stock stereotypes associated with black women of her generation, Michelle Obama's critics crafted and circulated numerous rumors, legends, and conspiracy theories that reinforced a message that the White House was no place for a black woman to be unless she was cleaning it.

ANGRY BLACK WOMAN AND AFFIRMATIVE ACTION BABY

In her autobiography, *Becoming*, Michelle Obama recounts her first brush with widespread public criticism.[3] It was the summer of 2008 and she was following the standard playbook crafted for the wife of a candidate. On the campaign trail, she, like most candidates and their spouses, relied on a tried-and-true stump speech largely committed to memory that she reused as she traversed the primary states. On the eve of the Wisconsin primary, the news media zeroed in on an abbreviated clip in which she said, "For the first time in my adult life, I am really proud of my country." And, to be sure, those fifteen words were in her stump speech, although creative editing had weaponized them. John McCain's wife Cindy introduced her candidate husband the next day by saying, "I am proud of my country. I don't know about you, if you heard those words earlier, I am very proud of my country."[4] She didn't mention Michelle by name and her husband's subsequent remarks did not unduly exploit the moment. Thus, the McCains, who had much to gain by disparaging the Obamas, took a rather tame approach to the matter. Either they realized that other conservatives and the right-wing press would capitalize on the incident, allowing them the perception of taking the high road, or they were disinclined to over-endow the moment with political significance.

If they assumed others would pounce, they were right. Members of McCain's party as well as media personalities voiced deep disdain for the implications they read into the simplistic and distorted abbreviation of Michelle's statement. Indulging in "if I were in her shoes" speculation, some commentators projected their own list of American milestones that they assumed ought to trigger pride in the wife of a presidential candidate, for example, the winning of the Cold War or the nation's leading status in science and research. Other writers were more focused on the changing status of blacks in America. They were irked that she didn't seem to find value in achievements construed as evidence of racial progress such as the passage of the Civil Rights Act or Shirley Chisholm's 1972 run for the presidency.

But it was Michelle (and Barack's) access to an Ivy League education that her first circle of critics most wanted her to acknowledge and appreciate as worthy of pride and thankfulness. The theme of a perceived absence of gratitude for her education surfaces in blogs such as *Hot Air*, which complains, "Nothing America has done in Michelle Obama's adult life, which at 44 goes back 26 years to 1982 has made her proud of her country? . . . Not the fact that she and her husband were able to go to Ivy League Schools before embarking on extremely lucrative careers?"[5] Or *Townhall*, where Rich Galen ponders, "When Michelle Obama received her undergraduate degree from Princeton and her law degree from Harvard . . . was she embarrassed by an America that gave her the opportunity to live up to her intellectual opportunities?"[6] A state Republican Party website notes, "While Mrs. Obama has trouble being proud of the country where she earned degrees from Princeton University and Harvard Law School and then became a multi-millionaire (there's no evidence that the Obamas were multimillionaires in early 2008), her husband makes statements that belittle average Americans' response to the difficulties of life."[7] And the respected and popular *Newsweek* opinionist Evan Thomas diverted the same questions as though it wasn't him but rather rank-and-file voters who said, "But a lot of voters did and will wonder: how could someone who graduated from Princeton and Harvard Law School and *won* (emphasis added) a job at a high-paying Chicago Law firm—who in some way was a beneficiary of affirmative action—sound so alienated from her country."[8]

This expectation of black gratitude dates back to the era of slavery when Southern slave owners countered abolitionist arguments by claiming that their slaves were happy and grateful for having been "rescued" from the heathen jungles of Africa and allowed to learn the ways of Christianity under the paternal guidance of benevolent plantation owners. The enslaved were often commanded to express their appreciation for whatever meager allotments they received at the hands of their masters. Enslaved Africans, and after emancipation, the African Americans who were their descendants, were expected to affirm a view of the United States as a place where access to anything of value—from basics like food to more abstract commodities like an education—was the property of whites and should only be meted out to compliant blacks willing to forever express their indebtedness. By focusing on her husband as a positive change agent for the nation, Michelle Obama had veered from the acceptable script for black female behavior.

In the hours, days, weeks, and months after the remark went viral, the Obama campaign and Michelle sought to contextualize her words. They made sure to provide the full context of her remarks, all of which had been available to any interested party with a search engine:

> What we've learned over this year is that hope is making a comeback! And let me tell you something for the first time in my adult lifetime, I'm really proud of my country. Not just because Barack has done well but because I think people are hungry for change. I have been desperate to see our country moving in that direction, and just not feeling so alone in my frustration and disappointment. I've seen people who are hungry to be unified around some basic common issues, and it's made me proud. I feel privileged to be a part of even witnessing this.[9]

She and Barack also answered interviewers' requests for clarification. But the die was cast. The perception that Michelle Obama wasn't proud of America or grateful to a country that bequeathed its bounty to her aligned with the notions that Barack Obama wouldn't sing the national anthem or pledge allegiance to the flag, rendering this couple unsuitable for the White House.

The frequent references to the Obamas' educations at Princeton and Harvard betray a concern about their shared history that would frequently resurface throughout the campaigns and Barack's terms in office. Whereas Ivy League educations have traditionally been counted as a plus for a presidential candidate and spouse, only some segments of the electorate considered it value added for the Obamas. There were clearly voters who were not only convinced that this Chicago-based couple didn't belong in the White House, but that they hadn't belonged in the colleges they attended either. The dismay expressed above about Michelle's supposed lack of gratitude for her postsecondary educational opportunities implies that her presence on these coveted campuses was not a result of the accepted formula of an intellectually gifted teenager financed by the checkbook of parents or a merit-based scholarship.

Attending Princeton in the 1980s, Michelle's matriculation coincided with an era when affirmative action policies were commonplace. *Affirmative action* refers to policies through which an institution acknowledges the past pervasive discrimination that a given people such as African Americans and Latinos have had to endure and designs remedies that encourage access and opportunities for members of that group. Many educational institutions developed and implemented affirmative action policies, and, as a result, the number of students from underrepresented groups increased on their campuses. Although many observers initially considered such policies a reasonable and fair mechanism by which to address the slow pace of social change, there were also quite a few critics who enumerated many possible problems with the policies. Most commonly, such critics invoked concerns about reverse discrimination, pointing out if seats at prestigious universities were already low in number, it was unfair to "innocent" white candidates to ignore their eligibility in favor of granting access to someone from an underserved group.

Affirmative action policies inspired the development of the term and accusation *reverse discrimination*. Further, since the beneficiaries of such policies often came from under-resourced schools, another of the most tenacious critiques alleged that the affirmative action students lacked the academic chops to make a success out of a highly competitive academic environment. The existence and promotion of affirmative action policies had an unintended consequence for virtually all students of color. There was a widely held assumption, and I experienced this personally, that any minority student on a college campus owed her slot to affirmative action. Even minority students who had all of the financial and educational attributes of their white counterparts were labeled, in the words of one of Stephen L. Carter, one of the more thoughtful commentators on the subject, "affirmative action babies."[10]

To many on the right, institutions that adhered to affirmative action policies were guilty of denying more academically qualified students their rightful place. The 1990s were characterized by very public law suits and legal actions challenging the ways universities and workplaces implemented their affirmative action policies, all with a supposition that underqualified minorities were seizing spots that belonged to whites.

For individuals sympathetic to the anti-affirmative action advocates, what they construed as Michelle Obama's lack of gratitude for her marquee education served as confirmation of her unworthiness. Before long, the "she's not proud to be an American" incident was followed by an even more manufactured allegation suggesting that her Princeton senior thesis could be read as evidence that she was unqualified. The Princeton brand as a venerable and rigorous undergraduate institution anointed to prepare the nation's leaders has long been linked to its senior thesis requirement. Each graduating senior is expected to submit a capstone writing assignment that reflects her ability to sustain a significant written argument about a topic embedded in a sophisticated understanding of her major. A sociology major with a track in African American Studies, Michelle's was titled "Princeton-Educated Blacks and the Black Community." With not one but two references to "black" and the naming of Princeton itself, the title piqued the interest of some of Obama's critics who wanted to scrutinize it.

But, initially at least, access to the thesis was restricted. As is so often the case, a kernel of truth can be extracted from the legend that circulated. Those who received an email or read a Facebook post saying that Princeton was embargoing the thesis until after the election were receiving accurate information. However, implicit or explicit in many of the inflammatory messages that quickly surfaced was a conspiracy motif that alleged that the leadership of Princeton was in cahoots with the Obama campaign. Their goal? To postpone the revelation of Michelle Obama's militant undergraduate rantings that critics were sure were so volatile that Barack's entire campaign would be undermined if the voting public knew about them. As the noise increased, the decision was made, presumably by the campaign, to authorize Princeton to release the thesis to the media.

The thesis didn't live up to the hype. It wasn't a malicious Michelle manifesto outlining a violent anti-white agenda. But soon, a second set of rumors circulated. Clearly dissatisfied that the thesis wasn't particularly incendiary, the distributors of these claims misquoted or took out of context statements within the thesis: "An email was circulated Obama's wife wrote a paper in college that said America was a nation founded on 'crime and hatred' and that whites in America are 'ineradicably racist.'"[11] In 2008 bogus quotes were uncommon in sources assumed to be legitimate. Although the thesis was/is available online, many recipients read this and accepted it at face value. No doubt many who received the email assumed someone else had done some fact-checking.

Did the twenty-one-year-old Michelle Robinson reveal any authentically anti-American statements in her senior thesis? Arguably the most problematic actual statement in the thesis is "blacks must join in solidarity to fight a white oppressor." This sound bite was cut and pasted into many an email and blog post as evidence that the husband of such a radical should not be elected. But the statement was *not* Michelle Obama's conclusion about race relations. She had interviewed black Princetonians and it is *their* views as submitted on her survey that she was summarizing:

> As discussed earlier, most respondents were attending Princeton during the 70's, at a time when the Black Power Movement was still influencing the attitudes of many Blacks.
>
> It is possible that Black individuals either chose to or felt pressure to come together with other Blacks on campus because of the belief that Blacks must join in solidarity to combat a White oppressor. As the few blacks in a white environment it is understandable that respondents might have felt a need to look out for one another.[12]

It is likely that understanding that the quotes were manipulated would have done little to appease many of those inclined to dislike Michelle Obama. Her undeserved presence at Princeton in the first place and her choice to write a thesis on the black community were sufficient grounds for rejecting her as an acceptable First Lady.

The incendiary thesis is one of the first of many building blocks that construct an image of the First Lady as a divisive radical. Chapter 1 documents and analyzes "I'd Like to Teach the World to Sing," a lengthy chain email that largely incriminates Barack. But most versions contain the statement:

We as a Nation, have placed upon the nations of Islam, an unfair injustice which is WHY my wife disrespects the Flag and she and I have attended several flag burning ceremonies in the past.

Of course now, I have found myself about to become the President of the United States and I have put my hatred aside. I will use my power to bring CHANGE to this Nation, and offer the people a new path. My wife and I look forward to becoming our Country's First black Family. Indeed, CHANGE is about to overwhelm the United States of America.[13]

For the remainder of the campaign the right-wing traditional and so-cial media reinforced the stereotype of the freeloading America-hating black female radical on Michelle Obama. The sanctity of her marriage was ridiculed when Fox News amplified what was being said in less visible outlets with a slide referring to her as "Obama's baby mama."

Enough voters did see what Barack saw that first day back at the Chicago law firm: a warm and polished black woman who belonged in a professional environment. But Michelle Obama, and those around her wise enough to know the tenacious hold stereotypes can wield, knew that she would continue to be subject to malicious rumormongering. This turned out to be the case and as those on the far right embarked on their campaign to make her a one-term First Lady, the arsenal of accusations grew.

FROM AFFIRMATIVE ACTION BABY
TO WHITE HOUSE QUEEN

On January 20, 2009, Michelle Robinson Obama became the First Lady of the United States and moved with Barack, their two daughters, and her mother into the White House. To Obama supporters, the ascendancy of a well-educated, beautiful black woman to the First Lady's East Wing offices was a cause for celebration. But the same segment of the population that was unnerved by an election that resulted in the presidency of Barack Obama was just as disappointed to see Michelle serving by his side. The stereotype of the ungrateful angry black woman that grounded the rumors about her before the election remained, and other familiar tropes (at least to those of us who study anti-black stereotypes) surfaced quickly.

Many of the rumors that circulated reflect a decided aversion to the mere presence of a black family in the White House, particularly in light of the fact that the house and other trappings simply come with the job. In other words, first families live rent free in a very high-end setting, complete with a full staff devoted to their needs. First families are expected to pay for their meals and personal expenses, although this aspect of the first family's contract is not well known. Monthly food and sundries bills aside, it's still a nice perk to have the White House, Camp David, a fleet of cars, presidential planes, helicopters, and all of the human resources needed to operationalize these taxpayer-funded assets at your disposal.

Implicitly or explicitly, the motif of "taxpayer funding" is one of the most frequent in the postinaugural rumors about Michelle. Six months into her husband's first term, emailed versions of this snippet began to appear: "There has never been anyone in the White House at any time that has created such an army of staffers whose sole duties are the facilitation of the First Lady's social life. One wonders why she needs so much help, at taxpayer expense, when even Hillary, only had three; Jackie Kennedy one; Laura Bush one; and prior to Mamie Eisenhower social help came from the President's own pocket."[14]

The rumor was submitted to fact-checking websites such as Snopes and FactCheck.org. Their researchers fleshed out the full story. In accordance with policy, the White House filed paperwork that detailed the size and salaries of the staff working there. TheLastCrusade.org, then took the information and posted a piece claiming that the First Lady had hired an "unprecedented number of staffers" to "cater to her every whim and to satisfy her every request in the midst of the Great Recession."[15] That piece was also posted on the conservative website Canada Free Press under the byline of Dr. Paul L. Williams, who runs TheLastCrusade.org. *That* post became a component of a chain email that expands upon Williams's post, falsely claiming that some recent First Ladies have had only one to three staffers.[16] The fact-checkers confirmed that Michelle Obama's staffing—paid for by the taxpayers—was consistent with that of Laura Bush—also paid for by the taxpayers.[17]

The Obamas were also subjected to unfounded accusations when they ventured beyond the stately chambers of the White House. When Michelle and her daughters attended the Olympics in London, a picture of the girls with their mother circulated showing them draped in towels imprinted with the national flag of South Africa. The posts that accompanied the photo falsely indicted them:

> Michelle and the girls at the Olympics
>
> Gee thanks for supporting the United States their country. What a bunch of losers.
>
> See your tax dollars at work!!! How patriotic!
>
> The Obamas display their colors at the Olympics . . . Really? South Africa? Gee ladies thanks for your support.[18]

As the fact-checkers verified easily, the picture was *not* taken at the London Olympics. Rather it dated to a visit to South Africa where the girls were gifted with the towels that they draped around themselves to stave off the chill of the evening. But the implication that while at the international games in England the first family, underwritten by American tax dollars, opted to root for teams from the continent of Africa further augmented the view of the first family as cavalierly diverting American resources to support African aspirations.

The Obamas were not the only first family to endure withering criticism about the costs of their travel. Because the safety concerns associated with having the president or his loved ones exposed to kidnappers or assassins run deep, extraordinary care and expense have usually been allocated to ensure that they are not put in harm's way. Frugal constituents of Republican and Democratic presidents have bemoaned the hefty price tag that accompanies what can seem to some as unwarranted self-indulgence. In recent decades the Bushes, the Clintons, and the Trumps have all faced at least some backlash regarding the costs of moving the president or members of his family from the White House to any other location.

But the Obamas had a bigger target on their luggage for two reasons. First, they, unlike any previous president's family, had to go through this with the internet as a daily portal through which commentary on their actions could be registered easily and quickly. And, second, that commentary was posted under pseudonyms or avatars, often triggering race-based associations. For example:

Yesterday, a White House source told the German Press Agency dpa that ~~Queen Marie Antoinette~~ Michelle Obama and daughter Sasha will spend 4 days next month vacationing in Spain's southern resort of Marbella. Reservation has been made for **THIRTY** rooms in a 5-star hotel near Marbella.

This is obscene.

The U.S. national debt is over $13.24 trillion, and counting. Millions of Americans are unemployed; 1 of 8 Americans are on food stamps. But Michelle and Sacha require **30** hotel rooms for a 4-day holiday, August 4–8.

The Sociopath will not be going even though his birthday is August 4. Interesting that Michelle won't be with her husband for his 49th birthday, isn't it? Not to worry: he has Reggie Love!][19]

Michelle and Sasha Obama did vacation in Spain, and they were booked at a nice hotel. As was the case with their predecessors, accommodations were required for the staff that accompanied the first family. But the post above and the comments that follow it are saturated with charged language picking up on the "Queen" reference with comments such as:

Queen Michelle has a staff of many, whose salaries come to $1.25 million a year.

What the hell is wrong with these people? I realize MO didn't grow up with a pot to pee in, but this is ridiculous. Thirty rooms for their entourage. I think a European hostel would be more appropriate.

The Obama's haven't impressed nor lived up to expectations, just more of the same. Why are the people complaining after their coronation/inauguration, it was like royalty being acclaimed, then we complain when they act like it. Ditch the pomp and ceremony, get down to business then we have aleg to stand on.

Michelle Obama is all ass, no class.[20]

A wide range of caustic sentiments are reflected in this exchange, with one observer arguing that the first family should be staying in a hostel and another using it as an opportunity to make an age-old anti-black slam with a reference Michelle's buttocks. But particularly noteworthy here, and it is true in numerous others I could cite, is the repeated references to royalty. The Obama's inauguration is likened to a coronation and commenters freely refer to the first lady as Queen Michelle. The conclusion that Michelle Obama thinks of herself as a monarch surfaces in postings that depict a profile view of her wearing a very formal purple (often the preferred color for royal vestments) dress and wearing a jeweled crown on what looks like a stamp. The messages that usually accompany the image imply that Michelle has lobbied the US Postal Service to have her face on a stamp, and this is the image she has chosen for it.

Two actual events were comingled to fuel the development of this contemporary legend. The first was the publication by a British magazine of an image in which they photoshopped a crown on a profile picture and then set it against the backdrop of a stamp usually reserved for the Queen of England. The image was created in March 2013 by Britain's *Sunday Times Style Magazine* after the publication named Michelle Obama the "Best Dressed Woman in the World."[21]

Meanwhile, back in the colonies, the First Lady was encouraged to work with the US postal service on updating the images that could be featured on postage stamps. The intention was to create stamps that would celebrate her campaign against childhood obesity, "Let's Move." Thanks to mischievous online pranksters, numerous individuals received the Queen Michelle image with none of this context.[22]

Taken together, the narratives about the size of Michelle's staff, the expenses accrued by her family's travel, and a crowned image of her all portray her as someone with an outsized sense of entitlement and delusions of grandeur. By suggesting that she longs to possess all of the frills and fancies of a well-heeled royal, those who perpetuate these beliefs are evoking the decades-old stereotype attached to black women, who, like Michelle, were from black urban enclaves. As adults they were said to have pursued paths that led them to a lifestyle funded by the taxpayers. "Welfare queens" became a fixture in the imaginations of many who were convinced that the tax rolls were being depleted by shameless black opportunists.

A little history may be helpful here. *Welfare* is a catch-all term usually referring to federally administered programs that provide monies to needy families. By the middle of the twentieth century, many observers on the right abhorred the existence of all such programs, characterizing them as nothing more than expensive government handout efforts, usually exploited by lazy individuals disinclined to work. Even during the era of slavery when overseers used brutal tactics to force labor from blacks, the proslavery contingent repeatedly tried to convince abolitionists, and those inclined to sympathize with them, that blacks were inherently lazy.

The architects and proponents of public assistance justified it on the grounds that a safety net ought to be provided, particularly for families, to prevent them from succumbing to the ravages of poverty. Welfare recipients came from all races but to many, *welfare recipient*, became synonymous with *African American*. Thanks to the publicity garnered by a few high-profile cases, the specter of welfare fraud eclipsed the laudable goals of the programs. The supposition was that blacks wanted to live lavish lifestyles at the expense of white taxpayers. Often welfare allotments were linked to the number of children in a household. Black women were accused of having children in order to boost the size of their checks. As Tom Mould has documented in great detail, in an early example of a politician attaching himself to a contemporary legend, Ronald Reagan made much of his plan to rid welfare rolls of "welfare queens," both in his campaign for governor of California in the 1960s and for president of the United States in the 1980s.[23] In reality, there were always more white recipients of welfare than black and most who turned to it were only on "the welfare rolls," for short periods of time as a result of an emergency situation.

As the price tag for providing public assistance increased, so too did the public's overall frustration with this line of the federal budget. Before they went to the polls, voters wanted to know what candidates wanted "to do" about welfare and the perceived rise of the welfare state.

As Gary Alan Fine and I pointed out in *Whispers on the Color Line*, numerous legends circulated alleging that an unscrupulous black woman had worked the system in order to haul in extraordinary amounts of taxpayer money.[24] This is not to say that individuals never abused the welfare system. It did happen. But the image of the welfare queen, often wearing ostentatious colorful clothes and driving a pimped-out luxury car, came to suggest that those who took advantage of the system were the rule and those who fairly met the criteria and received no more than the formula dictated were the exception.

Much to the dismay of many on the left, Bill Clinton, interested in swaying more right-leaning voters in his direction, campaigned on "eliminating welfare as we know it," and once elected, with his eyes on his reelection, he signed The Personal Responsibility and Work Opportunity

Reconciliation Act in 1994, effectively unravelling the safety net that had
been woven initially to combat the economic woes of the Depression in the
1930s. The title of the legislation catered to the erroneous perception that
if only financially strapped individuals took "personal responsibility," there
would be adequate jobs and opportunities for them.

The erosion of most public assistance programs did not result in the
disappearance of stories about despicable "welfare queens." The rumor
circuit remained alive with allegations, usually of black women, eschew-
ing work and capitalizing on monthly checks, even when monthly checks
ceased to exist. Just as blacks who fit every academic criteria for the college they attended were disregarded as affirmative action babies, so too
were black women whose hard-won incomes supported the purchase of
their cars and clothes mistakenly assumed to have cheated the government in order to get the finer things in life.

Perhaps it is not surprising, then, given this cultural backdrop, that
Michelle Robinson Obama, born to working-class black parents and
raised on the South Side of Chicago, a neighborhood from which whites
departed as the first black families moved in, was tarnished with the "she
thinks she's a queen," dig. Anyone—be they Eastern European operatives
paid to generate online social unrest in the United States or far-right extremists eager to make the Obamas a one-term first family—could play
the queen card by taking her expenses out of context and photoshop-
ping a crown on her head. By circulating or disseminating any or all of
this suite of rumors about Michelle Obama's unquenchable appetite for
the flourishes of a monarch's life, those who didn't want her husband reelected were hoping voters would see her as no different from the phan-
tom welfare queens.

FROM WELFARE QUEEN TO HOMICIDAL DRAG QUEEN

Although they were patently inaccurate statements, the anti-Michelle
folk beliefs that dominated during the first campaign and then the first
administration often contained one verifiable plot point—the familiar
kernel of truth element. Like First Ladies before her, Michelle Obama did
have a couple dozen folks in the White House who worked for her, and her

senior thesis was temporarily restricted. But Barack's election and reelection suggests that if these beliefs were intended to deter citizens from voting for him or buying magazines that had flattering pictures of her on their covers, they didn't sway a large enough portion of the electorate. As the Obamas entered his second term in office, Michelle remained a highly respected figure to Democrats, many independents, and even some Republicans, including former First Lady Laura Bush, who never missed an opportunity to heap praise on her successor.

The growing esteem with which so many held the Obamas was a source of even more annoyance and aggravation to their enemies who turned to absurdly outlandish accusations in their quest to delegitimize the first family and humiliate their supporters. In *Becoming*, Michelle notes, "I've heard about the swampy parts of the internet that question everything about me, right down to whether I am a woman or a man."[25] Just as she gives only glancing attention to the deployment of the "angry black woman," accusations, she does not explore just what these questions are about her gender identity in her best-selling autobiography. But understanding the gender speculations and their popularity—and unfortunately, they reached far beyond the swamp—is essential for comprehending just how much she and her family were hated and how much some voters wanted them and those who supported them to suffer. Their tool of choice was blatantly derogatory and hateful storytelling.

The conspiracy theories about Michelle's gender identity go hand-in-hand, so to speak, with those about Barack's sexual orientation. Also quite popular during Obama's reelection campaign, the Bathhouse Barry conspiracy theories are the first to allege that the Obamas and their minions stooped to murder to cover up their tawdry sexual histories. The earliest versions claim that Barack is either bisexual or gay and that in his early years he was so well known in Chicago's bathhouses that other devotees of these establishments knew him as Bathhouse Barry. Although Jerome Corsi never mentions Obama's alleged homosexuality in either his 2008 *New York Times* best seller *The Obama Nation* or its 2011 follow-up *Where's the Birth Certificate?*, he did aggregate the various gay rumors in a story for World Net Daily that was posted September 11, 2012, within two months of the November 2012 presidential election. Corsi's article methodically creates a story that incorporates all of the various motifs used in the rumors.

His talking points include: Larry Sinclair's self-published, grammatically disastrous 2010 book, *Barack Obama and Larry Sinclair: Cocaine, Sex, Lies, and Murder*; accusations that Obama was behind the death of a gay choir director at Jeremiah Wright's (himself a kind of gay ringleader in these stories) church; identification of former lovers including a Pakistani college roommate, personal assistant Reggie Love, and the former congressman and chief of staff Rahm Emmanuel.[26] Of course, those who were sharing stories about Barack's homosexual life style needed a good explanation for his attachment to Michelle. The conspiracy theories grouped under Michelle/Michael offered a plausible explanation.

Until the second half of 2014, the Michelle/Michael gender-identity rumors were largely contained to the swamp. They became more widely known, at least on the far right, in early July when a street reporter asked comedian Joan Rivers, identified on her television roast as the "Queen of Mean," if she thought a gay president would be elected before a female one. Rivers, who had just officiated at a same-sex wedding, responded by saying, "We already have it with Obama, so let's just calm down." Responding to the reporter's follow up she continued, "You know Michelle is a tranny, you know, a transgender. We all know. It's OK."[27]

Joan Rivers was to the sexual orientation and gender identity rumors what her longtime friend Donald Trump was to the birther beliefs. She was a celebrity magnifier, not a creator. To be sure, there's no evidence of premeditated maligning; instead, she seized the opportunity provided to her by the reporter. But her celebrity credentials ensured there would be press attention, and press attention there was.

Breitbart News, then one of the most visible and well-funded of the far-right wing outlets, covered the Rivers remarks with an ominous Fourth of July title, "Can Joan Rivers Survive Calling Obama Gay, First Lady 'Tranny?'"[28] Compared to middle of the road news websites, Breitbart News, is of course, extreme. But when held up against the more virulent profanity-laden, white supremacist websites, it is relatively tame. In this story, seemingly the first where Breitbart took up the gender identity of the First Lady, the reporter takes the perspective that "survival," meant Rivers's ability to continue her career as a performer and television host successfully without suffering undue backlash from pro-Obama types offended by her inelegant humor. It ends by saying: "Will Obama's defenders demand an apology from Rivers? Will such a statement be enough. . . . Rivers can survive if her reputation and time served in the comedy trenches come in to play. Like Don Rickles, Rivers' biting brand of comedy is more or less grandfathered in. If enough voices rise up to smite her and her comments, her long career faces a serious threat."[29] The reporter, Christian Toto, never implies that Rivers might have actually been sharing the truth. His focus is on the risk he thinks she has taken by daring to make a joke at the expense of the first family, who he suggests are humorless, but not homicidal. Toto limits his concern to her career, not the comedian herself. As is always the case, the rumors and conspiracy theories flourish in the comments that followed the story. Many of the 1,054 comments make various cases for believing Rivers to have shared the truth. For them, the sources are the even swampier parts of the internet:

> i forgot her head to shoulder ratio is that of a man NOT a woman . . . and he/she was born Michael LaVaughn Robinson in Chicago . . . google the name if dont believe me. http://disc.yourwebapps.com.[31 likes][30]

> Of course she [Rivers] wasn't kidding. Since bozo's turn for the worst, there's evidence surfacing that supports the facts that 1) bozo is gay and 2) moochey was born Michael Robinson. He is a transgendered she. Should this prove to be absolute truth, we should then offically be the 1st country to have a outwardly gay president and a man as 1st lady. What a pathetic country we've become. [224 likes][31]

In the days following the original posting of the story, Breitbart did not post any follow ups addressing the fact that thousands of their readers were claiming that their reporter had missed the mark, their audience was taking Rivers literally.

At that juncture, the mainstream media paid only cursory attention to Rivers's remarks, although the *New York Daily News* ran a very brief story that noted the incident focused on Rivers's track record for making scandalous comments by saying, "The octogenarian has a history of making outrageous remarks, including slamming stars from Miley Cyrus to Lindsay Lohan," but didn't seriously engage the legitimacy of the perceived sexual or gender identities of the first couple.[32] There were no breaking news stories on the nightly news revealing Michelle Obama's sex change operation and no one in the White House press corps asked Josh Earnest,

President Obama's press secretary, to verify that the First Lady was, in fact, a lady. Joan Rivers had been making sexually provocative comments for over sixty years and it is likely many reporters assumed this was just "Joan being Joan," always eager to get any press attention she could from making outrageous remarks. At the time of the street interview she was hosting and promoting a television show, aptly named the "Fashion Police," and was hawking a new book, *Diary of a Mad Diva*.

Rivers's comment emboldened those on the far right who hoped that stories about the gender and sexual identities of the Obamas would antagonize their followers and seed discord. The following contemporary legend systematically undercut every aspect of Michelle's life story:

> Michelle Obama, First Lady of the United States, was born Michael La-Vaughn Robinson in Chicago, Illinois on January 17th, 1964. He was the second son born to Fraser Robinson III, a well known cocaine dealer and union thug for Crime Lord/Mayor Richard J. Daley, and Marian Shields Robinson, a transient street prostitute who was diagnosed with the HIV virus in 1998. He was a popular high school athlete and in 1982, he accepted a scholarship to play middle linebacker for the Oregon State Beavers. After finishing a respectable rookie season with 88 tackles and 7.5 sacks, he suddenly dropped out of the school. Fellow teammates observed that Robinson could regularly be heard lamenting over how he is a "woman trapped inside a man's body," and on January 13th, 1983, he underwent sex reassignment surgery at Johns Hopkins University School of Medicine. To hide the shame of his new identity, Michael left Oregon State to attend Princeton University under his new legal name, "Michelle Robinson." Years later, he met Barry Obama Jr. a Kenyan immigrant who later became aware of Michelle's "true" identity. They subsequently married and adopted two children.[33]

Posted on July 4, two days after the Rivers interview, this contemporary legend distills many of the motifs discernible in the rumors that had been circulating. As of this writing, it is still available on the *Outrageous Minds* blog with the incongruous missions of trashing Obama and proving that the US government was covering up evidence of UFOs. The narrative fleshes out Rivers's quip and not only portrays the Obamas as total frauds, but also casts Michelle's parents into two of the most demeaning, deplorable, and detested stereotypical roles for African Americans of their generation, referring to her father as a thug and her mother as a prostitute. It provides just the kind of embedded details so often employed to give the aura of factualness to a legend; in this case, we get "Michael" Robinson's college football record and the actual date and location of his/ her reassignment surgery. Weaving in two of the Barack Obama rumors, it uses the "Barry" moniker to evoke the Bathhouse Barry rumors and defines him as an immigrant to trigger the birther accounts.

Other versions of the Michelle/Michael narrative focus more on her, grounding their evidence in Michelle Obama's physical appearance. There are several memes that depict Michelle in a form-fitting outfit revealing a bulge that is presumed to be a penis. Alex Jones, who made a good living out of peddling anti-Obama lore, opined, "Michelle appears in photos and videos to have a very large penis in his pants, her shoulders are wide, her face is very very masculine."[34]

One of the more distressing aspects of this posting stems from the use of a junior high school photo of Michelle that is used as some sort of proof of her masculinity. It is an unadulterated picture reminiscent of those typical of black girls. Beautiful black girls. But *USAReally* used an un-doctored girlhood picture to demonstrate that she was male. Jones wants his readers to look at prepubescent Michelle Obama and see a boy, not a girl; to see Michael, not Michelle. The need to deny the femininity of black women stems from one of the most enduring of anti-black stereotypes.

Much older than the angry black woman and welfare queen stereotypes, the masculinized black woman images date back to the era of slavery. By depicting enslaved women as devoid of any of the then cherished markers of femininity—pale white skin, delicate facial features, a petite frame—pro-slavery forces could both justify the backbreaking physical labor expected of enslaved women and counter accusations that white male slave owners were turning to them for sexual satisfaction.

The association remained long after slavery was abolished. In the popular stage shows of the early twentieth century as well as in early movies, large dark-skinned black women were aggressors, often using physical force to prevail over black men. Postcards and print materials often endowed them with the shape and look of animals, usually primates. For most of the twentieth century, the few black women who were deemed to be attractive were those whose physical features mirrored those of the white women who were considered appealing. Tall or stout women with darker complexions and pronounced facial features were rarely touted as beautiful. But by the end of the twentieth century the standards of attractiveness began to expand. More and more fashion editors and casting agents were placing a much wider range of black women (and white women for that matter) against backdrops in which they were rendered as the alluring one. Coming into the public eye within the first few years of the twenty-first century, Michelle Obama was a test case. Many Americans—white and black—easily agreed with Barack's original assessment, "She was tall . . . and lovely," but some did not and reverted to a disturbing outdated standard.

The Michelle/Michael and the Bathhouse Barry conspiracy theory cycles are proudly toxic narratives. Michelle/Michael casts Michelle, Barack, and the Robinsons in the lead roles. But the minstrel rewrite of their auto-biographies is an assault on all African Americans who have carved a satis-fying niche for themselves in twenty-first-century America. If the Obamas or any other African Americans read these narratives and experience any emotional pain, from the perspective of the haters, that's a good thing. The goal is to invalidate the real Obama and Robinson narratives as well as the stories of so many other black families who, like them, successfully pursued economic mobility. The timing of its posting and the ways in which other references to Michelle/Michael began to proliferate in July substantiates the conclusion that Rivers herself didn't create the rumors but that her saying them aloud gave permission to anti-Obama zealots to take them out of the swamp.

Joan Rivers died unexpectedly about two months after making her com-ments about the Obamas. Even though she was eighty-one years old, her death was sudden and unexpected. She was still very much in the lime-light, and her whole career had been marked by frequent and successful sojourns to medical facilities, most typically for cosmetic surgery. On this occasion, suffering from a throat disorder that was interfering with her ability to speak, she followed her doctor's advice and underwent an en-doscopy during which her vital signs plummeted causing her brain to be denied oxygen. An investigation was conducted that found that the clinic that performed the endoscopy, typically a low-risk outpatient medical pro-cedure, was responsible for the numerous irregularities that caused her death. Joan's daughter, Melissa Rivers, filed a malpractice suit against the clinic and settled out of court for an undisclosed amount of money.

When polarizing figures in the public eye meet untimely and hard-to-explain deaths, conspiracy theories can quickly develop. Virtually all of the assassinations of 1960s political figures were fodder for conspiracy theorists, and the official explanations for the deaths of performers such as Elvis Presley, Tupac Shakur, and Biggie Smalls were all questioned. So when Joan Rivers, a proud serial plastic surgery enthusiast, succumbed to such a low-risk procedure, it is probably not surprising that the impulse to unearth a grander explanation for her death took hold in some of her followers. Her comments about the Obamas seemed to provide a motive for foul play.

Several versions of the original exchange with the reporter were posted in various places, including YouTube. At one time in 2015 there were over a million hits with thousands of comments, most linking Rivers's death to the Obama comments. The themes that were outed in early July resurfaced with significant attention to the anatomically absurd claim that her head-to-shoulder ratio was that of a man's. Even though Breitbart's story on Rivers's death, titled "RIP Joan Rivers: No One Will Ever Call Michelle Obama a 'Tranny' Again," the reporter, this time John Nolte, continued to limit his argument to accusations of a political double standard.[35] He devoted several paragraphs to the claim that while jokes about women on the right such as Sarah Palin were endorsed and rewarded, jokes about Michelle Obama or Hillary Clinton were pilloried as racist and sexist. The comments section for the article certainly contained definitive proof that people actually would be calling Michelle Obama a tranny: within the fifty-three comments there were plenty doing just that: "Obama is bi he belonged to that gay club in Chicago and Michelle does look like a Tranny *shrug* I doubt the children are theirs anyways."[36]

In light of the mysterious circumstances surrounding Rivers's death, as well as her celebrity acclaim, the media continued to run stories related to her demise for well over a year. Four days after her death her lavish funeral—attended by a who's who of the political, comedy, and fashion worlds—was covered in print, on television, and on internet news sites. As results of the investigation into her death and the autopsy were made public, there were multiple stories about the findings. When her daughter Melissa Rivers settled her malpractice claims and when she published a remembrance of her mother's career, she was interviewed widely. All of the official explanations for Rivers's death focused on the negligence of the clinicians charged with her care. A damning accusation surfaced that in pursuit of souvenirs with their famous patient, medical staff took selfies with a sedated Rivers. The findings were, in layman's terms, that Rivers's death was the result of a botched procedure undertaken by staff who didn't follow the protocols that would have protected their patient's well-being. None of the mainstream media coverage drew any connections between her remarks about the Obamas and her untimely death. But in any story that had a comment section following it, the rumors were prominent and pervasive. For example, "She was snuffed, Obama administration lol" (162 likes).[37]

Even when Rivers's daughter plainly placed the blame for her mother's death at the hands of the clinicians who cared for her, comments continued to reference the conspiracy theory: "Predictable complication???????if only joan had shut her mouth she would be alive now!!!!!!!"[38] To those who subscribed to the conspiracy theories, Melissa Rivers's decision to lay the full responsibility at the door of the clinic was easy to explain. The grieving daughter knew better than to connect her mother's death with the Obama administration because if they could get away with killing her mother, they could also do harm to her and her son.

Just over a year after the results of Rivers's autopsy were issued and within a month of the 2016 presidential election, Rivers's death was the subject of a cable network documentary. Each installment of *Autopsy: The Last Hours of . . .* , is a forty-two-minute investigation into the circumstances of a celebrity's death. Rivers joined the ranks of Whitney Houston, Michael Jackson, Bruce Lee, and others whose cause of death were dissected by supposed medical experts eager to enumerate the many missteps taken by those with whom the deceased spent their final hours. The Rivers episode clearly laid the blame for her death at the hands of her personal physician as well as the incompetent staff at the clinic where the procedure took place. As its title suggests, *Autopsy* feeds on audiences who are fascinated by the sensational aspects of celebrities' lives and deaths. The visual trademark that unites all of the episodes depicts a morgue and features the bare feet of a corpse with an identification toe tag hanging from it. The more outrageous the circumstances of the celebrity's death, the better for this kind of sensationalist programming, but at no juncture do the filmmakers ever hint that Rivers's death had any connection to her remarks about the Obamas.

The Rivers incident coincided with the second half of the second Obama administration. Barack was a lame duck, and presidential politics was largely about the 2016 election. Once she finally declared her interest, Hillary Rodham Clinton was always the likely Democratic candidate. Initially fairly large, the field of candidates for the Republican nomination ominously narrowed in the direction of the candidate with the least political experience, Donald Trump, who, incidentally, had cast Joan and Melissa Rivers on his reality television show. In most of the more public circles, Michelle's star was as bright as ever. Although she always adamantly denied any personal political aspirations, there was occasional speculation that she should consider running for president or vice president. Michelle continued to fulfill her responsibilities as First Lady and further the agendas she had established in her first years in the White House. In March 2015 she made an appearance on the popular Ellen DeGeneres afternoon talk show. As always, Ellen and her studio audience were enchanted by her demeanor. In support of the fifth anniversary of her popular anti-obesity Let's Move campaign, she and Ellen previewed a dance she intended to roll out at her last White House Easter Egg hunt.[39] Other television shows quickly shared the clip of a soulful First Lady who could hold her own while dancing with people half her age. When the clips were shared on YouTube or on the network's websites, the comments section were replete with claims that the clip proved that Michelle was Michael. There were accusations that the network's editors had eliminated the bulge in the white pants she wore. Many commenters simply identified the First Lady as, "Big Mike," a label frequently used for her on the far-right blogs and websites. Others retold aspects of the conspiracy theory, linking her to Rivers's death. Given how mean-spirited some of the comments that remain posted are, it is hard to imagine how vulgar those that were deleted must have been. Some of the postings of these clips, and many others that feature Michelle and/or Barack Obama, have the ominous line, "Comments for this story have been turned off," suggesting that the conversation had spiraled into such noxious verbiage that it all had to be scrubbed.

Most of the original clips of Rivers making her now-famous dig have been deleted, but other clips featuring the actress making absolutely no references to the First Lady are followed by assorted articulations of the conspiracy theory. As I write this, six years later, it is still easy to find newly posted commentary linking Rivers's death to her quips about Michelle Obama.

MICHELLE MATTERS

The trajectory of the anti-Michelle lore reveals much about the intractability of racist stereotypes and their hold on a significant segment of the American voting public. The first rumors used to discredit Michelle Obama falsely alleged that she had written an incendiary college thesis and that she had disdain for the American flag. But these did not prevent her husband from being elected, and thus a black woman moved into the family quarters of the White House. After his first election, even more fictional stories circulated alleging that his wife had delusions of grandeur. Extremely distasteful caricatures and images of her were created and circulated widely to ensure that recipients would be able to picture Michelle as needy and demanding. But then her husband was reelected to a second term in office. Her cultural capital seemed only to increase; in 2013 she and Sarah Palin were tied in the Gallup Most Admired Women poll, and in 2014 she edged the former vice presidential candidate out, although Hillary Clinton continued to top the list. Talk show hosts continued to fawn over Michelle and magazines could count on more sales when they put her on their covers. Adoring crowds assembled whenever she spoke publicly. Authors were writing flattering books about her. At this juncture the most pernicious and painful stereotypes in the arsenal were called upon in attempts to hijack her image and to antagonize those who admired her.

Within two weeks of the 2016 election of Donald Trump, Pamela Ramsey Taylor, then the director of the Clay County Development Corporation outside of Charleston, West Virginia, celebrated the change of first families by posting the following on her Facebook page: "It will be so refreshing to have a classy, beautiful, dignified First Lady back in the White House. I am so tired of seeing an Ape in heels."[40] One of her Facebook friends, Beverly Whaling, the mayor of Clay, replied, "Just made my day,

Pam."[41] It was far from the first time that Michelle Obama was defined as a primate on social media and not even the first time the slur was hurled by an elected official. But coming after the election of Donald Trump, Taylor and Whaling faced a more pronounced and public shaming than their kindred racist predecessors. Following the fall out, both women eventually resigned, and Taylor was ultimately convicted on an unrelated matter— embezzling disaster-relief funds.

From hardcore supporters on the far right to apoplectic activists on the far left, and just about every voter in between, the election of Donald Trump was a powerful signal about racial politics in America. Assuming they wanted to keep their tax payer–supported positions, Taylor and Whaling must have believed that there would be no repercussions for posting derogatory remarks in plain view of their constituents. It was folks like them whose votes had ensured that Trump, clearly the candidate who had shown the most hate for the Obamas during the campaign, was the president-elect. Of course, they didn't realize that those who had supported the Obamas (and even perhaps Republicans who were not Obama fans but who would find it offensive to equate a black woman with an ape) were scrutinizing the channels of communication with more care. Comments that prior to the election were dismissed as the unfortunate musings of an extreme but small fringe of the American voting public were taken much more seriously because their candidate had prevailed at the polls. There were a lot more Pam Taylors and Bev Whalings out there than people realized.

5 Pandemic Levels

In August of 2020, following Joe Biden's long-anticipated announcement that Kamala Harris would be his running mate, in her very first speech, the forthright California senator compared the COVID-19 pandemic—then about six months into its international wrecking spree—with the Ebola outbreak in 2014: "It didn't have to be this way. Six years ago, in fact, we had a different health crisis. It was called Ebola. And we all remember that pandemic, but you know what happened then? Barack Obama and Joe Biden did their job. Only two people in the United States died. Two. That is what's called leadership."[1] Right-wing critics ready to pounce on all things Harris—the first vice presidential candidate with African American lineage—were quick to contradict and condemn her for insinuating that Barack Obama had triumphed over a public health threat comparable to the one that emerged on Donald Trump's watch. Several of the conspiracy theories that would stalk her candidacy also were posted in comments sections under the speech. For instance, her constitutional eligibility for the presidency was cast in doubt and accusations that she traded sexual favors for political ones were commonplace.[2] Clearly, there was a segment of the electorate dismayed by the prospect of another black candidate in the vicinity of 1600 Pennsylvania Avenue.

Selectively critiquing the Ebola outbreak several years after it had run its course and eager to short-circuit Harris's credibility, right-leaning journalists and pro-Trump tweeters poked holes in her statement where they could. They cited sources that defined Ebola as an epidemic and COVID-19 as a pandemic. They claimed that because COVID-19 can be spread by asymptomatic carriers and that Ebola transmission requires direct exposure to the bodily fluids of a carrier, the threat from Ebola to Americans had been minimal. They argued that Ebola had been largely contained to a handful of epidemiologically underprepared West African countries, an argument that also could be used to validate Harris's words.

Less than a week after Harris's speech, former First Lady Michelle Obama incorporated a plug for the Obama/Biden handling of Ebola 2014–2016 into her opening-night remarks at the virtual Democratic National Convention: "Our leaders worked hand-in-hand with scientists to help prevent an Ebola outbreak from becoming a global pandemic."[3] As was always the case when the former First Lady spoke publicly, her fans were ebullient in their praise for everything from her necklace (containing the word VOTE and selling out immediately) to the content of her comments, while her detractors wheeled out the legends about her gender identity, referring to her as Michael and pointing out what they perceived as evidence of her masculine anatomy.

Missing from all of these comments was any attention to the racially charged backdrop that developed as President Obama labored in 2014 to convince indifferent Americans and their elected representatives that it would be short-sighted and dangerous to leave the bare-bones African public health system to its own devices. Ebola had posed far more complicated problems for the Obama administration than the upbeat speeches suggested. A 2014 article in *The Hill* opined, "The Ebola crisis in the United States has become an anchor threatening to sink the Obama presidency."[4] Numerous commentators suggested that Ebola would be to Barack Obama what Hurricane Katrina had been to President Bush. Erupting in 2014, Ebola cast a shadow on the midterm elections, which were devastating to Obama and the Democrats. The Republican Party retained and indeed increased its majority in the House of Representatives and won back control of the Senate. Without a majority in either house of Congress, Obama's last two years were, from a legislative point of view, lackluster and disappointing. In an unprecedented abuse of power, the US Senate, under the leadership of Mitch McConnell, refused to hold the constitutionally required hearings that would have enabled the president to fill a vacancy on the Supreme Court.

THE HIV/AIDS LESSONS

When it comes to infectious diseases, Barack Obama was dealt a really bad hand. Not only did conspiracy theories about Ebola complicate his second administration, his initial bid for the White House in 2008 was nearly capsized when it was discovered that his pastor, the Reverend Jeremiah Wright, had subscribed to well-known conspiracy theories about HIV/AIDS. Wright's pronouncements articulated a then almost twenty-year-old conspiracy theory that had long been challenged, including by my own 1993 book, *I Heard It Through the Grapevine*. As is so often the case, those of us who offered up scientific evidence that contradicted the theory were disregarded by many people unpersuaded by our reasoning. As long as the notion that HIV/AIDS was a product of an anti-black, genocidal impulse made more cultural sense to Reverend Wright and others, any fact-checking by academics would fail. Barack Obama's predicament in the HIV/AIDS conspiracy situation was a familiar one to many African Americans of his ilk in the twenty-first century. In order to earn the respect and trust of many white Americans, he was expected to condemn black Americans who came to unpopular conclusions about the world. For African Americans who have some measure of success in terms of social and economic mobility, the request to forever rationalize, contextualize, and in some instances, impugn other black people, comes with too much regularity.

HIV/AIDS conspiracy theories were well entrenched in the black community in the early 2000s and remain commonplace even today. Looking at the time period when Reverend Wright was repeating these theories and Barack Obama was purportedly listening to them, polls suggest the good reverend was certainly not an outlier. An abstract for an article in the well-respected *Lancet* reported that 16 percent of African Americans surveyed found credible the view that the government created AIDS to control the black population. More than half of blacks believed that the government was guilty of holding back "a lot of information," about the virus.[5] These numbers indicate that suspicions regarding the official narratives about AIDS were not just the musings of a small fringe group of paranoid black people.

There is much that can be learned from the early days of HIV/AIDS and the ways in which people react to sometimes contradictory and always complex news and speculation. For those who came of age toward the end of the twentieth century, HIV/AIDS was the most significant "new" disease of their lifetimes. It really rocked our world and set the standards by which many of us would digest and process subsequent infectious disease outbreaks. In retrospect, we can see that some maladies exhibit characteristics that increase the likelihood that racially specific lore will take off. Infectious disease outbreaks that exhibit several of the attributes listed below are virtually guaranteed to inspire the circulation of conspiracy theories.[6]

Inventory of Conspiracy Theory Activators: Infectious Diseases
1. A commanding newness
2. Opaque or delayed disease naming
3. Atypical and unstable media coverage
4. Incomplete or contradictory medical theories
5. Marked patients/marked authorities
6. Graphic symptoms including contaminating bodily fluids
7. Geographic (non-Western) and/or ethnic etiology/involving animals
8. Long incubation period
9. Always or often fatal

We can see in HIV/AIDS examples how virtually all of the factors identified coalesce, laying the ground work for the human tendency to weave strands of information into narratives that contain all of the basic elements we crave in a good story that matches our worldview. These factors all lent themselves to interpretations regarding racial dynamics as they were playing out at the end of the twentieth century. At the end of the twentieth century we also see that while every color and kind of Americans was sculpting the news to fit their worldview, the Russians were watching and scheming.

Commanding Newness

A " commanding newness" gets top billing for a reason. Discussing contemporary legends about Snapple Iced Tea as well as other commercial products in the introduction, I noted that when a previously unknown product claws its way into the limelight and displaces the tried and true, the new kid on the block can generate an outsized amount of very speculative talk. In the case of infectious diseases, it's the new enemy in the emergency room that triggers the speculation. Part of the explanation for the rumors about Barack Obama stem from his status as a prominent "first" in so many ways.

A commanding newness in a disease can seem even more alarming than in commercial products or politicians. We think of diseases as rooted in nature, which we assume has given us enough diseases already. Famed virus researcher Peter Piot described the reaction his faculty mentors had to his desire to conduct research on infectious diseases in the mid-1970s: "Infectious diseases weren't considered interesting or cutting edge in 1974. They had just about all been conquered by advances in antibiotics and vaccines. My professor of social medicine grabbed my shoulder firmly, to make sure I was paying attention. 'There's no future in infectious diseases.' He stated flatly, in a tone that bore no argument. 'They've all been solved.'"[7]

Most people agreed with Piot's social medicine professor. Those of us in the baby boom generation, can't help but wonder why it is that our parents' generation experienced a stable and known inventory of diseases, while we have to worry about epidemiological crises like HIV/AIDS, Ebola, and COVID-19. And while our early to mid-twentieth-century ancestors certainly saw new products emerge and politicians from diverse backgrounds flourish, newly minted diseases weren't in the mix. As a result, any "new" disease is going to be met with suspicion.

Naming/Media Coverage and Incomplete Medical Theories

The public probably has unrealistic expectations both for journalists and scientists. If there's a chance we or our loved ones might succumb to a new disease, we want the scientific community to isolate it, tell us if we are likely to "catch" it, and quickly repurpose their labs to find therapies, or, better yet, a cure. The media is expected to provide accurate and unchanging advice and updates. After all, that's how it unfolds in a medical thriller or a feel-good, scientist-as-hero movie.

Real-life scientists and journalists rarely measure up to such an unreasonable standard. Before naming an emergent disease, scientists need to understand it well enough to determine how to categorize it. That takes time and research. But humans prefer our threats—everything from hurricanes to wars—to be named. In the case of HIV/AIDS, both medical researchers and the general population came up with labels that contributed to the stigma that soon became a debilitating force for early sufferers. One early appellation was the *Haitian disease*, another was *gay cancer*. The latter led to the quasi-official *gay-related immune deficiency syndrome (GRID)*. Even some in the scientific community used the 4H disease, the Hs referring to its supposed targets: Haitians, homosexuals, hemophiliacs, and heroin users. Eventually, the scientific community redirected attention from the victims' demographic characteristics back to the particularities of the disorder itself. Their research concluded that it was an "acquired immunodeficiency syndrome" which was quite a mouthful, hence the easy-to-remember acronym AIDS that became the recognized shorthand. After even further research, scientists came to understand that AIDS was actually the last stage of a disease caused by a virus that could be appropriately labeled human immunodeficiency virus, so then the moniker became HIV/AIDS.

Medical journals have never been a source of information for the public-at-large and in the 1980s most Americans relied upon television and print journalism for their news. As a result, all of this back-and-forth within the medical community was played out in the popular media, resulting in the kind of confusion that engenders the construction of alternative explanations. If you have been led to believe that homosexuals have something to worry about from gay cancer and then soon after are told that a heterosexual who has had blood transfusions is at risk, you may lose faith in the medical and journalistic communities.

In the 1980s—and some will argue that this is still the case—the scientific and journalistic spokespeople lacked any significant racial diversity. Thus, in some African American communities, white-coated white doctors were seen to be scrambling around about a mysterious new disease in ways that implicated communities associated with the African diaspora.

Marked Patients/Marked Authorities

From the beginning, HIV/AIDS had a disproportionate impact on select communities. Clearly, homosexual enclaves endured tremendous losses and other studies have documented the conspiracy theories that were common in gay circles. The list of likely HIV/AIDS patients also included several classifications that explicitly or implicitly identify black people. Sub-Saharan Africa's human losses were quickly staggering in number. Closer to the United States, early outbreaks in Haiti resulted in a tenacious association between that nation—one long riddled with the problems of abject poverty—and the disease.

Intravenous drug users and prostitutes held a place on the list of sufferers, and in the minds of many, blacks were overrepresented in these groups. In those days it was hard to identify another disease that was so capricious in its targets. An unavoidable common denominator linking all of these groups stemmed from their relatively low status in mainstream society. Gays, drug abusers, Africans, and the rest were marginalized and often unwanted populations. Could it truly be a fluke of nature that a new disease was diminishing their numbers?

The authority figures, individuals, and entities that wielded the power to do something about the disease were marked as well. Although it can now be traced to the 1950s, HIV/AIDS debuted as an ominous disorder during the administration of Ronald Reagan, a Republican president with a reputation for disinterest in, if not hostility toward, the groups—blacks, gays, drug users—most associated with the disease. Remarkably quiet as the death toll increased, President Ronald Reagan's minimal response was considered a cruel and callous expression of his preexisting disdain for the afflicted. His critics hypothesized that had HIV/AIDS plagued more socially influential Americans, he would have dispatched federal economic and research resources more generously. Presidents George H. W. Bush, and even Bill Clinton, who was certainly considered more liberal and inclusive than his Republican predecessors, were also criticized for under-investing in HIV/AIDS research. "The government" and numerous governmental agencies such as the Centers for Disease Control (CDC), the Federal Bureau of Investigation (FBI), and Central Intelligence Agency (CIA) were frequently found at fault for inadequate enforcement of policies that would protect HIV/AIDS patients from discriminatory practices and were key figures in the conspiracy theories that alleged the intentional or inadvertent manufacture of a deadly disease.

Although Anthony Fauci did not become a household name during the HIV/AIDS crisis, at least not in households oblivious to the developments in research laboratories, his stature as a renowned specialist in infectious diseases was established in the 1980s and 1990s and this is when his voice became one of the most respected ones on the disease. The well-known tennis great, public intellectual, and activist Arthur Ashe was one of the first highly visible African Americans to be diagnosed with AIDS. In his remarkable autobiography *Days of Grace: A Memoir*, he recalled being pressured by a caring friend to insist that Kemron, an anti-AIDS treatment developed in Kenya, be included in his treatment plan.[8] According to a common conspiracy theory, the Western medical establishment was unfairly discouraging the use of Kemron because it had been developed in Africa and would not therefore bring profits to American pharmaceutical companies. In more sinister versions, the allegation was made that the American government didn't want Kemron interfering with the desired genocidal outcomes of AIDS. When Ashe's own physician eschewed the effectiveness of Kemron, Ashe met with Fauci, who then led the Office of AIDS Research for the Centers for Disease Control (CDC). Fauci described Kemron's poor performance in clinical trials and predicted that it would not receive FDA approval.[9] Ashe accepted the science, like virtually all who had full-blown AIDS in that era, and later died from AIDS-related causes. Fauci and the medical community's refusal to sanction Kemron remained controversial at least until viable AIDS treatments became an option. Little did we know then that the good doctor would continue to be a vital supporting character in subsequent infectious disease narratives.

*Geographic (Non-Western) and/or Ethnic
Etiology/Bodily Fluids/Animals*

In order to develop effective treatments for HIV/AIDS, scientists needed to trace its origins, and lay persons trying to make sense of its novelty needed to situate the disease in a specific setting. Before long, scientific theories established that the disease was rooted in Africa, and that humans there must have been contaminated by the blood of African green monkeys. Several decades later, and after a multitude of research studies, it remains the prevailing scientific theory that blood from a chimpanzee infected a human from the Democratic Republic of Congo, thereby causing an animal disease to jump to a human, resulting in a virus harmful to humans. To laypeople, the revelation that so much human suffering in the Western world had been spawned by the blood of an African monkey commingling with the blood of an African man seemed extraordinarily implausible—more like the plotline of a science fiction novel rather than a bona fide research-based conclusion.

The combination of Africa as the geographic epicenter, monkeys as carriers, and bodily fluids as the mode of transmission was a trifecta of triggers for the development of counternarratives. To some African Americans, this seemed like just another excuse for whites to continue the painful stereotyping of blacks as ape-like in behavior and appearance. Since this association was reviewed in the last chapter, I will not go over it here. What conformed more to their worldview was the possibility that the scientists involved were incompetent or evil actors in the dissemination of HIV/AIDS.

Long Incubation Period/Fatal

The HIV/AIDS narratives are part classical tragedy and part modern horror story. In those early years, once a definitive diagnosis was established, there were no upbeat plot twists. When the hero contracted HIV/AIDS, he and his loved ones were in for an unhappy ending. Of course, the hero doesn't start out feeling, looking, or acting sick. HIV/AIDS has a protracted incubation period, meaning that infected individuals could (and did) infect others by practicing what we now call unsafe sex, by donating blood, and by sharing needles. Several folklorists have documented the once extremely well-known contemporary legends that reflect the public's anxieties about the prospect of "catching" the deadly virus as a result of a casual sexual encounter. In many versions a young man meets a fetching young woman at a party or in a bar. They have sex, usually in his hotel room. In the morning, he can't find "Mary" but does discover "Welcome to the World of AIDS," scrawled in her red lipstick on the bathroom mirror.[10]

Race is not a strong theme in most versions of AIDS Mary but the cautionary tale showcases the attitudes that have developed about carriers and the risks that unsuspecting folks needed to be aware of. A widely known and believed legend, it signals the ongoing concerns that innocent, albeit indulgent, behavior, enabled by a contaminated and corrupt individual, could have fatal consequences.

Once they did surface, the symptoms of HIV/AIDS were not ones that a sexual partner or anyone else could miss: patients often lost a great deal of weight; they suffered hair loss; they became pale; they developed unsightly lesions on their skin; they vomited frequently and robustly; and they endured endless bouts of crippling diarrhea. Unable to stave off other illnesses, patients were frequently in and out of hospitals, regularly adding other diseases to their list such as pneumonia and Kaposi Sarcoma. More so than with invisible, airborne diseases or ones in which the fluids are microscopic, humans fret about the toxicity of substances we can see, touch, and smell such as pus, semen, urine, and blood. The body of an AIDS patient became a map to the extent of their suffering; death was a certainty for all afflicted. Nothing is more ominous than an inelegant fatal disease.

AIDS STORIES

HIV/AIDS clearly exhibited enough characteristics to prompt conspiracy theory formation in impacted communities. Others in addition to AIDS Mary surfaced and within the gay community a subset of these theories flourished. For many African Americans, the individual components of the AIDS crisis would soon coalesce into a story that better jibed with their sense of place in the world than the official explanations. As I reviewed in *Grapevine*, rumors and conspiracy theories spread in which the scientists themselves, at the direction of government agencies, were the ones who actually created HIV/AIDS in top secret laboratories. Nature hadn't made a new disease; it had been created by man. Diligent scientists designed the biological weapon but failed to anticipate just how powerful it would become—the havoc that ensued was not a part of the experimental design. In other versions, the scientists were more evil and their game plan had been to test their weapon by using marginalized populations such as homosexuals, drug users, and blacks during their trials. Again, they underestimated its potency and were unable to stop its stampede. The most diabolical threat, and this is the one that was repeated by Reverend Wright in 2008, alleged that the goal had not been to develop a weapon for potential deployment against a foreign adversary, but a genocidal tool that would annihilate blacks once and for all. With additional permutations, all three of these conspiracy theories were widely circulated, and some African Americans continue to find these explanations more credible than anything linking the disorders to African monkeys.

Reverend Wright refused to back down from his statements; like so many others, he supported his belief in AIDS as a genocidal weapon by citing the most well-known authentic example of medical experimentation with black bodies, the notorious Tuskegee Experiment. Arthur Ashe recalled that the unfortunate history of the Tuskegee Experiment had surfaced in his conversation with Fauci, and it was a constant reference point during my HIV/AIDS interviews in the 1980s and 1990s. For four decades, doctors affiliated with the Public Health Service (PHS), a precursor to the CDC, methodically charted the progress of syphilis on the bodies of 399 black men who had been told that they had "bad blood." Even after new drugs were approved that could have mitigated their suffering from syphilis, the researchers did not administer it to their subjects, as that would have ruined the design of their experiment.[11]

As is so often the case with conspiracy theories, individuals whose experience of everyday life differs from that of the believers find the stories flawed and nonsensical, and they often disparage anyone who doesn't see the same holes in the story they see. In order not to appear as a paranoid black man, Barack Obama had to disassociate from Jeremiah Wright and ensure that white voters understood he did not believe HIV/AIDS was a genocidal weapon. In order to be elected, Barack Obama could not risk alienating potential voters who would reject claims that in late twentieth century America, blacks were victimized at the hands of the government or its agencies. Once again, Barack Obama's predicament was shared by other African Americans who were expected to denigrate any of their sister or brother blacks who gave credence to the HIV/AIDS conspiracy beliefs.

SOVIET SUBTERFUGE

If the attributes of HIV/AIDS didn't already hit enough criteria for the spread of conspiracy theories, there was one more propelling force at work. During my research for *Grapevine* in the late 1980s I became interested in just what the "government" had to say about the fact that it was being blamed for spearheading the development of a genocidal weapon. After all, if it was being falsely charged, wouldn't it behoove the powers that be to try and disabuse African Americans of the notions that they were its prey? Not surprisingly, governmental documents and various agencies did categorically deny any wrongdoing. They didn't, however, suggest that blacks were unduly paranoid, as I expected. Rather, they assigned blame to foreign agitators. At the request of the US House of Representatives, the United States Information Agency (USIA) prepared a report in 1988 that included references to a Soviet campaign accusing the United States of working with either the South Africans or the Israelis to design an "ethnic weapon," that could be used to kill blacks but not whites. Tracing this campaign back to "at least 1980," the report informed the Congressional committees that, "The Soviet goal in this campaign seems clear: to make it appear as if the United States and its alleged collaborators are pursuing racist, genocidal policies."[12] Speaking to AIDS more specifically, the report informs its congressional readers that "the largest Soviet disinformation campaign in recent years has made the totally false claim that the AIDS virus was created in a U.S. military facility at Fort Detrick, Maryland."[13]

Crafting an old-fashioned business letter, I took it upon myself to reach out to the CIA to ask for their position on the AIDS (this exchange and research predate the HIV discovery and labeling) conspiracy theories and heard back: "We believe that rumors linking the CIA with the development or the spreading of the AIDS virus especially in Africa, may be the result of what we would call "disinformation" efforts of hostile intelligence services to damage the United States. The CIA has had absolutely nothing to do with either the development nor the spreading of AIDS or any other virus. The CIA is not carrying out experiments in this regard and you can document by corresponding with either the House or Senate Select Committees on Intelligence which monitor Agency operations."[14]

Back in the 1980s, I was disheartened by Washington's approach to the conspiracy theories. I thought it was naive for the CIA representative to suggest that anyone who took seriously the belief that the CIA had its hands in the formulation of AIDS would think that Congress wasn't in ca-hoots with them. Consequently, staff to intelligence committees certainly wouldn't acknowledge their misdeeds to a mild-mannered university-based black folklorist. I also thought there were missed opportunities to point out that the US government would find the prospect of a genocidal weapon morally reprehensible and profoundly counter to all of the prin-ciples of the Bill of Rights and the Constitution. I was also bothered by the underlying assumption that had the Soviet Union's agents not planted the conspiracy theories, then blacks would not have suspected the govern-ment of malfeasance.

I was willing to accept that our intelligence community had secured proof that the Soviets were actively and aggressively throwing accelerant on the flames of racial discord in the United States. But nowhere in the reports, or in my correspondence, could I find any references to an action plan. What were our agencies doing in turn to neutralize or undercut this Soviet campaign? If the Soviet Union had mobilized its Navy too close to an American military installation, the United States would have been quick to send in our own ships to protect our terrain. So if the Soviets were send-ing agents to antagonize African Americans, where were our government's counterforces, and why weren't they trying to thwart this plan? Did they have any scenarios that involved actually letting Americans know what was going on, maybe share with African American leaders information on the sources of these stories? The message I got at the time was that the pow-ers in Washington acknowledged that while it was unfortunate that Soviet manipulation was exacerbating racial tension in the United States, that was somehow a necessary evil, given the geopolitical agenda at that time. Assuring black people, and other Americans for that matter, that their government was not pursuing a genocidal agenda was not a high priority.

The takeaway of the "AIDS is a result of intentional governmental machinations" conspiracy theory is that the well-being of blacks is un-important to the US government. But the government's silence and in-activity on dispelling these beliefs is similarly supported by virtually the same message—that it is acceptable to have foreign intelligence operatives manage and manipulate the attitude some of its citizens hold toward its home government. Perhaps this explains why those who accept the current scientific explanations for the origins of AIDS get a bit weary at having to defend our friends and family who aren't as convinced.

As long as there is any level of relevance to their content, conspiracy theories do not disappear. Given that those in power took no steps to debunk the theories, and that the overall circumstances of blacks in America changed only minimally, it is not surprising that the original theories as well as new ones about HIV/AIDS therapies retained their persuasiveness and many are still in vogue.

Much to the dismay of many on the far right, Obama's association with Reverend Wright didn't prevent his election. But that didn't mean Obama received a get-out-of-Trinity-Baptist-Church-free card. He made his way to the oval office during a time in which HIV/AIDS was still a significant problem for a sitting president. Domestically, it exemplified the different scenarios experienced by Americans with access to reliable health insurance and those who lacked that safety net. Americans who were privy to the most current information about the disease and the always improving pharmacological options on the market did not have to consider HIV/AIDS a terminal disease. On the other hand, those on the lower end of the socioeconomic and educational spectrum faced far more uncertainty, and their less rosy health outcomes demonstrated the gap between the haves and have-nots. As always, there were a disproportionate number of blacks in that "have-not" category. Internationally, HIV/AIDS dominated the needs list of sub-Saharan Africa and Barack Obama's status as the son of an African father lent itself to a multitude of cultural complexities that had not been faced by his predecessors.

EBOLA, 2014

If the race-based conundrums posed by HIV/AIDS in the United States were not enough of a challenge for President Obama, the medical news coming from West Africa was ominous and introduced a potentially catastrophic problem into his agenda for his second term in office. A clearly contagious infectious disease was making its way from one West African community to the next, leaving scores of dead behind it. The timing was not fortuitous—once again, a situation bound to attract conspiracy theorists had developed on the eve of a significant election. His name wasn't on any ballots in 2014 but attitudes about President Obama and his policies were bound to influence voters in the midterm elections.

In 2014, Ebola wasn't as new as AIDS had been in the 1980s, but it was relatively new, certainly when compared with familiar diseases such as malaria or smallpox. The first cases appeared in 1976 in Sudan, soon followed by another outbreak in Zaire. In his autobiography, Peter Piot—one of the first researchers on the scene—recalls that in the naming process the scientists resisted the obvious geographic identifier because they didn't want to unduly stigmatize Yambuku, the site of the first cases. Instead, they opted to use the name Ebola, the reference point being a nearby river. In this instance, Piot and his colleagues—all the kind of courageous doctors who willingly made their way to rural Africa out of a humanitarian impulse to minimize the damage of a disease outbreak—may have underestimated how unlike other Westerners they were. To those unfamiliar with or hostile to all things African, the exact locale within the continent had little meaning, all that mattered was that Africa was the source of an ugly affliction. Ebola had a built-in mnemonic component, like *Africa* and *Obama*, the word *Ebola* had three syllables and began and ended with vowels. Yambuku wasn't stigmatized but Africa was and Obama would be. Piot acknowledges that they were drawn to the name in part because Ebola means "black river," in the local language. While I concede that the perpetuators of the many conspiracy theories and memes that exploit the Ebola name probably are not aware of this translation, the name is a starting point for a thorough trashing of the disease as a blight inflicted on the rest of the world by Africans.

In terms of the media, Ebola went from being a minimally covered disease to a near household name in the United States, even with very few Americans actually contracting the virus. When it was first discovered in 1976, there was some minor coverage, but in the year of the US bicentennial, Africa's health problems were not going to get a lot of ink in the mainstream American press. The presumption was that what happens in Africa, stays in Africa. But a decade later when national boundaries and large bodies of water seemed to mean nothing, as we learned from the spread of HIV/AIDS, more cautious thinking prevailed. Suddenly it made sense to be attentive to the emergence of an infectious disease, no matter how far from the United States it erupted.

Ebola got a second and very impactful look, thanks to Richard Preston's runaway 2004 best seller, *The Hot Zone: The Terrifying True Story of the Origins of the Ebola Virus*. A sharp-penned science writer with storytelling skills that would be the envy of many novelists, Preston created a page-turner that would sell more than a quarter of a million copies and be translated into thirty languages. Ten years after its original publication date, the 2014 Ebola outbreak provided Preston with a boost in sales. That year *The Hot Zone* reached number seven on the *New York Times* bestseller list and number twenty-three on Amazon.[15]

Few in the book publishing business would have predicted the popularity of *The Hot Zone*. The book is tantalizing for the same reasons that the Ebola conspiracy theories became appealing. *The Hot Zone* focuses on several aspects of Ebola that are also components of the inventory of conspiracy theory activators: the extensive damage that can be wrought during Ebola's two- to twenty-one-day incubation period; the fact that it is so often fatal; the naivete with which some medical researchers as well as politicians treated the disease; the day-to-day life of the West African peoples that accelerated the spread of the disease; and how the virus jumped from bats to humans. He was particularly adept at prose that reinforced the untidiness of the symptoms:

> He leans over, head on his knees, and brings up an incredible quantity of blood from his stomach and spills it onto the floor with a gasping groan. . . . The only sound is a choking in his throat as he continues to vomit blood and black matter while unconscious. Then comes a sound like a bedsheet being torn in half, which is the sound of his bowels opening and venting blood from the anus. The blood is mixed with intestinal lining. He has sloughed his gut. The linings of his intestines have come off and are being expelled along with huge amounts of blood.
>
> The other patients in the waiting room stand up and move away from the man on the floor, calling for a doctor. Pools of blood spread out around him, enlarging rapidly. Having destroyed its host, the hot agent is coming out of every orifice, and is "trying" to find a new host.[16]

Charles Monet, the pseudonym given to the patient described above, was actually suffering from Marburg virus, but since the title of the book contains *origins of the Ebola virus*, it could be expected that this was one of the many descriptions of the utter physical devastation wrought by Ebola.

Most credentialed infectious disease experts concluded that Preston had exaggerated the potency and sloppiness of the virus. After acknowledging that the book was one of the motivations for her career in infectious disease research, Tara Smith noted in 2014, "The clinical picture of Ebola that people take away from *The Hot Zone* just isn't accurate and with 3.5 million copies sold, is certainly driving some (much? most?) of the fear about this virus." Smith further notes that Preston's prose inaccurately suggests that Ebola is an airborne disease, that one is in danger from the virus drifting across a room.[17] This mischaracterization of the modes of transmission greatly contributes to the Western anxiety about Ebola. With its relentless and grisly descriptions of a hyper-contagious, profoundly aggressive virus capable of squeezing, curdling, toxifying, and projecting any fluids out of the body of its host, *The Hot Zone* guaranteed that anyone uneasy about being exposed to a deadly disease would pay attention.

The title of the book emphasizes that it will be about *The Terrifying True Story of the Origins of the Ebola Virus*. In the pages of the "true" story, Preston provides a list of eleven "main characters," with Ebola itself appearing as a twelfth anthropomorphized character on the list. All eleven human characters are white Westerners and the settings are either the African locales to which they traveled or laboratories in Virginia or Maryland. Much of the book focuses on the potential threat to the white scientists who are conducting research on imported monkeys that have contracted a frightening and infectious disease that mimics the behaviors of the Marburg and Ebola viruses. The "main characters," about whom the reader is intended to worry, are white men and women who might succumb to this Africa-rooted virus wreaking havoc in US-based enclaves that are an easy drive from the nation's capital. Preston draws much less attention to the humans victimized by the disease in Africa, although one might reasonably expect that *the True Story of the Origins of the Ebola Virus* might take that topic on. Preston doesn't ignore them entirely, but their predicament alone would not have prompted so many book sales.

With a diabolical and inelegant disease as its main actor, *The Hot Zone* cemented the origins story for Ebola in the United States. Between 1995, when Preston's tale of the dangers of American research on Ebola insinuated itself into the American psyche, and 2014, there were several outbreaks of the virus, all confined to rural sections of West Africa and all eventually contained. But when Ebola surfaced in 2014, the conditions were stacked in favor of the opportunistic filovirus. Appearing first in rural southeastern Guinea, it quickly spread to the much more densely populated capital. Once the disease made its way from the more sparsely populated homogeneous environs to sprawling capital cities traversed by visitors from neighboring countries, its stature as the most deadly Ebola outbreak was sealed. Ironically, Westerners who still had their copies of *The Hot Zone* on their bookcases (I did) knew much more about the disease than the impoverished urban-based residents and the political leaders of these West African nations who continued to engage in practices that enabled the disease to spread with abandon.

Neither the local political nor the public health infrastructures in Africa were poised to manage a severe health crisis. Unfortunately, overwhelmed governmental leaders were loath to go public with the bad news befalling their countrymen and women. So black men, women, and children were dying, and they were dying with visceral disfigurement. Neither family members who were caring for the afflicted nor medical workers—who were in short supply—had access to personal protective gear and were themselves dying in large numbers. These were cultures that vested deep spiritual significance in the ritualistic washing of the bodies of the dead. Those baths and subsequent burials provided a playground for the virus and led to many more deaths.

By the middle of 2014, the international public health community had sounded the alarms, noting that if these under-resourced countries did not get significant help and get it quickly, the death rate would accelerate, precipitously. Further, Ebola wouldn't be an African problem, it would be an international one. Once again Dr. Fauci's voice becomes a key one as Americans began to shape their views on the crisis itself and the role the United States should take or not take in its mitigation. Frustrated by the pace of the American response, Fauci went on record saying: "The community of nations—European nations, other developed countries that have resources to do it, the UN, the African Union—if they get involved in a very aggressive way to do infection control, we can put an end to this, I'm confident." But if we have a lot of motion but no action, a lot of signing of resolutions with no resources, it's not going to happen. We're not going to control it."[18]

There were two prevailing views of what exactly the Ebola problem was and what would constitute a path to resolution. President Barack Obama, Fauci, members of the public health community, and many on the left were operating from a problem/solution statement that can be summarized in the simplest terms as follows: Ebola—the debilitating disease depicted graphically in *The Hot Zone*—was killing Africans again and moving quickly. In partnership with other concerned governments and the World Health Organization (WHO), we have the financial resources and the public health know-how to quash this outbreak and ensure fewer lives are lost. To Obama and members of his team who understood the competing perspectives of the electorate, the corollary to this problem statement was that 2014 was an election year, and those unhappy with his decision would show their dissatisfaction on social media, and, more importantly, at the polls in November.

On the right, the problem/solution statements went something like this: Ebola—the debilitating disease depicted graphically in *The Hot Zone*—was killing Africans again and threatening to move beyond that continent. The citizens of the United States would be safe if all travel from these countries was forbidden and any Americans who may have traveled to those regions were prohibited from returning. If the president and Congress took a different direction, the November congressional elections were approaching.

Ultimately, President Obama endorsed sending both military and medical personnel to administer aid to stricken Africans and he eventually allocated a significant amount of money—approximately six billion dollars—to anti-Ebola efforts. To those on the left who advocated a strong response to the needs of Africans and to infection control, the president's action was too long in coming. To those on the right whose only concern was to prevent any Americans from suffering, Obama's decision to not stop all flights and to send money and personnel to assist Africans on the ground was an egregious misuse of presidential power.

The objections were quick to surface. Between August and November of 2014, Donald Trump used his Twitter account to repeatedly criticize Obama's decisions. For Trump and his followers the only thing worse than welcoming more Africans to the United States was enabling sick ones to enter. Over and over again his comments reflect dissatisfaction with black mobility and indicated a belief that danger from the virus could be curtailed by prohibiting anyone in Africa from traveling to the United States and anyone from the United States from traveling to Africa. His disgust with the prospect of the arrival of a patient suffering from Ebola is clear from the first of his over ninety tweets issued before the midterm elections: "Ebola patient will be brought to the U.S. in a few days—now I know for sure that our leaders are incompetent. KEEP THEM OUT OF HERE!"[19] Before long, his voice became more confrontational. One of his most retweeted comments read: "President Obama-close down the flights from Ebola infected areas right now, before it is too late! What the hell is wrong with you?"[20] Trump was just as incensed over the Obama administration's decision to send American military and health care personnel to assist local governments in impacted regions: "Why are we sending thousands of ill-trained soldiers into Ebola infested areas of Africa! Bring the plague back to the U.S.? Obama is so stupid."[21] Trump harshly disparaged the experts Obama relied upon during the crisis: "Obama just appointed an Ebola Czar with zero experience in the medical area and zero experience in infectious disease control. A total joke."[22] From time to time, he drew tenuous connections between Ebola and Obama's health care initiative, often referred to as Obamacare: "Do you notice that because of Ebola, ISIS etc. ObamaCare has gone to the back burner despite horrible results coming out. A disaster!"[23]

As his comments on the American military suggest, Trump offered no support for humanitarian-based interventions. The unnecessary deaths of African peoples were not a part of the problem statement for him and the voters who would soon comprise his base. They considered the expenditure of American dollars on African peoples as unnecessary and wasteful.

Compared to his tweets on President Obama's eligibility to be president and religion, the Trump Ebola corpus fall a bit short of actually promoting the conspiracy theories that were in circulation. However, virtually all of the themes discernible in those theories resonate with the Trump tweets. The anti-Obama/Africa venom in articulations of the conspiracy theories is striking. Many of them incorporate the already established anti-Obama motifs; the misspellings of his name; the assumptions of his allegiance to Muslims; his purported hatred for America and the Second Amendment; his manipulation of FEMA; and his sexual preferences. Obama's approach to Ebola showcases how, having elected and reelected such an individual, Americans have set themselves on track for annihilation because the president wants them all dead.

Just as written anti-Obama lore often riffed off of the Obama autobiographies or his actual quotations, many successful visual images repurposed iconography that had been used in his campaigns. Here we can really see just how disastrous the choice of the word *Ebola* for the name of the virus proved to be for Obama. The linguistic and visual symmetry of the words Ebola and Obama is one of the most common connections exploited in the images. The image in figure 1 was not only circulated on the internet, but was also manufactured as a bumper sticker. The font and colors were used by the 2008 and 2012 presidential campaigns. Intended to be suggestive of the American flag and to convey the sun rising over the horizon of a new day the middle "O" was the Barack Obama political logo. The message was clear that those posting it on their social media accounts or attaching it to the bumpers of their cars wanted to communicate a negative association between the president and the outbreak.

Intended to more directly link Obama with ill will toward his country, another version, shown in figure 2, contains the sentence, "Enjoy Barack Obama's Legacy America." Here each letter from EBOLA is used to decode an embedded message.

The most common corruption of the spellings of Obama and Ebola replace the "E" in Ebola with an "O." The image in figure 3 morphs the iconographic "Hope" poster designed and disseminated by street artist Shepard Fairey in 2008. It is hard to imagine that the original image was unfamiliar to any voter seeing it in 2014. Considered one of the most successful visual representations of a presidential candidate, it is also one of the most manipulated.

Sometimes rendered separately, sometimes as a triptych, the first image transforms the ubiquitous flag lapel pin into a shape slightly reminiscent of the image of the actual Ebola virus. In the second, the flagged virus is missing from his lapel and a traditional health care mask has now been added to the visage of the president. The health care mask might be construed as a signal of humanitarian efforts, but that message is discarded

Figure 1. Obama campaign iconography embedded in Ebola bumper sticker.

Figure 2. Ebola converted to anti-Obama acronym.

and the third situates the look of a full gas mask, a stock piece of equipment for a soldier in danger from gases or other toxins. The message moves from Obama as someone wearing the virus with the same pride he has for the flag to someone protecting himself from the virus to someone militarizing the virus.

Some of Obama's critics continued to use prose to make a case. One of the most coherent written articulations of the Ebola-as-genocide beliefs followed an article on a right-wing website advancing unsubstantiated rumors about a single African Ebola patient being brought to the United States. According to this commentator who claimed to be writing from Houston, Texas:

A couple of years ago Obama made the statement while in Egypt that by 2016 America would be a Muslim nation. In order to do that he has to move hundreds of millions of Muslims to the United States. But before he can do that he has to get rid of hundreds of millions of Americans living here now. He planned to collect all the guns owned by Americans and then incarcerate them into Fema prisons to be exterminated at his leisure. Well, gun confiscation has not gone his way. Americans have been buying guns ever since he hit the White House and it has not stopped yet. Millions and millions of Americans are not going to buy that many expensive firearms just to hand over to the Federal Government. It is evident that we are not going along to the death chambers peacefully like the Jews did in Germany. Plan two! He will simply introduce Ebola in the United States and let it do his dirty work for him. Remember he had the first two Ebola cases brought to Dallas, Texas. He also sent hundreds of our soldiers over there to be infected. And he refused to let Ebola patients be excluded from entering the United States. This is all his plan to destroy America as we know it today and turn it into a Muslim hell hole.[24]

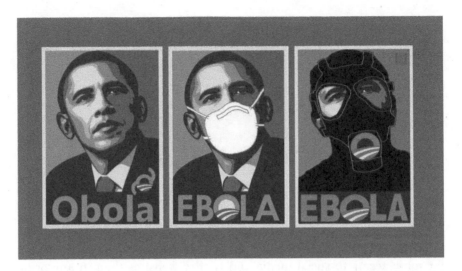

Figure 3. Obama/Ebola: Variations on a theme.

Dispassionate and methodical, this narrative moves through the anti-Obama tropes that would be familiar to similarly inclined thinkers, building a case that the president was intent on genocide. Most of the underlying messages had both visual and written versions.

Obama's decision-making regarding Ebola had implications for the 2014 election. This becomes clear in comments in which an accusation of genocide is followed by voting advice such as:

> We can't seal ourselves off from disease when we have a traitor who wants to intentionally infect Americans as Obama does want to do. Obama is literally a mentally ill racist hater. He is psychologically unstable. Look at what he does, not his non-stop lies. Obama is the worse person possible to be in charge of other peoples lives. Obama needs to be sealed off from any influence on America. Vote the democrats out of the Senate on election days will help do just that.[25]

Using images (figure 4) intended to provoke fears of both the Ebola virus and crime, the caption also encourages voters to make their dissatisfaction with President Obama known at the polls.[26]

For better or for worse, the range of internet communication pathways increased steadily in the twenty-first century; by 2014, voters had

Figure 4. Anti-Obama midterm election meme.

far more access to social media and sundry websites than in any prior election. Using Facebook as an example, in the 2012 election season, the world's most popular social media platform had 979.75 million users—by 2014 the figure was 1.33 billion, a 35.75 percent increase. The Republican Party was making sure its candidates were turning Obama's handling of Ebola into an issue that would undermine their Democratic opponents. According to an early October 2014 CNN story, "GOP officials . . . internal polling finds 60% of voters believe that if a single case of Ebola arises in the U.S., it should be treated as a major crisis by the federal government."[27] While Republican candidates and strategists were keeping Ebola in the mainstream news, their grassroots allies, cantankerous internet trolls—a new breed of computer savvy malcontents eager to generate pandemonium—and probably Russian bots as well, were keeping the Obama/Ebola conspiracy theories prominent on the computer screens of voters.

As a rule, there are no winners in epidemics and pandemics. The figures for Ebola in 2014 are sobering. In Guinea, Liberia, and Sierra Leone there were just under thirty thousand cases with just under twelve thousand deaths. Twenty percent of the deaths were of children, and the epidemic had a crippling impact on health care workers in all three nations. Along with international partners and the WHO, the United States devoted resources to building laboratories in Africa and training local communities in infection prevention and control practices. The medical and military personnel who returned from offering humanitarian assistance in Africa did not unleash Ebola in the United States. There were a total of eleven cases of Ebola in the United States and according to the CDC, one death.

The Obama administration certainly earned the praise that Kamala Harris and Michelle Obama offered during the 2020 Democratic convention. But the Obama administration and the Democratic Party were victims of an Ebola panic.[28] Much of this panic was manufactured by an increasingly emboldened right-wing cohort of opponents skilled in the tools of meme-making and social media. They largely operated without scrutiny from the press and the Democrats, or even checks from administrative agencies. Donald Trump—now known for his disastrous oversight of the COVID-19 pandemic—was relentless in his desire to tell his Twitter world about Obama's incompetence. It is probably the case that the efforts to malign Obama's handling of the epidemic was aided by trolls and Russian bots—although pinpointing the exact level of interference in the 2014 election season is difficult. Ebola beliefs shifted the nation to the right in the midterms and that shift signaled the direction the country would take in 2016.

COVID-19

On April 26, 2020, the popular actor Brad Pitt donned a wig, a suit, and glasses to appear on *Saturday Night Live* as Dr. Anthony Fauci. In the frequently re-telecast clip, Fauci/Pitt attempts to justify several optimistic assessments that President Trump had made about the fight against the pandemic. After the last gag, Pitt removed his wig and glasses and thanked Fauci for his "calm and clarity in this unnerving time."[29] But not everyone wanted to show the love to Fauci that weekend. On the same day, former mayor of New York City and Donald Trump's most fervent wingman, Rudy Giuliani, posted a tweet, which was retweeted at least twenty-five thousand times, posing the question, "Why did the US (NIH) give 3.7 m to the Wuhan Lab in China? Such grants were prohibited in 2014. Did Pres. Obama grant an exception?"[30] In other interviews during that time frame, Giuliani more specifically indicted Fauci as the decision maker on this award by saying, "Dr. Fauci gave 3.7 million dollars to the Wuhan laboratory."[31] The seeds for a conspiracy theory linking former President

Barack Obama and Dr. Anthony Fauci to the invention of COVID-19 in a laboratory were germinating.

The supposition that Barack Obama and Anthony Fauci were really at fault for the spread of COVID-19 was not the first nor the last of the cavalcade of trash talk generated by the pandemic. Those conspiracy theories that supporters of the forty-fifth president used to blame the forty-fourth president and his administration are the ones I will consider here. The building blocks of the anti-Obama theories can be better understood by analyzing the characteristics of COVID-19 data points as viewed through the lens of the conspiracy theory activators. Having come to understand the cultural consequences of ill-considered disease naming, the public health community designated this disease the "novel (new) coronavirus" as a placeholder name for a new virus. Once its composition was more fully understood, it got its own name, sans any geographic markers. In this case, COVID-19, referring to its membership in the coronavirus family with the "19" referring to the year of its discovery, 2019. According to most researchers, it was identified in a laboratory in Wuhan, China; it was brand-spanking-new, having jumped from a bat to a human in an exotic locale. In fact, it was soon clear that as much as the scientific community wanted to avoid the potential for geographic slurs, more xenophobic observers were going to reject their efforts: in this case, the president of the United States, who repeatedly and unapologetically used "China Virus" to refer to the disease and had no reservations about assigning blame to the Chinese people for the outbreak.

In addition to having a long incubation period, COVID-19 was also uneven in its wrath. Some patients were asymptomatic but contagious, meaning that a person who looked completely healthy could spread the disease easily. Although COVID-19 is rarely fatal, the rate of contagion is so high that even a small percentage of deaths is a high absolute number.

From its earliest days the media coverage of the virus was deemed problematic. Against the backdrop of a highly acrimonious and polarized presidential campaign, the epidemic became politicized, and coverage of it was criticized accordingly. Media outlets that were construed as paying overly close attention to the epidemic and statistics such as hospitalizations, positive test results, and death rates were accused by the right of overreacting. Media outlets that were perceived as privileging economic stability over the pandemic cautions were accused by the left of disregarding the wisdom of the scientific community. Fauci and other scientists, doctors, and members of the public health profession were pilloried by the right when they initially discouraged widespread use of masks by the public at large, only to reverse themselves several weeks later, suggesting that masks would be a prime tool in slowing the spread of the virus.

COVID-19 patients were not marked in the ways that HIV/AIDS and Ebola ones were and the disease's symptoms are less visible and unsightly. More members of the African American and Latino community were likely to be diagnosed with COVID-19, but that stems from their disproportionate representation in high-risk occupational settings. In the very early days there were some rumors that blacks would not develop COVID-19, but those dissipated quickly. Individuals with preexisting health conditions and the elderly were vulnerable but as the disease spread, it counted victims in every age group, ethnicity, and social class. COVID-19 could manifest with symptoms similar to a common cold or profoundly debilitating breathing issues. Although it is transmitted via fluids, they are microscopic respiratory droplets. Whereas Ebola tended to make its presence known on the outside as well as inside of a patient, COVID-19 limits itself more to internal manifestations including severe body aches and shortness of breath.

But if the patients who succumbed to COVID-19 were not marked, those who were positioned as authorities certainly aroused the suspicions of many on the far right. Giuliani's accusations about Dr. Fauci and Barack Obama should not be surprising. Still in place as the director for the National Institute of Allergy and Infectious Diseases (NIAID) and a prominent member of the White House Coronavirus Task Force, Fauci often appeared with President Trump at the daily press briefings on the pandemic that occurred in the spring of 2020. Fauci's task was to put the pandemic in laymen's terms, explaining to the public what was known about the disease and what steps could be taken to mitigate its impact. From the beginning, Fauci's messages were often at odds with those of the president. The more some members of the public embraced Fauci, the more the president distanced himself from him.

As is so often the case with individuals who find themselves prominent in conspiracy theories, Dr. Fauci provoked extreme reactions from the public. Americans either loved or loathed him. More so in the United States than elsewhere, the COVID-19 pandemic engendered public debates about the value of science itself and the wisdom of scientific and medical professionals. Urging a cautious approach to the virus and favoring ongoing mitigation strategies, Fauci was perceived by some on the right as an obstacle to efforts to reverse the economic impact of the pandemic.

Rudy Giuliani, Donald Trump, and their inner circle also had routinely found creative and spurious ways of blaming problems that emerged during the Trump administration on President Obama and his administration. Journalists from a variety of media outlets penned follow-up stories on the Giuliani interview and tweet. A headline in the *Washington Examiner* read "'Paid for the Damn Virus That's Killing Us': Giuliani Rips Fauci over Grants to Wuhan Laboratory." The article goes on to say, "According to a report [no specific report is cited], the U.S. intelligence community has growing confidence that the current coronavirus strain may have accidentally escaped from the Wuhan Institute of Virology rather than having originated at a wildlife market, as the Chinese Communist Party first claimed."[32] Another headline read, "Dr. Fauci and Obama Administration Gave Wuhan Lab 3.7 Million Dollars after Its Top Dr. Shi Zhengli Had U.S. Project Shutdown and She Was Sent Back to China." After claiming with no substantiation that Dr. Zhengli's papers acknowledged that she had isolated and experimented with COVID-19 in a laboratory in 2013, the article states, "This information provides a basis that contradicts the theory that COVID-19 is a variant that just magically mutated in a bat in the wild and then jumped to a human when they ate a delicious bowl of bat soup."[33]

Other journalists, including ones that specialize in fact-checking, dissected the tweet and the interview claim by claim. These sources all reported the same set of facts. The National Institute of Health did appropriate $3.7 million to EcoHealth Alliance, a nongovernmental research group that conducts research on new diseases that may stem from contact between humans and animals. Some, but not all, of that money was dispersed to the Wuhan Laboratory. And some of that money was actually allocated during the Trump administration. Given the number of grants that scientific agencies distribute, it seems extremely unlikely that President Obama even knew about this long-term investment in increasing the research community's understanding of the threats that come from human/animal interactions. Dr. Fauci, as head of NIAID, may or may not have been familiar with the grant, but it was not an inappropriate use of resources intended to study diseases.

On that same fateful April weekend as Giuliani's tweet, Robert F. Kennedy Jr. reinforced another motif in the growing conspiracy theory about Obama and Fauci. Well-known for his deep-seated anti-vaccination stance, the nephew of the late John F. Kennedy implied that Dr. Fauci was motivated by greed. With no chain of evidence to support his claims, Kennedy alleged that Dr. Fauci and his agency would reap a huge financial reward from an approved vaccine because they had a vested interest in the patent. Kennedy also incorporated references to the Bill and Melinda Gates Foundation, perpetuating the accusations that they had sinister and selfish reasons for their well-known efforts to make vaccinations widely available in the developing world.[34]

Bill and Melinda Gates of Microsoft fame are frequently cast as evil actors in conspiracy theories. One reason for this dubious distinction likely stems from their status as one of the wealthiest and most successful couples in the world. In 1985, folklorist Gary Alan Fine coined the term "Goliath Effect" to describe the evidence he had gathered indicating that "a larger percentage than would be predicted by chance [of rumors and legends] refer to the most dominant corporation or product in a particular market."[35] The Goliath effect translates to people as well. In the days when television was the dominant media portal, talk show giants such as Phil Donahue and Oprah Winfrey were frequently identified in contemporary legends.

But, in the case of the Gateses, there are other factors that likely led to the role they have both played in COVID-19 beliefs. Under the mantle of their well-funded Gates Foundation, Bill and Melinda have been ardent activists on behalf of peoples in the developing world, particularly women and children. They have directed tens of millions of dollars to campaigns to bring medical care to underserved communities in what was commonly called the "third world," with a concentrated emphasis on administering vaccines. Funneling the Microsoft millions into Africa and into vaccination ramp-up programs incurred the wrath of anti-vaxxers and Americans distraught over the prospect of American dollars going to Africa. It was

Figure 5. Intentionally misidentified photo.

bad enough that taxpayer dollars were being directed to relief efforts for African famines, droughts, and disease, now the profits from consumer money spent on the ever-growing suite of Microsoft products was headed in that direction as well.

Of course, the best way to give traction to a conspiracy theory is with a compelling visual. In July of 2020, a modified version of the conspiracy theory developed when a picture purportedly depicting President Obama, Anthony Fauci, Melinda Gates, and a Chinese researcher in a WuHan [*sic*] laboratory surfaced and went viral through social media (figure 5). The picture was dissected by fact-checkers who determined that its setting was a laboratory in Bethesda, Maryland, not Wuhan, China.[36] Both President Obama and Fauci were present in the Maryland laboratory. But maybe all women look alike, as both women in the photo were incorrectly identified. The woman next to the president is Nancy Sullivan, chief of the Biodefense Research Section. Standing next to Fauci is Sylvia Burwell, who bears a slight resemblance to Melinda Gates. But given that Burwell was the Secretary of Health and Human Services, it was probably more likely that she would be in the lab than Gates.

After mis- or dis-information campaigns were linked with the election results of 2016, the titans of powerful social media outlets were strongly rebuked for allowing patently false information like this viral image from being spread on their platforms. They began to develop and deploy algorithms capable of identifying ill-intentioned foreign actors who were setting up bogus Facebook pages, Twitter accounts, and mechanisms to automate "likes" and shares in ways that would inflame segments of the electorate. In the case of the Wuhan Lab picture, it was widely circulated in the first few days of July 2020. However, once it was determined to be Bethesda and not Wuhan, with two of the individuals incorrectly identified, many platforms either removed it or labeled it as false. A Facebook search for the picture turns up either accurate posts that attest to the fact that the picture is inaccurate or a message conveying: False Information: The same information was checked in another post by independent fact-checkers.

But other social media outlets proved to be more porous than Facebook. With news stories about the ongoing threat from COVID-19 and the upcoming presidential election, versions of the picture continued to be posted on Twitter, often with comments such as "What were Fauci, Gates and Barack Obama doing in the Wuhan Lab in 2015—planning their strategy? (November 2) An October 27 post read, "I agree 100% and just to show my support I have sent a few images of Oscama and friends on a visit to China—I hope the people who are wondering about the virus will put 2 and 2 together and make 4." The next day another poster responded with the Snopes assessment of the picture, but the original poster offered no mea culpa. This was a frequently repeated pattern, one poster would evoke the conspiracy theory and the picture while another sought to educate them with a reference to one of the fact-checking websites. To those who reference the picture, the actual facts are not relevant. They express a faith in the underlying idea that power-hungry business people and money-grubbing scientists assembled by Barack Obama are guilty of pursuing any path that will further enrich and empower them.

These already murky waters were further muddied by research suggesting that such posts were not all made or circulated by disgruntled American citizens. They could have been generated by Russian or Chinese bot farms intent on generating civil unrest among communities in the United States. The numbers are telling. Carnegie-Mellon is one of one of many research universities to document the role of bots on Twitter. In 2021 they analyzed over 200 million tweets. "Of the top 50 influential retweeters, 82% are bots, they found. Of the top 1,000 retweeters, 62% are bots."[37]

Whether the source was an authentically disaffected citizen or a well-crafted Russian imitation of one, in the early days of anti-Obama lore, the fledgling social media outlets had no accountability for the mistruths circulated on their websites. Skeptical consumers were expected to do their own follow-up; if they questioned the veracity of a post they needed to either do some research or take the step of going to one of the fact-checking websites. If they discovered, for example, that the image of Barack Obama's Kenyan birth certificate was inauthentic, they had to decide if they wanted to antagonize the original poster and set themselves up for barbs from a network of friends and strangers. Determining if something originated on a Russian bot farm was even more complex; as a researcher, I continue to be perplexed as to how it's done. It wasn't until the volume of mistruths was so large and impactful in 2016 that the CEOs of the large companies were asked to assume some responsibility for assessing the accuracy of potentially damaging information on their websites. It seems to me that the sundry variations on the message imposed by Facebook—False Information—has some heft to it and provides those who become embroiled in a "it's true/it's not true" battle some artillery.

But the continued circulation of the false narratives that place Barack Obama (and Fauci, the Gateses and George Soros) as responsible for the COVID-19 outbreak are reminders that retractions rarely work. COVID-19, like HIV/AIDS and Ebola, is an infectious disease outbreak that displays a suite of confusing characteristics, demanding speculation from those who find them unfathomable. Once someone who already thinks the worst of Barack Obama sees a picture that seems to clearly indict him, it is unlikely that they will accept any corrections. Nonetheless, I have no interest in returning to the days when social media companies absolved themselves of any responsibility for fact-checking. The mainstream online portals such as Facebook and Twitter are patronized by many individuals who do not operate at the extremes. These are the individuals who might conclude that a post doesn't ring true, but because they trust the poster, they give that person the benefit of the doubt. When Facebook comes along and declares something False Information, such an individual can accept that assessment.

FROM HIV/AIDS TO COVID-19 AND BEYOND

When it comes to firsts, there's an obvious list of ones checked off by Barack Obama. First president to navigate the consequences of three infectious disease outbreaks—one occurring as he was running for office, one occurring during his presidency, and one developing during the administration of his successor—isn't usually on the list that focuses on his identity as a black man. But Obama, whose identity and characteristics ensured that his leadership would prompt conspiracy thinking, had the misfortune of being in the spotlight during an era that coincided with an unprecedented series of widespread disease outbreaks, themselves bound to engender conspiracy thinking. With each successive outbreak, Obama's detractors had more assets with which they could construct an image of him as a monster. The initial HIV/AIDS controversy enabled his critics to depict Reverend Wright, a man he had described as a friend and mentor, as a hate-filled, ungrateful black man inclined to view whites as capable of genocide. It fell to Obama to do all of the damage control, and his speech "A More Perfect Union," delivered in March of 2008, stemmed some of the negative tide, but it was inadequate to the task of truly contextualizing the ways conspiracy thinking had infiltrated the black world in the first place.

As disease outbreaks go, Ebola was very different from HIV/AIDS. The genocide accusation was flipped; now Obama was seen as an elected president who aspired to kill all white Americans. The memes and postings alleging this diabolical agenda were allowed to proliferate. Although it was clear that Ebola was not going to threaten the health of Americans, voters in 2014 used their ballots to put Republicans in office. The Republican majority Congress then prevented Obama from filling a vital seat on the Supreme Court.

When COVID-19 surfaced, it was not difficult for Trump supporters to connect Obama with another insidious plot, this time to profit from the deadly pandemic. By now, the folly of allowing social media outlets to be used to spread such conspiracy theories is more apparent, but after more than a decade's worth of wanton and unchecked Obama bashing, it is very difficult to stymie the false stories of his complicity. Unlike Ebola, COVID-19 caused enormous harm and death throughout the United States. The faux Wuhan laboratory picture is used to castigate and condemn establishment entities such as the government, as repre-sented by Obama, the business community as led by the woman presented as Melinda Gates, and the scientific community in the form of Fauci and Nancy Sullivan. Rather than assuming that these three communities might be working in the best interest of the public at large, segments of the electorate presume they have the worst of motives. Although compari-sons between Ebola and COVID-19 have to be made with care, it is worth noting that Donald Trump mercilessly and relentlessly used his Twitter account to condemn every aspect of Obama's handling of Ebola and then proceeded to offer slipshod and incompetent management of the far more consequential COVID-19 outbreak, exactly the kind of inept oversight he would have skewered Obama for. As I will show in chapter 6, the presence of Donald Trump in the political world guarantees that anti-Obama lore will be ubiquitous in the world, even when the forty-fourth president is no longer in a seat of political power.

6 Obama Legends in the Age of Trump

On July 25, 2016, Michelle Obama addressed an audience of devoted delegates at the Democratic National Convention (DNC). Although she was there to affirm her support for Hillary Rodham Clinton, the First Lady reflected on the mantra she and Barack developed to enable their daughters, Malia and Sasha, to cope with the never-ending chorus of false accusations leveled at their parents:

> That is what Barack and I think about every day as we guide and protect our girls through the challenges of this unusual life in the spotlight, how we urge them to ignore those who question their father's citizenship or faith. How we insist that the hateful language that they hear from public figures on TV does not represent the true spirit of this country. How we explain that when someone is cruel or acts like a bully, you don't stoop to their level. No, our motto is when they go low, we go high.[1]

The last sentence was the biggest applause line of her speech.

Traditionally, refusing to "stoop" and respond to meritless personal accusations is considered a mark of a good upbringing and a sign of class. But is complete silence in the face of unfounded and destructive rumors really in the interest of the greater good? In the case of the Obamas, when going high translated to silence or minimal engagement with correctives, there were consequences beyond their nuclear family. In this case, members of an electorate were also hearing "hateful language," not just Malia and Sasha. In the summer of 2016, when Michelle delivered this rousing speech, the trash talk was not just about Barack's citizenship or faith. In addition to these vintage staples of anti-Barack lore, low blows included accusations of genocide and treason. Michelle's gender identity was questioned, and she was being derided as complicit in the death of a celebrity. Right-wing television programs baited their audiences with some of the tamer accusations, but it was World Net Daily, Breitbart News, and numerous threads on increasingly popular social media platforms such as Reddit, 4Chan, and many others that enabled and amplified an endless stream of invective aimed at the Obama's and their admirers. These vitriolic comments endlessly mocked and castigated anyone who refused to understand that Michelle Obama was a recklessly extravagant, unattractive, anti-American man, and that Barack was a gay, murdering, Muslim-loving thug who was eager to convert his country from democracy to socialism. The Obamas likely didn't realize that their decision to go high served the needs of their opponent's agenda.

There was an abundance of ways to disseminate and perpetuate the low stories and to be rewarded for doing so, but the same could not be said for promoting accurate information. By 2016 it should have been clear that leaving it to fact-checking websites, however thorough and professionally run, and interested users to set the record straight doesn't work with a large enough segment of the population. The Obamas—and the press that covered them, their political party, and other supporters—had been going high since 2004. While they as a family had prevailed, the policy of ignoring trash talk empowered and emboldened their opponents by failing to call out the smears and correct false information. Hillary Clinton, whom Michelle was there to support, was facing off against a candidate who had optimized conspiracy thinking in order to successfully commandeer his way to the top of the Republican ticket. As the internet became more democratized and accessible, it was increasingly easy to circulate brazenly inaccurate statements. Savvy internet entrepreneurs were monetizing conspiracy theory dissemination, making it in their financial interests to "go low." Because of their efforts, more and more members of the public were willing to believe increasingly incendiary rumors, legends, and conspiracy theories.

The rumors about the Obamas didn't subside. Many of the classics were rehashed in the comments section of YouTube postings of the famous speech at the DNC.[2] But some of the oldies would metastasize and new ones that bolstered the shifting political order would emerge. Over the next five years, the low was going to reach new depths. By the summer of 2020 when Michelle would be delivering her next rousing speech at the DNC, going low was manifesting in more than just evil words. Purveyors of conspiracy thinking were about to start acting, in addition to just posting, in support of their misguided thinking.

WELFARE PRINCESSES

Starting with familiar themes, the list of contemporary legends intended to reinforce the welfare queen stereotype, which had so tainted Michelle herself, more directly implicated the daughters. Now teenagers, Malia and Sasha Obama were not as safe from unsubstantiated stories as they were during the first Obama administration. One common tale erroneously claimed that the taxpayers had picked up the $40,000 tab for the evening gowns the girls had worn to a state dinner for the prime minister of Canada. Just as so many of the rumors, legends, and conspiracy theories about their parents were based on the premise that the first couple was intrinsically undeserving of the perks of American privilege and ought to stay in the places reserved for blacks, so too were the daughters condemned as aspiring for more than was appropriate for two young black women.

The approach to that story exemplified the range of conversations about the Obamas in early 2016. It is a case study of a compliment-to-condemnation pattern that was now going to ensnare the daughters as well as the parents. Since moving to the White House in 2008, the president and the First Lady had been very cautious about putting Sasha and Malia in the public eye. But, as the final year of the Obama presidency was winding down, they may have concluded (perhaps aided by their daughters' lobbying) that grown-up invitations to a sought-after social extravaganza was recompense for the years spent enduring a Secret Service detail that shadowed them from malls to slumber parties. Because the sisters were so rarely seen in public, their presence at the formal dinner turned out to be newsworthy. The mainstream coverage tended to be flattering and complementary; conventional entertainment and fashion websites covered the girls' attendance with headlines such as *E! Online*'s "Malia and Sasha Obama Look Stunning at First State Dinner," or *InStyle*'s "Malia and Sasha Obama Look All Grown Up at Their First State Dinner," and featured attractive pictures of the girls in their posh evening gowns.[3]

Consequently, individual social media posts and right-leaning websites were quick to contradict and condemn. A Twitter user posted: "I could pay off a college loan with how much Sasha Obama's state dinner dress cost and my taxes paid for that thing."[4] A Gateway Pundit headline read, "Sasha and Malia wore $20,000 Dresses to State Dinner Paid for by US Taxpayers."[5] The first sentence of the article proclaimed, "The girls are growing up to be just like their mother." Interestingly, the mistaken implication that the taxpayers had underwritten the costs of the dresses was never mentioned in the brief article, it was solely noted in the headline.

But references to that taxpayer-dollar belief permeated the 143 comments appended to the article, reflecting a multitude of opinions on the presidential lifestyle of the Obamas and other first families. More than one poster noted that in the 1980s, Republican Nancy Reagan endured merciless criticism for the price tags associated with her designer wardrobe. Other reasonable voices pointed out that fashion designers cognizant of the public relations value of having the first family wear their clothes often strategically donate their frocks—their designs—that eventually go on to reside in the textiles collections of the national archives. But less reasonable comments dominated this thread. From his purported gay lifestyle to Michelle's unbridled spending, almost all of the anti-Obama rumors and legends get a shout-out from the posters, no doubt some of whom could be considered trolls or perhaps even bots.[6]

Regarding the girls themselves, one writer poses the question, "Is it just me or do Malaria and Sharia look absolutely nothing like Michael and Barry?"[7] Disputing a rare poster who commented positively on the girls' looks, another mean-spirited commenter wrote, "No matter what they wear they still ugly inside and out."[8] At a couple of intervals within the chain, the message "This comment was deleted," is registered. While there is no doubt that this is the kind of cruel comment that Michelle Obama encouraged her daughters to ignore, there was a downside to this approach.

Should anyone have wanted to determine if the taxpayers paid for the dresses, the Snopes fact-checking website posted the results of its research on March 16, six days after the dinner. Their conclusion? Yes, the two designer dresses would have retailed for about $40,000. No, the American taxpayers didn't pay for them.[9] As was always the case at that juncture, only individuals who took the time to probe a rumor's veracity would have found that it was indeed inaccurate.

In many respects, the dress rumor was a classic example of the state of anti-Obama rantings in 2016. The list of targets was expanding. After their social debuts, Malia and Sasha were no longer merely fetching little girls; now there were more Obamas to compliment or condemn. It was still the case that their more ardent followers gravitated to feel-good stories illustrated by elegant photographs of their favorite first family. But there remained plenty of critics who were infuriated by the media outlets that carried positive stories about them and the Obama-besotted readers who showed appreciation for such coverage.

The list of available social media outlets through which the naysayers could make their voices heard had never been longer; Twitter had more users than ever before and those users were taking advantage of its options. A few months before the state dinner, a Twitter account entitled Trump-American: Make America Great Again! was established. Following the state dinner, a tweet was posted reading: "LET THEM EAT CAKE! Obama girls wear 20K dresses to state dinner while nation struggles."[10] Given that the American economy was actually quite strong in March of 2016, the French Revolution reference is ill-fitting, although there's no doubt the poster was more interested in connecting images of a self-indulgent female monarch with the Obama women. The playing of the "welfare queen" card itself is depressingly familiar. What was new in 2016 is that Trump-American had access to a powerful communications portal and the ability to attract and influence thousands of followers. Erected in the first quarter of 2016, TrumpAmerican came about when Twitter had over 310 million accounts, a 21.5 percent increase over even two years earlier when there were a mere 255 million Twitter accounts in existence.[11]

It is unclear whether TrumpAmerican had any official role with the Trump campaign or was just a well-organized and tech-savvy supporter. Certainly, no one from the official Trump campaign was going to intercede and discourage such a fan from promoting conspiracy theories. There would be no John McCain/Gayle Quinnell moments for Donald Trump. Despite his own daughters' devotion to high-end fashion, he was never going to try and dial back the rhetoric by acknowledging that if tax-payer money wasn't at play, the Obama daughters could wear $20,000 evening gowns if they were so inclined.

In those days, posts on social media were not removed for being inaccurate—most outlets only took down posts that were profane or that violated pornography-related criteria. There were no banners or pop-ups with language from the websites notifying readers of mistruths, no algorithms employed to catch misinformation in real time. Even if the student who complained on Twitter about her college loans looked at Snopes on the day of her posting, she would not have found anything relevant, as the editors were still doing their fact-checking. The Obamas themselves, as Michelle would say at the Convention, refused to "stoop to their level." No statement—official or informal—was issued from the White House.

In the last months of the second Obama term, virtually no rumors or conspiracy theories about members of the first family had disappeared. No fact-checking websites, and no amount of contradictory behavior resulted in the eradication of any anti-Obama beliefs. While some folks forgot the details of a particular narrative, the underlying stereotype it reinforced remained. People didn't post narratives claiming that Michelle expressed disrespect for white oppressors in her Ivy League senior thesis (and a similar text would soon surface about Malia once she matriculated at Harvard), but she was still subject to accusations that she hated whites. The lists had only grown longer and the unfounded accusations more damning, extreme, and implausible. In 2008, Obama's critics made a big deal out of his alleged refusal to sing the national anthem. Eight years later in 2016, right-wing websites alleged that the president had signed an executive order allowing the US military to engage in combat with US citizens.[12]

Given her and her husband's long and bumpy political careers and her proximity to Barack Obama and his campaigns, Hillary Rodham Clinton in her 2017 book *What Happened* comes across as being very under-informed and late to the game in terms of understanding the potency of misinformation. Describing a wholly inaccurate video alleging the misuse of funds by the Clinton Foundation, she says: "At the time, I was barely aware that such silly Russian smears were circulating on American social media. And yet, according to a U.S. intelligence assessment, that one RT [Russian Television] video alone was viewed more than nine million times, mostly on Facebook. . . . Even if I had known that, it would have been hard to believe that many voters would take any of it seriously."[13] She and her campaign gurus should have been taking it very seriously. The Clintons' experience with rumors, legends, and conspiracy theories dated back to her husband's first presidential campaign and persisted throughout their years in public service. If she, or anyone in her campaign, had been paying close attention, they would have been well aware of how frenzied and prolific the anti-Obama folks had become and how impervious they were to evidence that contradicted their preconceived notions. They would have realized that a candidate like Donald Trump who knew exactly how to exploit contempt for Barack Obama, would pursue an agenda of enraging and increasing the number of Hillary haters.

PIZZAGATE

Three months after Michelle Obama's speech on behalf of the Democratic nominee, Hillary Clinton and the head of her campaign, John Podesta, were featured at the center of an elaborate and insidious conspiracy theory. Known as Pizzagate, the core story claims that emails stolen from Podesta's account offered coded proof that he and Secretary Clinton were active participants in a child sex-trafficking ring that used the basement of a popular Washington, D.C., pizza parlor, Comet Ping Pong, as its base of operations.[14]

In the world of twenty-first-century, anti-leftist conspiracy theories, Pizzagate was at least as significant as the Obama birther cycle, if not more so. Versions of the core story, some casting President Obama, Jeffrey Epstein, and George Soros as pedophilic pals of Hillary and Podesta, received quick and widespread attention. It was disseminated by both manipulative operators who were well-versed in internet dissemination strategies and contrived to prevent Hillary's election as well as naive believers who wanted to make sure their personal Facebook sphere was warned about Hillary and company. From InfoWars and Breitbart to the *New York Times* and the *Washington Post*, Pizzagate came to receive more attention from journalists than any other conspiracy theory in the second Obama administration. Numerous journalists and academics conducted exhaustive research on Pizzagate, documenting its emergence on an almost hourly basis, starting in October of 2016. It was likely responsible for the summoning of the leaders of Facebook, Google, and YouTube to testify in front of Congress and to pledge to revisit their long-standing practice of allowing false information to remain on their websites.

Why did the stories that the basement of Comet Ping Pong (which actually doesn't have a basement) was a sexual playpen for the rich, political, and famous garner so much more attention than the ones about the Obamas? Equally outrageous was the conspiracy theory that President Obama and Michelle had arranged for Joan Rivers to be murdered. But there were several reasons why Pizzagate stood out.

First, there was Donald Trump. Pizzagate emerged when the Republican Party's nominee was in the last weeks of his campaign, and even though he never tweeted a version of the core Pizzagate theory on his feed, this outlandish story owes much of its prominence to the stature and maliciousness of the man who would become the forty-fifth president of the United States. To Donald Trump, a good conspiracy theory about an opponent was as welcome an addition to his campaign toolkit as a no-strings-attached, seven-figure donation from a Political Action Committee (PAC). He had secured the Republican nomination for the presidency in no small measure as a result of his willingness to embrace and echo any conspiracy theory that had the potential to draw more votes his way.

In the case of Pizzagate, he let his opponents connect the dots. In his Twitter feed and at his campaign events he never passed on an opportunity to stoke anti-Hillary flames. He frequently referred to the former First Lady, former senator, and then secretary of state as "Crooked Hillary." Referring to her use of a private email server for government business, he demanded that she be prosecuted, and his crowds responded enthusiastically with chants of "Lock her up." Within two weeks of Pizzagate, he framed a retweet of a story from the *National Review* with the statement, "We've all wondered how Hillary avoided prosecution for her email scheme. Wikileaks may have found the answer! Obama!" The tweet contains a picture of Barack Obama and Hillary Clinton, and shows the title of the *National Review* article as "Podesta Leaks: The Obama-Clinton Emails."[15] On November 2, 2016, within a week of the election, Trump's campaign advisor General Michael Flynn—the same Mike Flynn who would go on to be named as Trump's first national security advisor only to be forced to resign in less than a month after pleading guilty to a felony and who was ultimately pardoned by President Trump during Thanksgiving week 2020—that Mike Flynn—tweeted: "U Decide—NYPD Blows Whistle on New Hillary Emails: Money Laudering [*sic*], Sex Crimes with Children, etc. . . . MUST READ!"[16] General Flynn's tweet was liked more than eight thousand times and retweeted more than 9,000 times. As Pizzagate unfolded from Trump's inner circle and in sources often praised by Trump—InfoWars, Breitbart, etc.—readers could easily conclude that Donald Trump, who loved to hear "Lock her up," was not uncomfortable if sex trafficking was the crime they wanted her locked up for.

Timing was everything in the unfolding of Pizzagate. The initial rumors began to swarm at the end of October 2016, just days before the national presidential elections. Hillary Rodham Clinton was ahead in most respected polls. However, then FBI director James Comey announced that the Bureau was reopening its investigation of the security issues related to email traffic when Clinton served as secretary of state. This was prompted by the FBI finding emails related to Hillary Clinton's assistant Huma Abedin and her estranged husband, the now-convicted sex offender Anthony Weiner, on Weiner's laptop. So, while mainstream news sources were reporting on an FBI investigation into job-related emails from Hillary Clinton on a sex offender's computer, less reliable news sources were claiming that the damaging emails confirmed her participation in a sex trafficking ring. Hillary Clinton herself has claimed that the Comey announcement cost her the election. That may be only partially accurate; it could well be that the combination of the Comey announcement and the widespread rumor-mongering about Comet Ping Pong were aligned factors.

But what really made Pizzagate the game changer in the world of conspiracy theories was the specificity of the allegations and the actions enabled by information about an exact geographic location. Unlike other conspiracy theories, Pizzagate pointed interested parties to a supposedly *ongoing* illicit activity and offered a *concrete address* where the perpetrators and their victims might be found. Jack Posobiec, one of Donald Trump's alt-right fans, went to the pizzeria one night in November 2016 and live-streamed his visit on Periscope.[17] Although the video offers nothing more than would be found in a typical high-end pizza parlor, it was wildly popular with followers predisposed to believe the worst about Hillary Clinton. According to research conducted by Amanda Robb in *Rolling Stone*, the day before the Posobiec visit there were six thousand tweets about Pizzagate. But the day after there were fifty-five thousand. Alex Jones, the perpetually unhinged editor of InfoWars, delivered one of his breathless videos exhorting, "When I think about all the children Hillary Clinton has personally murdered and chopped up and raped, I have zero fear of standing up to her. . . . Yeah you heard me right, Hillary Clinton has personally murdered children."[18]

Concerned about the welfare of his employees and customers, James Alefantis, the owner of the restaurant, unsuccessfully appealed to Twitter and Facebook to remove the posts, which they refused to do. A Reddit thread was taken down after personal information was posted, a practice known as doxing. Alefantis notified the police and FBI when he and his employees started getting death threats. Local police stepped up their surveillance of the restaurant, but employees of Comet Ping Pong, as well as neighboring businesses, were bombarded with threatening messages.

During the next two weeks, the *New York Times* and other outlets published exhaustive articles discrediting the conspiracy theory. But, numerous right-wing websites and message boards continued to circulate supposedly true versions of the story, sometimes falsely citing the *New York Times* as evidence of their accuracy. Consumed by the "news" he was reading and distraught over the possibility of innocent children being sequestered for sex games with Democrats in a pizza parlor, Edgar Maddison Welch packed his assault rifle, pistol, and a knife and made his way to Comet Ping Pong. Once inside, he found cooking supplies, fresh pizza dough, and children playing ping pong with their parents. He opened every door and found nothing related to a child sex ring. During the course of his mid-Sunday afternoon "self-investigation," he fired three shots from his AR 15. No one was physically hurt and he surrendered to the police without incident.

The Welch shooting was the proverbial wakeup call that signaled to the law enforcement community, the social media giants, politicians, journalists, and others that there could be devastating consequences to the unchecked circulation of conspiracy theories. Prior to the Welch incident, the assumption prevailed that words were the weapons of the conspiracy theorists, and many liked to think that more persuasive, reality-based words were counterforces that could be used to discredit the falsehoods. And yet, on that Sunday afternoon, a month after the election of a willing and reckless purveyor of conspiracy theories, a purportedly religious man with a young family walked away from his keyboard to take tangible and deadly weapons into a public space—the kind of space presumed to be safe for a family eating out. Welch became the most visible of what proved to be a growing number of right-wing individuals to shift from the "supporter," category to the "activist" one. Going low had moved from online speculations to real-world armed threats.

Suddenly, lots of people in high places were thinking that a more hands-on approach to discrediting conspiracy theories was in order. Journalists and academics meticulously fact-checked every claim related to Pizzagate, and articles were written reviewing every component of the conspiracy theory, exposing every hand that was involved in its dissemination. The head honchos of social media companies seemed genuinely unnerved by the possibility that the next person to conclude that a Facebook (or Twitter or YouTube) post warranted taking an assault rifle into a public place might actually kill innocent people. The likelihood that misinformation strategically and systematically circulated on their forums might have tipped a presidential election caused the corporate leadership to revisit their laissez-faire approach.

If the movers and shakers who bent themselves to the task of debunking Pizzagate in print or video—or by curtailing online conversations—assumed that such reasonable actions would thwart its dissemination, they were dead wrong. Alex Jones may have posted an apology, but his motives were more likely driven by concerns about lawsuits than a genuine change of heart. Pro-Pizzagate enthusiasts had a rejoinder for every piece of evidence cited by the many journalists who probed the story. Right-leaning journalists were not immune from searing criticism. Megyn Kelly, a celebrated anchor on Fox News at the time, was ruthlessly shredded in the vitriolic comments that followed her sympathetic interview with Comet Ping Pong's owner James Alefantis.[19] There was a lesson in the skewering of Megyn Kelly: right wingers tended to be very unforgiving of anyone who questioned the conspiracy theory du jour.

Post-Welch shooting, Pizzagate's ongoing promoters included General Flynn's son, Michael Flynn Jr. a member of Trump's transition team. Flynn Jr. tweeted, "Until #Pizzagate is proven false, it will remain a story. The left seems to forget #Podesta Emails and the many "coincidences" tied to it."[20] Flynn Jr. did lose his job with the transition team after that tweet. Even if the scrupulously fact-checked articles and the removal of posts and videos did not convince the hardest-core of Pizzagate believers of its falseness, the fact that there were now more powerful parties invested in discrediting conspiracy theories represented an overdue move in the right direction.

Hillary Rodham Clinton and her campaign did not comment on Pizzagate when it started to gain traction in the weeks before the election. *What Happened* was released in the fall of 2017, and in it, she starts and ends her account of Pizzagate with the Welch shooting incident and describes her reaction by saying, "I was horrified."[21] Within a month or so of her book's release, Clinton's horror must have intensified as she continued to be named on a list of Democratic politicians, prominent business people, and A-list celebrities who had sex with minors and participated in cannibalistic Satanic rituals as revealed by a conspiracy theory spreader known as QAnon.

MOVING ON

For Barack and Michelle Obama, the last ceremonial moment of the 2017 inauguration festivities was their walk down the Capitol steps, accompanied by President Donald and First Lady Melania Trump, to Marine One. It would be easy to imagine that as the Air Force helicopter lifted off, the Obamas looked forward to a life away from the harsh limelight of the presidency, one that might also mean an end to the rumors and conspiracy theories about their family. If they harbored such optimistic notions of a disinformation cease-fire, they would soon learn that their status as convenient enemies of the far-right remained unshakeable. Like Hillary Rodham Clinton, John Podesta, and others, they too would be smeared by QAnon, but there would also be a few others to contend with along the way.

The post-presidency Obamas remained fodder for conspiracy theories because they remained visible to the public, vulnerable to attacks from conservatives, and newsworthy even after leaving the White House. As a black former first family, they were still moving in directions that infuriated many on the right who were profoundly annoyed to see them enjoy the finer things in life.

Michelle and Barack were able to supplement the pension that comes to former presidents by signing lucrative contracts to write books about their White House years. Like many individuals with marquee name recognition, they were sought after on the public speaking circuit and commanded hefty honoraria. They bought a large and lovely home in Kalorama, one of D.C.'s most coveted neighborhoods, so their younger daughter Sasha's high school years would be uninterrupted. They also purchased a spacious and inviting vacation spread on Martha's Vineyard, long a summer playground for the rich and famous. The Obama daughters pursued academically challenging internships and attended respected and competitive institutions of higher learning: Harvard for Malia, a private university often at the top of any college rankings report, and the University of Michigan, a very highly ranked public university for Sasha after her high school graduation. In short, all four of the Obamas were leading productive and financially comfortable lives that lent themselves to periodic news stories. Those same stories inevitably generated a wide range of comments, including disparaging and spurious ones from critics who didn't think that this black family had earned the lifestyle of high-net-worth individuals.

No longer the first family, the Obamas were still guilty of being "elites." Within the parlance of right-wing Trump followers—let's call them the MAGA (Make America Great Again) crowd—the label "elite" is a damning one. "Elites" are portrayed as affluent, left-wing globalists who move too smugly and comfortably through a world financed by mysterious corporate shenanigans, and who entertain themselves with undecipherable yet still objectionable art and music. The MAGA crowd disliked all elites, but black elites were more distasteful than others.

This presumption was evident immediately following news stories about the purchase of their first post-presidency home in the Kalorama section of the District of Columbia. A popular tweet showed a photo of an art moving van outside the stately brick home. The verbiage accompanying the tweet is short and to the point, "Moving van outside the Obama's new home in Kalorama. Good riddance!" Reply tweets included: "He made himself a millionaire selling our country. An African with a America made fake birth certificate, nowadays you can make a birth certificate yourself using the graphics in paint shop, heard he had his own grandmother killed to keep her quiet." And: "Check Obama's moving van for White House historical artwork." Under a Twitter advisory stating, *Show additional replies including those that may have offensive content*, the following can be found: "Why not go back to Chicago and set an example for the people in the inner city." And: "He hasn't done bad for an unAmerican piece of trash."[22] The anti-black stereotypes being lobbed at President Obama in the comments are familiar, and so too are themes. For instance, along with Michelle, he is presumed to be a crook willing to take public property (chapter 4), to misrepresent his African birthplace (chapter 3), and to flaunt his unpatriotic beliefs (chapter 1).

Even if Hillary Clinton had won the 2016 election (or even one of the other Republican candidates), I suspect that the post-presidency, anti-Obama lore would still have adhered to the well-rehearsed, racially tinged themes that surfaced during his initial campaign and his two terms in office. Inaccurate stories associating the family with bogus accusations that have long plagued African Americans would have erupted intermittently in response to public attention to positive or profitable things happening to him or his family. The publications of his and Michelle's autobiographies—both of which proved to be runaway best sellers—would have resurrected the attacks on their patriotism, faith, sexual preferences, substance abuse, and so on.

But it *wasn't* Hillary Clinton who walked back to the Capitol after he and Michelle took off in Marine One. Donald Trump—who had jumped on the birther wagon and seized its reins—who had decried his handling of the Ebola outbreak—who implied that his fabricated Muslim heritage had prevented him from serving the best interests of America in any Middle East negotiation—was going to be tweeting from the White House, not

Trump Tower. The exploitation of conspiracy theories had been a key factor in Trump's success, and he was predisposed to use any strategy—respectable or disreputable—to ensure that he enjoyed a successful presidency and to queue himself up for a second term in office.

Over the course of the prior six years, Donald Trump and his supporters had assembled and polished a rumor and conspiracy theory "manual" with which they could proactively shape the messages that best served their goals.

Trump Conspiracy Theory Manual

1. Use the voice of Trump to direct and inspire followers—Trump Twitter Feed (global)/Trump Speeches and Rallies (local).
2. Encourage first-rung magnifiers to use their platforms to denigrate Trump opposition. Don't discourage them from profiting from this activity.
3. Refrain from antagonizing Russian agents or any trolling communities smearing Obama.
4. Rely on passionate followers to express their anti-Obama sentiments on all social media outlets.
5. Characterize any disappointing story as fake news or a hoax. Sustain pressure as long as the story is in the news cycle.
6. Do not discredit any loyal individual or segment of the Trump base.
7. Demonize any former friend who shifts from a Trump-purist stance.
8. Rewrite all stories from a Trump-as-hero point of view and characterize any pro-Trump allies as heroes, all others as villains.
9. Condemn any media sources not conspicuously sympathetic to Trump.
10. Coin and repeat buzzwords/hashtags that encapsulate the conspiracy, e.g., "deep state," "globalist" "#Obamagate."

While I don't think that Team Trump sat down in a series of formal meetings with three-ring binders and white boards to identify the techniques they would deploy in rumormongering strategy sessions, by the time he was president, he and his followers had a shared understanding of how to support Donald Trump by methodically redirecting any negative attention to Obama and other Democrats.

The post-second-term reality was that not only was Barack Obama going to remain prominent in rumors and conspiracy theories, but the former president was actually going to have to endure an overall uptick in them. Emergent rumors on the Kalorama post above signal the new arena in which Obama was going to be situated. Exemplifying number 4 on table 2, Trump's passionate followers indicated that Barack had behaved inappropriately, not just because he moved his family into an expensive house, but because he had set them up in a fancy house inside the Washington, D.C., Beltway, too close to the hub of American politics for the taste of some of his critics: "Unfortunately, Obama will live in DC to continue to undermine Trump. A smooth transition is the farthest thing from his mind." "Anyone else curious to the reasoning the Obamas are staying DC? There must be a globalist reason."[23] With these and other dog-whistle comments on the Obama/Trump transition, a new cycle of rumors, legends, and conspiracy theories about Barack Obama were being seeded.

The Snopes website, which fields inquiries on tens of thousands of rumors per year, declared that "Obama's Shadow Government" easily earned its way onto the list of the most frequently repeated conspiracy theories of 2017.[24] The suite of conspiracy theories that fit within the "shadow government," also known as the "deep state" framework constitute one of the more complicated cycles of anti-Obama beliefs to surface.

The latest in a series of labels such as "military-industrial complex," the "shadow government," and "deep state" predate the election of Donald Trump by several years. Not surprisingly, there are multiple definitions of them, and no two are exactly alike; in fact, many are quite contradictory. Prior to the Trump election, the term *deep state* was, for the most part, in the vernacular of journalists with political beats, social scientists, and others whose livelihood stemmed from the world of national or international politics. First applied to Turkey in the 1990s, the term originally was intended to describe that country's reality in which powerful career politicians and military leaders worked invisibly and illegally with more criminally bent members of their society to shape a self-serving nationalist agenda, usually completely circumventing the will of democratically elected officials.

The *deep state* term soon became an attractive one for describing any bureaucratic situation in which large numbers of career staff remain in place while democratically vetted leaders shift with elections. At least one aspect of the reimagined deep state paradigm does seem relevant to the American government. Few observers would deny that many bureaucracies in its agencies can be illegible and that the presence of career staffers and cumbersome policies can, at the very least, impede efficiency and generate unnecessary expenses. Democrats and Republicans alike would agree that bureaucracies do become bloated and the government payroll does include some slackers. Whereas a fair amount of solid proof suggests that in Turkey there was actual premeditated and widespread corruption at work, many Americans would make the case that comparable evidence of widespread, politically motivated, blatantly illegal behavior on the part of American civil servants has not been documented.

But other Americans would quarrel with that assessment. Indeed, Trump and many of his followers embraced the notion that the processes and people he inherited from President Obama were every bit as corrupt as those in Turkey. Throughout his campaign, he had aroused crowds by promising to "drain the swamp," a chant almost as popular as his promise to "lock her up." Overall, Trump attracted followers who shared his disregard for virtually all aspects of government. Many cabinet-level offices—Labor, Education, the Environment, and others—were unnecessary obstacles to free enterprise, according to their perspectives. Since this branch of the far right didn't think such offices should exist in the first place, any employees dedicated to the mission of the office were considered guilty of being anti-Trump.

The message that Barack Obama had erected and established a deep state network of Trump obstructionists was very appealing to his first-rung magnifiers. These are the business-attire-wearing folks who enjoyed some name recognition as prominent and persistent Obama opponents, for example, Rush Limbaugh, Sean Hannity, Dinesh D'Souza, Maria Bartiromo. Using the full spectrum of traditional and online communication channels—tweets, books, videos, documentaries, social media posts—they insist that Trump voters must remain diligent, else the willful and wily pro-Obama crowd, still safely ensconced in their Beltway offices, will continue to thwart any conservative inroads. In the capable and always busy hands of these and other pro-Trump acolytes, *deep state* was reshaped into an easy-to-remember conspiracy essay prompt—one that could be used to trigger the articulation of a story in which former President Obama was the evil commander of clandestine forces, and President Trump and his noble team were the underdogs endeavoring against all odds to save loyal supporters who wanted to make America great again. A list of deep-state conspiracy theories of considerable length could be assembled—here are just a few examples:

- Barack Obama tapped Donald Trump's phones during the 2016 campaign season.
- Embedded Obama bureaucrats sustained Obamacare after Trump's election.
- Obama hacked Fox News and other reporters allegedly sympathetic to the right.
- Obama concocted the Russia hacking the US election story.
- Referred to as Obamagate, in a January 5, 2017, meeting attended by President Obama, Vice President Biden, Sally Yates, and James Comey, the subject of "unmasking" government employees identified in a report was raised and endorsed.
- Valerie Jarrett (senior advisor to President Obama) covered up fraudulent Clinton Foundation activity.
- Upon leaving the presidency, Barack Obama planned to become the secretary-general of the United Nations.
- Barack Obama was a part of a plot to assassinate Donald Trump.

The deep-state framework was an extraordinarily useful conspiracy theory because it could be articulated as a single sweeping statement— Obama's hidden army of bureaucrats is out to sabotage Donald Trump—or it could be used as a supporting statement for a more specific accusation, for example, Donald Trump was impeached because Obama's hidden army of bureaucrats are out to sabotage him.

THE RUSSIANS ARE HACKING! THE RUSSIANS ARE HACKING! 2017–2020

Having operationalized the full range of practices in the manual of perpetuating conspiracy theories, the pro-Trump posse kept the specter of the deep state plot in the minds of right-leaning members of the American public for his entire term in office. In the first year of the Trump administration, the most prominent anti-Obama conspiracy theory accused the former president of concocting a false story that Russia had interfered with the 2016 presidential election in order to cement a victory for Hillary Clinton. Pro-Trump advocates would summarize it as follows: Having created this entirely baseless narrative, the conniving President Obama then conspired with FBI and other intelligence agency leaders to formally investigate Russian meddling, including the possible collusion of Donald Trump and his campaign representatives, with a goal of sabotaging the reelection of the forty-fifth president.

As was customary in such situations, Trump effortlessly glided into number 5 (table 2) immediately assuming a belligerent, offensive stance. In press conferences, on Twitter, and at any opportunity that arose, President Trump decried the core story of Russian interference as "fake news" or a "hoax." All the while, copious evidence was being revealed that substantiated the veracity of claims that the Russians had indeed inserted themselves into the American electoral process. In December 2017, PolitiFact declared, "that Russian Interference is a 'made-up' story is the lie of the year."[25] But the more legitimate sources documented evidence of Russian involvement, the more Trump stuck to the script his followers had come to expect, refusing to back down.

The most comprehensive documentation of the chain of actual events is contained in the now infamous *Report on the Investigation into Russian Interference in the 2016 Presidential Election*, better known as the Mueller Report. Coming in at 508 pages, the Mueller Report is itself prima facie evidence that an investigation was authorized during the Obama administration, albeit after the election, and it was completed during the Trump administration. In other words, the Obama administration initiated an investigation, that fact is irrefutable. The reasons for this investigation were entirely justified, and President Obama was fulfilling his responsibilities as president by authorizing it. The suggestion that he was out of recognized presidential bounds is false.

To the satisfaction of many who read and understood the report, Mueller provided solid evidence that the Russian intelligence community, often creating or amplifying conspiracy theories on social media, sought to seed chaos among American voters and shift support to Donald Trump. The report itself and its author, Robert Mueller, never definitively indicted Trump as a participant in malfeasance. But the report does contain documentation that many journalists, Democratic politicians, and political watchdogs interpret as tracking some collusion to Trump and his family. To summarize what is widely accepted about the matter: Yes, in response to compelling information from the intelligence community, Barack Obama authorized an investigation; and respected professionals, with no clear reason to micromanage the outcome, did uncover a cyber trail that led to Russia. It was neither fake news nor a hoax.

From the earliest days of the investigation until long after the Mueller Report was issued and vetted, Trump maintained that not only was he completely innocent of any wrongdoing, but that the evidence of any Russian intervention was completely bogus, a fabrication traceable to Obama and the deep state. In complete alignment with number 8 (table 2), he transformed those doing their jobs appropriately—Mueller, Obama et al.—into the disloyal criminals and insisted that those whose behavior lapsed into actual criminality—Michael Flynn, Roger Stone—were the unsung patriotic heroes.

At the highest level, Trump could continue to rely on several tried-and-true right-wing pundits—the magnifiers—to use their rhetorical prowess and media resources to disparage Obama. Many of the same players were on the front lines, and, as they had in the birther days, they figured out ways in which they or their organizations could reap financial or reputational gain from luring others into the world of conspiracy thinking. Without so many capable individuals across a full spectrum of media outlets, it is hard to imagine that the deep-state lore would have proliferated with such ease.

Advancing deep-state thinking was a well-paying gig. Once again, Jerome Corsi, who profited enormously with a 2011 best-selling book entitled *Where's the Birth Certificate? The Case That Barack Obama Is Not Eligible to Be President*, continued to line his own pockets by writing and promoting books that framed conspiracy theories about Barack Obama. In early 2018, eight months or so before the midterm elections, he published *Killing the Deep State: The Fight to Save President Trump*, and just two years later, several months in advance of the 2020 presidential elections, he published *Coup d'Etat: Exposing the Deep State and the Plan to Reelect President Trump*, complete with a shadowy picture of Barack Obama on its cover. Within the context of other anti-Obama entrepreneurs, the Harvard-educated Corsi assumed a more erudite voice, determined to sound learned and academic: "After eight years in in office, Barack Obama had set the stage for a Hillary Clinton presidency that would once and for all time recast the American charter with new legislation and Supreme Court decisions that would transform what Obama had achieved into a final rewriting of the American covenant. Where our Founding Fathers desired to limit government power to protect and preserve individual liberties, the Democrats under Obama and Hillary sought to establish a Marxist-leaning social welfare state consistent with globalist one-world-government ambitions."[26]

A number of well-compensated news and opinion personalities from Fox News were willing to give considerable air time on the network to stories about the perils of the deep state. Perhaps the shrewdest of Corsi's fans in the Fox family was Sean Hannity, who took up the deep state mantra early in 2017 and stuck with it through the publication of his own August 2020 *New York Times* best seller, *Live Free or Die: America and the World on the Brink*. Two chapters of the book promoted the deep-state conspiracy theory, chapter 5, Deep State I: Russian Collusion—The Hoax of the Century, and chapter 6, Deep State II: Impeachment—The Failed Attempt to Decapitate the Trump Presidency.[27] Hannity himself used the Trump election and his nonstop support for the forty-fifth president to negotiate the highest salary—estimated to be $36 million in 2018—of any news anchor at the time. Like Corsi, Hannity endeavored to maintain a veneer of journalistic credibility. Neither resorted to insulting nicknames for Obama, and they did not directly encourage their audiences to ready their weapons. Instead, their demands are more focused on supporting Trump by using the power of the pink slip and firing just about any government worker hired during the Obama presidency.

Just as it had during the Obama administration, Breitbart News continued to play its part in creating and perpetuating conspiracy theories. It was largely responsible for the accusation that Obama had ordered the phones in Trump Tower wiretapped—purportedly to connect Trump with Russia and prove collusion. On March 3, 2017, less than two months into the Trump administration, Breitbart ran a story whose only source was a far-right radio broadcast floating the idea that Obama had enacted a "silent coup"—probably in hopes that the term would become a buzz-word—in order to thwart Trump's election. Breitbart reporter Joel B. Pollack concluded that: "In summary, the Obama administration sought, and eventually obtained, authorization to eavesdrop on the Trump campaign; continued monitoring the Trump team, even when no evidence of wrong-doing was found; then relaxed FSA rules to allow evidence to be widely shared within the government, virtually ensuring that the information, including conversations between private citizens, would be leaked to the media."[28] The next day, the always important @realDonaldTrump Twitter feed was doing its part to spread the news: "Terrible! Just found out that Obama had my "wires tapped" in Trump Tower just before the victory! Nothing found. This is McCarthyism!"[29]

As Snopes pointed out in its exhaustive research on this conspiracy theory, President Trump never identified the source that information.[30] Obama's spokespeople, and others familiar with the rules and guidelines regarding phone surveillance, were emphatic in their statements denying that Obama or anyone in his administration violated these rules. Over two years after the series of tweets, Trump acknowledged to Sean Hannity that his proclamation had been based on "a little bit of a hunch." Silent coup did not become a popular buzzword, but Trump's March "Twitter vortex," as folklore experts Ryan M. Miller and Whitney Phillips described his unique use of Twitter, contributed to the casting of Barack Obama as disreputable and manipulative.[31]

Several of the players squarely in the Trump magnifier camp found their actions on his behalf with Russia did not stand up to legal scrutiny—Michael Flynn foremost among them. Although a few individuals served in both the Obama and Trump administrations (usually briefly for the latter), Flynn is a rare one whose job performance was very problematic for Obama and much appreciated by Trump. A career military professional who had worked his way into positions of increasing importance, Michael Flynn was named by President Obama as director of the Defense Intelligence Agency in 2014. But the forty-fourth president was dissatisfied with Flynn's allegedly undisciplined and erratic leadership style and came to believe that Flynn's statements could not be counted on to be accurate and factual. Under pressure, Flynn resigned from the Obama administration and embraced the Trump campaign with unbridled vigor.

Flynn's formal employment in the Trump administration was actually less than a month in duration. The man who had fallen out of favor with Obama for playing fast and loose with the truth was quickly caught lying and accepted a plea deal for "making false statements." The false statements were to Vice President Mike Pence, regarding contact that he had with Russian leadership in the wake of the Trump campaign. Even though Flynn was clearly guilty of lying to the vice president, Trump and Flynn remained fiercely loyal to one another. Flynn was always willing to do his part to expand any anti-Obama (or any other) conspiracy theory that could be of use to Trump.

But in May of 2020, when Flynn was still grappling with the legal consequences of his lies to Pence and others, then attorney general William Barr announced that the Justice Department would be dropping the prosecution of former national security advisor Michael Flynn. In what was then a rare instance of Obama's commenting on the Trump administration, the former president was recorded as saying: "There's no precedent that anybody can find for someone who has been charged with perjury just getting off scot-free. . . . That's the kind of stuff where you begin to get worried that basic—not just institutional norms—but our basic understanding of the rule of law is at risk."[32]

Always hypersensitive to any press coverage regarding Barack Obama, Donald Trump was clearly incensed that the former president was criticizing his administration at all and further irritated that he was challenging the decision-making around Flynn. Within a day or so, Trump had activated his Twitter account with the starter dough for the next version of a Russian deep-state conspiracy theory aimed at his predecessor. Using the tried-and-true formula of adding "gate" to any potentially contentious matter, Trump pontificated about "Obamagate," which became #Obamagate and was ultimately one of the most successful conspiracy theory triggers of the second half of his administration.

On May 10, 2020, Trump tweeted Obamagate as though it was recognizable terminology that would be deciphered by readers in a common fashion.[33] It wasn't, and over the course of next several days and weeks Trump was asked to explain what he meant by it. In the usual minimally coherent Trump fashion, he responded to queries and, of course, continued to tweet.

Over time, he and his enablers came up with a narrative. When used most specifically, Obamagate came to mean a well-attended White House meeting on January 5, 2017, after Donald Trump's election but before his inauguration. Attendees included, besides the president, Deputy Attorney General Sally Yates, US Ambassador to the United Nations Susan Rice, Vice President Joe Biden, and other high-level members of the Obama administration. The ongoing investigation into Russian interference with the 2016 presidential election was the topic of the meeting and attendees learned, among other things, that Michael Flynn had engaged in inappropriate conversations with the Russian ambassador to the United States. During the course of the meeting, Biden asked that Flynn be "unmasked," a common term understood in the intelligence community as removing anonymity from a person not currently identified by name in a report.

The January 5, 2017, meeting has been extensively dissected by both Trump and his acolytes as well as by fact-checking websites and the mainstream press. Although Trump and his followers argue that there was more embedded criminal activity in Obamagate than in the original Watergate cover-up, and that virtually all of those who participated in the meeting merited prison sentences, no one in a position of authority to pursue such an agenda has found anything irregular about the meeting. "Unmasking" is a fairly routine occurrence in the national security world, and there's no reason why Flynn's identity couldn't be known. Everyone in the office was acting in ways commensurate with their job descriptions. Nonetheless, among far-right adherents, "Obamagate" was a marker of the former president's power in the deep state that retained potency from mid-2020 forward. The unsubstantiated notion that Michael Flynn was unfairly targeted in the Russian interference investigation explains why so many Trump followers supported the pardon issued to General Flynn in the last weeks of Trump's administration.

QANON

On the 4th of July, 2020, and in clothes suitable for an outdoor barbecue, Michael Flynn recorded himself and five others, presumably family members, with their right hands raised taking an oath. The language is all vaguely familiar to anyone who has heard the oaths taken by newly elected officials when they are sworn into office. It ends with the pronouncement: "I will and faithfully discharge the duties of the office on which I am about to enter. Where we go one, we go all. God Bless America."[34] The first part is generic, but "Where we go one, we go all" is the motto of QAnon.

In its earliest incarnation, QAnon was the new landing pad for Pizzagate believers and conspiracy-oriented disciples of Donald Trump. The first visible manifestation of Q came on October 28, 2017, and appeared on a thread in the 4chan message board where an "anon" (anonymous poster) identified himself as a "Q clearance patriot" and used the Trump reference "calm before the storm" to forecast that Trump was about to orchestrate massive arrests of legions of child-eating pedophiles. Pizzagate had identified Hillary Clinton and John Podesta as running a sex-trafficking ring out of Comet Ping Pong; Q, who claimed to be embedded in Trump's national security orbit, alleged that there were thousands of other members of the ring who took pleasure from having sex with and eating children. The leaders of these libertines comprise a who's who of Democratic Party leaders, business tycoons, and A-list celebrities. All could be indicted by the right-wing as "elite," but, of course, they were being accused of much more than preferring avocado toast to bacon and eggs. Former president Barack Obama is prominent on the list, and he's joined by Ellen DeGeneres, Oprah Winfrey, Bill and Melinda Gates, George Soros, Chrissy Tiegen and her husband John Legend, and Tom Hanks—to name the folks with the most star power. Q implored "his" followers to support President Donald Trump, as he needed all the help he could get to fight the deep state and fulfill his calling to "save the children" by apprehending and punishing these evil elites.

The evolution of QAnon speaks to the enormous potency of internet communication avenues in the late twenty-teens. For many media consumers, message boards such as 4chan, 8kun, and Reddit were uncommon online destinations. The 4chan message board was aligned with the kind of vitriolic speech Q became famous for. Writing in 2019, journalist Rob Arthur said of his research on 4chan: "On the heavily trafficked 'politically incorrect' board slurs against racial, ethnic, religious or sexual or gender minorities have increased by more than 40% since 2015 while neo-Nazi propaganda has proliferated. And users on the forum are increasingly making violent threats against minority groups: comments that include hate speech and violent language have increased by 25% over the same period."[35]

Three clever, young, right-wing online entrepreneurs discovered and promoted "Qs" posts methodically, bringing them from the margins to the mainstream. Thanks to their internet know-how, within three months, QAnon had a visible and growing presence on the more mainstream and familiar social media outlets of Facebook and Twitter.

Paul Furber, Coleman Rogers, and Tracy Diaz were the magnifiers in this case, and, like the boss birthers and other deep-state magnifiers, there was financial gain for them in this effort. Again, it was financial benefit 2017 style. For Jerome Corsi, who briefly invaded the QAnon universe and quickly retreated, making money off of rumormongering about Barack Obama first came in the form of traditional book sales. Much to the eventual dismay of some other early QAnon supporters, Furber, Rogers, and Diaz realized the kinds of profits that stem from attracting thousands of subscribers to online channels, setting up donation buttons that enable fans to fuel your "research" through PayPal or cryptocurrencies, avenues of large profit unheard of ten years earlier. According to an ABC News exposé in 2018 quoted in *COVID-19 Conspiracy Theories: QAnon, 5G, the New World Order and Other Viral Ideas*, Diaz was able to fully support herself from her QAnon peddling work.[36]

Furber, Rogers, and Diaz understood that the voters known as Trump's base were eager for the campaign promises to punish the Democrats to be fulfilled. Initially, the deep-state theories partially answered questions about Trump's initial effectiveness or lack thereof. Whereas he had promised to replace the Affordable Care Act, also known as Obamacare, with a better health care plan, he hadn't done so. The belief that embedded bureaucrats were undermining President Trump's efforts was only satisfactory up to a point. The MAGA crowd yearned for evidence that President Trump would enact his most extreme negative campaign promises. They supported him with the hopes that he would finally be the one to put Barack Obama in his place—preferably jail, where black men belong—and also take down his immoral socialist pals.

From its earliest days until this writing, QAnon has either predicted Barack Obama's arrest or suggested that it has already happened. The first predicted occasion was at the funeral of George H. W. Bush on December 5, 2018. Purportedly, Justice Department agents planned to do a full sweep of deep-state leaders at the funeral, arresting the Obamas along with George W. Bush and both Bill and Hillary Clinton. All of them were going to have to face the consequences for their participation in the child sex-trafficking ring. In the days leading up December 5, Q followers used "D-5" to reference the anticipated mass arrests. However, December 5 came and went and the biggest news story to come out of the funeral was George H. Bush sneaking a hard candy to Michelle Obama. Undeterred, Q adherents continued to be assured that it was only a matter of time before the former presidents would be brought to justice. The following month, a YouTube video titled "Soros Arrested: Bush Pleads Guilty to 9/11—Obama Begs for His Life" was posted, piling up over seven hundred thousand views. In this and similar versions, Obama is being held at Gitmo, a well-known nickname for the detention facility in Guantanamo Bay, Cuba. QAnon followers embraced the irony of having the former president incarcerated at a prison he had once vowed to close. In all of the versions of the conspiracy theory in which Obama's arrest has already happened, he is at Gitmo and because QAnon devotees have cast him as a coward, there are always references to him being terrified.

Of course, the problem with saying that he's already been arrested is that he (and other Q targets as well) can be clearly seen out in public. The next round of rumors alleged that Obama and others were under house arrest or forced to wear ankle bracelets while the Justice Department wrapped up the loose ends that would result in them being taken to jail. When George Bush wore an ankle boot after an injury, memes were circulated claiming that it was a cover-up for an ankle monitor. The stay-at-home orders that accompanied the COVID-19 outbreak provided a convenient explanation for spring 2020 versions of the theory in which it was said that Obama was wearing the ankle monitor at home, and, of course, since he was following the Centers for Disease Control (CDC) recommendations to stay at home, no one was able to claim to have seen him elsewhere. This worked for other celebrities whose names were tied up in the QAnon mythology. Upon learning that QAnon was boasting about her being under arrest, Oprah Winfrey tweeted that she was "being trolled for some awful FAKE thing. It's NOT TRUE. Haven't been raided or arrested. Just sanitizing and self-distancing with the rest of the world. Stay safe everybody."[37]

Figure 6. QAnon manipulation of Obama campaign image. *Joe Raedle/Getty Images.*

From 2004 until this point in 2020, the smears about Obama position him as a ruthless politician who has duped gullible segments of the American public, poor saps who are loyal to him and his family despite misrepresentations about his faith, his patriotism, and his sexual preference. He almost succeeds in spreading Ebola through the United States and was one of the architects of the COVID-19 pandemic. But the QAnon theories that Obama "will be/has already been" arrested positions then president Donald Trump as the all-powerful one. The faith that the MAGA crowd (figure 6) has shown in the reality star tycoon has been borne out—in obliterating Obama, he has done what no other politician was willing to. Even though Obama is never actually arrested, the hardcore Q followers accept the always-dubious explanations and expect that soon the storm will come.

BACK IN POWER

On the evening of November 3, 2020, it became clear that Joseph Biden, once Barack Obama's vice president, and a prominent figure in most deep-state conspiracy theories, would likely deny Donald Trump a much-coveted second term as president of the United States. As that prediction was confirmed over the next several days, President Trump and many of his supporters were adamant that the Biden victory was manufactured. Trump and his legal team mounted over sixty legal cases and pursued every possible legitimate and illegitimate remedy in their attempt to nullify the election. Rumors and conspiracy theories undergirded their reasoning throughout; they claimed erroneously that a water main break had caused a distraction in a key Georgia precinct enabling Democratic operatives to stuff the ballot box, and they claimed that the most commonly used voting machines were rigged against them.

For the social media outlets, the relentless sharing of false information posed a problem. Trump was using his Twitter feed to circulate his spurious claims, almost all of which were followed by a disclaimer in Twitter blue colors! *This claim about election fraud is disputed.* Virtually every Trump tweet from November through early January was accompanied by that language. The same rules were applied to other supporters tweeting false information and other social media outlets took similar steps. Unfortunately, the comments sections suggested that the MAGA crowd was unmoved by these disclaimers.

During the week of December 20, 2020, Smartmatic and Dominion, the makers of the software and voting machines most frequently besmirched by Trump and his magnifiers, went on the offensive and notified many parties of their intention to take serious legal action against them.[38] In response, Fox News, home network to three of Trump's most ardent media magnifiers—Maria Bartiromo, Lou Dobbs, and Jeanine Pirro—quickly offered contrite statements dialing back their earlier unsubstantiated accusations about the voting systems. Those hosts, as well as conservative pundits on other networks, removed the allegations about American-made voting systems from their playlist of voter fraud allegations.

On or about January 5, 2021, accusations surfaced that the man responsible for diverting Trump votes to Biden was Barack Obama. Even for a conspiracy theory, the reasoning is convoluted, but, in a nutshell, President Obama had orchestrated a Biden win before leaving office in 2016. Italian voting machines, satellites, and complicit international agencies all had a hand in making sure that Biden secured enough votes: "The political level of the plan was basically conceived by Barack Obama who was allegedly helped by his Italian counterpart, Matteo Renzi, the former Italian Prime Minister . . . the Chairman of Nations in Actions claims that what happened was 'a really brilliant plan orchestrated by Obama with the help of Renzi.'"[39] This conspiracy theory places Barack Obama at the heart of a four-year-old, international plot to replace Trump with his own vice president, further solidifying his desire to run the world indefinitely. In a Twitter exchange on Italygate, as some MAGA types referred to it, one poster summarized: "You seen the story coming out of Italy Nigel? Obama seems to be in a bit of trouble. He's only just got the Italians switching votes for Biden! Paid them $ 400 mill for the treasonous act too, tax payers money! Google 'Italygate Leonardo US election' people for details."[40] Italygate illustrates several points regarding anti-Obama lore at the beginning of 2021. First of all, with Trump now vulnerable and unlikely to assume a second term in office, the QAnon theories that Obama was under arrest and disempowered seemed inaccurate. The idea of an autocratic and evil Barack Obama who had the power to control leaders of his own party as well as international heads of state remained a fixation for MAGA followers.

In terms of the overall evolution of contemporary legends and conspiracy theories, Italygate is also informative. Now international actors could turn anti-Obama smears into a profit center, just as domestic ones had. Maria Strollo Zack, who issued the first interview, has a website for her organization, Nations in Action, which has a button to click on so that concerned individuals can donate money to help her with the research that will fill in all the missing pieces on Obama's culpability.[41] Italygate also demonstrates the ways in which new narratives develop when older ones become dated. Even though some of Trump's more reckless followers continued to risk the legal liability that stemmed from libeling Smartmatic and Dominion, most of the media pundits put that one on the shelf. The notion that foreign-born interference was responsible for a disappointing election result was a convenient replacement theory. Italygate also signals a newly cautious world of social media companies. Against a backdrop of increasingly tight social media oversight, Italygate texts would surface and be deleted by websites or users within hours. As a researcher, this I found my job infinitely more difficult—I never had that problem in the early days when I was looking at "Obama is a Muslim" beliefs, or even in his second administration when he was being accused of intentionally exposing the

US military to Ebola. Italygate also demonstrated just how quickly texts could move in 2021. According to *USA Today*, five days after Italygate theories were first posted, "The three videos have amassed a combined 100,000 views and 7,000 shares on Facebook. An interview with Strollo Zack on *American Can We Talk* on YouTube has garnered over 400,000 views."[42]

WHEN THEY GO LOW

After leaving the White House, the Obamas continued to live in a bifurcated world where they enjoyed enormous popularity with most of the voters who had campaigned for them in the first place but were hated by most of the voters who put Donald Trump into office. According to Real Clear Politics, Barack Obama's final approval rating was 49.8 percent. And, as they left the White House, Michelle Obama came in at second place in the most admired woman polling. But for so many of the people who put Donald Trump in office and were determined to have him serve a second term, the Obama administration represented America at its worse. Marjorie Taylor Greene, elected to the House of Representatives from the fourteenth district of Georgia, was unabashedly proud of her association with QAnon and during her run for office had even proclaimed, "Yes, I do believe he (Obama) is a Muslim. . . . Obama opened up our border to an invasion of Muslims." She is representative of the Trump followers who abhorred an Obama-driven agenda that took the needs and concerns of our international allies seriously, that sought to work in partnership on climate change, that looked for ways of increasing the economic and social mobility of underrepresented groups, and any number of other progressive stands pursued by Obama.

The election of Joe Biden, Obama's two-term vice president, and Kamala Harris—whose name and identity overlapped in distressingly similar ways with Barack Obama's—represented an intolerable return to power of Obama's values. Throughout November 2020 and into January 2021, Joe Biden made announcement after announcement of high-level positions that would be held by appointees he knew through his years in the Obama administration. Flattering images of Kamala Harris on the cover of *Vogue* magazine were circulating. It was well known that Trump and the MAGA base bitterly resented the fact that Michelle Obama had graced the cover three times and Melania Trump had never been deemed cover material. These undeserving, un-American, ethnically challenging elites were back.

With its Confederate flags, Southern Crosses, ropes and nooses, the January 6, 2021, storming of the US Capitol exposed the extraordinary overlap between white supremacist affiliates and pro-Trump supporters. The domestic terrorists deployed a long list of anti-black slurs to intimidate and insult the African American Capitol police officers who were defending the halls of Congress and the legislators and legislative staff on hand to certify the results of the election of Joseph Biden. Reversing the outcome of the 2020 election would further advance their goal of abolishing the changes in American culture they associated with the two Obama administrations and feared from a Biden/Harris one. In their America, neither blacks in the uniforms of law enforcement nor ones bearing the labels of president or vice president belonged. Other "snowflake" Americans had enabled Barack Obama to get beyond his place and they had been made to suffer for it. The ignominiously self-named "patriots" would stop at nothing to Make America Great Again and "greatness" constituted an America white-washed of the Obamas, other uppity blacks, and their disloyal countrymen who enabled them access to positions of authority.

Epilogue

American elections reveal a great deal about the ways in which citizens understand and seek to codify or nullify power. The timeline for *Trash Talk: Anti-Obama Lore and Race in the Twenty-First Century* begins with the 2004 presidential election, marked by Barack Obama's searing speech, which thrust him into the public imagination, and ends with the 2020 inauguration of Joe Biden, who, although once a political opponent, was ultimately his two-term vice president. Every national election between those two benchmark dates is taken up in this book. The progression at two-year intervals from 2004 to 2020 is stunning to consider. During the 2004 election season a segment of the population immediately became enchanted by the unanticipated story of Barack Obama. As progressive Democrats proudly steer him and his family on the road to the White House, a completely oppositional choir of reactionary voices begin to use tools of misinformation to minimize the likelihood of this half Kansan/ half Kenyan, Ivy League–educated, left-leaning candidate, and his formidable wife becoming the President and First Lady of the United States.

For the most part, Obama's 2008 opponent, John McCain, sticks to the conventional political playbook of presidential elections and wages a campaign based on divergent policy platforms, not the personal attributes that make Obama an unconventional opponent. Obama wins. Clearly stunned by this outcome, the anti-Obama forces double down in the next two years and with the help of increasingly sophisticated mastery of the internet and the self-serving antics of conspiracy theorists for hire (and possibly Russian bots), they succeed in depriving Obama of a House of Representatives majority. In 2012 the Republicans select Mitt Romney, a traditional conservative candidate who campaigns by the rules familiar to all at the time. He too focuses on the considerable policy differences that would distinguish a Romney presidency from an Obama one. But lurking in the background and taking measure of the public is Donald Trump, a defiant Beltway outsider, who ridicules any rules that might get in his way. Romney's platform fails to inspire a sufficient number of Republican voters and Obama is reelected. Two years later, the anti-Obama lore is more prevalent than ever, and after the 2014 midterm elections Republican majorities rule in the House and the Senate. In contention with Hillary Rodham Clinton, who had served in the Obama administration, Trump, armed with a Twitter feed and unfettered by a moral compass, violates just about every recognized campaign protocol and defeats her in 2016. The left becomes as astounded and agitated as the far right was in 2008. Anti-Obama smears continue to be convenient for the Trump side as the one-term forty-fifth president and his followers assign blame for any failure on the forty-fourth president. An energized and electorally shrewd Democratic party manages to oust him from the White House by focusing its human and financial resources on persuading enough voters in the swing states that they want to be "ridin' with Biden." Georgia-based Stacey Abrams becomes a Democratic Party heroine of the first order. There was a time when I assumed that the 2020 election would be the logical marker at which to end this book. It wasn't meant to be.

Much of the typically dull sojourn between election day and inauguration day was consumed by an unprecedented attempt on the part of Trump and his followers to upend the November election results. Although Biden was the actual opponent and winner of the election, the lore about Barack Obama continued to have currency. This time, the deep state under his leadership was impugned for stealing the election. During the two-week lead up to the inauguration, a whole new conspiracy theory about him emerged, proving once again that his rent-free residence in the imagination of the MAGA crowd was much in place. The final conspiracy theory I document, Italygate in chapter 6, will probably not be the last rumor to afflict Obama. But it is the last one for this book, I am truly done as of January 20, 2021.

Although the name "Obama" is in the title and it is probably the most frequently used noun in the book, *Trash Talk* is not really about the Obamas. It is about which Americans thought the Obamas belonged in the White House and which ones thought they weren't staying in their place. It is about what twenty-first-century Americans, from sea to shining sea, read into the Obamas and what possibilities they saw as available to black Americans. Throughout the book, I have endeavored to make the case that plenty of Americans of all stripes warmed to the family immediately and maintained a respect and affection for them. He was, after all, elected twice.

But the wrath of the folks who would evolve into the Trump base, the MAGA crowd as I refer to them in chapter 6, intensified with each passing year. Part of their venom was directed at the Obamas themselves, that's for sure. But they were equally furious with their fellow Americans, who, blind to the faults that were so apparent to them, twice elected him president of the United States. They didn't like the black man whose serious face was the centerpiece of the Shepard Fairey image, and they didn't like the people who wore T-shirts, buttons, and baseball hats inscribed with it. Eager to personally and professionally capitalize on both conventional media outlets as well as emergent ones, entrepreneurial Obama foes along with Russian bots and trolls packaged and perpetuated stories designed to intensify disrespect for the first family and Americans who wore T-shirts and affixed bumper stickers to their cars.

The only thing worse than an Obama/Hope T-shirt was one that read Black Lives Matter. Throughout the first couple of decades of the twenty-first century, examples of race-based antipathy extended beyond the first family. I wish there were fewer examples with which to make this point. Toward the middle of Obama's second term, an unarmed African American male teenager, Trayvon Martin, was fatally shot by George Zimmerman, who interpreted Martin's demeanor in a nice neighborhood as "suspicious." Claiming to perceive himself at risk, Zimmerman fired and subsequently invoked Florida's stand-your-ground laws in his own defense. His trial and the not-guilty verdict it rendered received extensive media coverage. Asked to comment, Obama opined, "If I had a son, he'd look like Trayvon Martin." In a later speech he said, "Trayvon Martin could have been me thirty-five years ago."

Although many members of the black and progressive communities considered Obama's remarks too little, too late, Obama's foes indicted him for racializing the moment. Ensconced in his mother's home in South Carolina, Dylann Roof sought to understand why Trayvon Martin's case was dominating the news. His online research led him to a plethora of white power websites and he quickly concluded that George Zimmerman had done the right thing and that "niggers are stupid and violent."[1] Inspired to take arms, he drove his car, complete with a Confederate flag insignia, to Emmanuel African Methodist Episcopal Church. He was welcomed in and sat for a while during the choir practice before he opened fire, shooting and killing nine African American worshippers. Roof justified his actions by portraying himself and "white people" as the victims and his targets as aggressors. In her award winning *Algorithms of Oppression*, Safiya Noble uses the Dylann Roof case to meticulously delineate the inherent biases built into search engines that lead searchers to inaccurate, racist, and inflammatory information, information that in this case can be linked to a mass shooting of innocent church-goers.

Pondering the devastating massacre and other senseless assaults on black Americans, Michael Eric Dyson queried: "Could it be that unarmed blacks who were dying across the nation were urban proxies for the black presidency and the change it had brought? Those who can't aim a gun at Obama take whatever black lives they can?"[2]

The Black Lives Matter hashtag first surfaced following the murder of Trayvon Martin, and as subsequent assaults on unarmed blacks unfolded, what started as a hashtag morphed into a movement—a movement complete with its own T-shirts, posters, and lawn signs. Showing an unwillingness to position Black Lives Matter in the context of the police brutality that engendered it, many on the far right expressed disgust with those three words and those who embraced them.

In turn, those on the left were repulsed by the Trump supporters whose wardrobe also came to symbolize the rift between the groups: cargo khaki pants and clothes with camouflage patterns became associated with the Proud Boys, a white supremacist group touted favorably by Trump himself; and the red, white, and blue ensembles favored by groups such as Moms for Trump and Women for Trump. The investigations into the attempted insurrection of January 6, 2021, proved that a disturbing number of its participants had military and law enforcement uniforms in their closets. White-collar Trump supporters who probably eschewed the ubiquitous MAGA gear garnered even more criticism, as leftists presumed that Ted Cruz or Nikki Haley ought to know better than the QAnon shaman.

It is easy to lose sight of the fact that many American voters have neither right- nor left-wing T-shirts in their wardrobe. A local small businessman to whom I have turned for professional reasons many times is a Republican who voted for Trump. But politics is of minimal importance to him and he would never spend his hard-earned money on a campaign contribution or a shirt. There will never be a sign in his yard or a bumper-sticker on his car. He would never tune into a political convention; Sports is the most important section of the news to him. When told politely that the picture someone had emailed to him of Obama and Fauci was *not* taken with Chinese scientists and Melinda Gates in a Wuhan lab, and instead was an innocent snapshot from a lab in Bethesda, he didn't become defensive or protest, and he was appreciative of the insight. I am well-acquainted with many Democrats who voted for whomever the party put forward and are just as disinterested in the nuts and bolts of politics as my Republican contact. By keeping this segment of the population in mind, it is a little easier to consider whom to target in efforts to curtail the impact of rumors, legends, and conspiracy theories. These are the people who are open to evidence-based persuasion.

When I wrote *Grapevine* and coauthored *Color Line*, the genres focused on were rumors and contemporary legends. Many of the anti-Obama texts are most precisely labeled conspiracy theories. As pointed out in the introduction, conspiracy theories are also rumors if they are short and vague, or contemporary legends if they are more fully formed narratives. They fit as conspiracy theories because they concern an unsubstantiated, secretive, organized agenda of some sorts. But my point here is that twenty-plus years ago, none of these labels were commonplace in the news. It was a rare thing for someone to characterize a prominent public figure as a conspiracy theorist or to in any way suggest that they dealt widely in the spread of inaccurate information. In the past five or so years, that has changed, largely, but not exclusively, because of the election of a president who trafficked in conspiracy thinking. And it proved to be contagious. As I am writing this in early 2021, it feels as though it has been years since I watched a news broadcast or read a newspaper in which the term *conspiracy theory* was not evoked. Is it possible to have an information reset? At the very least it will require a cultural full-court press.

In order to delineate my notions about how we could diminish the spread of trash talk (as well as how hard it will be), I will use a couple of examples taken from earlier in the book. "Obama is a Muslim" in chapter 2, as well as "Obama conspired with Fauci, Gates et al. to make COVID-19 in a Wuhan lab" from chapter 5 are useful. When confronted with an articulation of the Muslim/Arab rumor on the campaign trail, McCain seemingly did the right thing by contradicting the speaker, telling her "he's not." Of course, that had a bit of a shaming effect that may have backfired on him, as she was already convinced of the validity of her position.

What if, long before that awkward moment in the campaign arena, both the Republican and Democratic Party leaderships had negotiated a concrete agreement to reject any patently false information about the other candidate? Reporters discovered that Gayle Quinnell and other volunteers had been passing around the "proof" of Obama's Muslimness for weeks. What if the political parties themselves had to protect the reputation of their opponents? In order for a candidate to get the party's blessing, he or she might be expected to say something akin to "I'm Pat Turner and neither I nor my campaign will directly or indirectly incriminate my opponents with unsubstantiated information." In order to mitigate the chances of having a rogue candidate such as Trump who would have probably signed such a paper without altering his verbiage, the parties themselves would have to agree to discipline their own and to refuse to enable such conduct. I realize that this represents a dramatic departure from a political ecosystem in which all serious candidates invest money in opposition research, but the times may call for such a challenge.

Using that same example, it would also be important for Obama himself to have taken steps to set the record straight. After the rumors that Michelle Obama had written an incendiary thesis took off, his campaign added the "Fight the Smears" tab on their campaign website. Once he was president there was no "go to" place where someone could determine that

Barack or Michelle Obama themselves rebutted the accusations being leveled at them. As Nicholas DiFonzo and Prashant Bordia point out, the lack of a rebuttal contributes to the believability of a rumor.[3] I know that the counter argument to this is that by him even saying "I am not a Muslim," or "I didn't conspire with Fauci et al." it plants the idea in the minds of folks who haven't heard it, but it should be remembered that others will forever wonder why someone wouldn't deny a blatant mistruth about themselves. Perhaps the job descriptions of the White House staff should be expanded to include inhouse debunking. Constituents and the press could have access to the first family's confirmations or denials.

Although I have criticized some of the social media websites for their sporadic and ineffectual approach to correcting information on their websites, I don't envy them, and I certainly acknowledge that sustaining a philosophy that supports the American value of free speech while preventing irresponsible speech from creating concrete harm is fraught with the potential for missteps. As someone who was long a high-functioning adult before there was such a thing as social media, and who now marvels at Facebook's ability to know when I am in the marketplace for patio furniture and that I gravitate toward faux wicker, I suggest they invest in the problem of misinformation on their platforms with the same singularity of purpose as they invest in targeting just the right ads to their customers. Yael Eisenstat, who was a former CIA agent and national security advisor to Joe Biden when he was vice president and who spent a few frustrating months as Facebook's global head of Elections Integrity suggests that by adjusting the algorithms used to determine what political advertisements show up on feeds, Facebook, and presumably others, could do a great deal of preemptive damage control.[4] Based on her rocky tenure with the company and subsequent research, she is pessimistic that the company will be willing to make a choice that is not in their best financial interest. I'm not sure how Facebook users might self-mobilize, but perhaps if we did we could be persuasive on this front.

In early 2021, Facebook, Twitter, YouTube, and others took the previously unimaginable step of permanently blocking some of the more controversial account holders. Clearly Donald Trump was at the head of that class, but QAnon devotees and other groups that traffic in conspiracy theories found themselves blocked as well. But capitalism is a strong force, and niche social media websites saw an uptick in accounts from right-wing users who believed themselves to have been betrayed. Folks who want to communicate with others who share their perspectives usually find a way to do so. The development of pedagogical tools that would enable K–12 teachers to find age-appropriate ways of instructing students on how to evaluate online information would be helpful.

By now it should be clear that I am a big fan of the fact-checking websites. However, they do have their limitations. Their value is tethered to the supposition that a user knows they exist, recognizes when they should be consulted, and then reads and accepts their full assessment. Someone sees a Facebook post from a friend indicating that Barack Obama, Melinda Gates, and Anthony Fauci were in Wuhan together. There's a picture with it. But the fact that their friend is telling them this and the news has managed to miss this story leads them to invest the time to check it out. If they go to Snopes, the picture is described as "miscaptioned."[5] If a diligent user just reads the assessment and not the narrative, they could easily continue to assume that there was some truth to it. Given the stakes embedded in the issues that have come forward in the past ten years, it seems unreasonable for the public to expect these operations to be the sole sources of truth or fiction. Most of these websites operate on a financial shoe-string. Currently exploring a membership model, Snopes is dependent on ads and volunteers to make its model work. For many publications, fact-checking was always an internal process implemented to prevent misinformation from being published in the first place. Now, more and more media companies are investing in fact-checking for after-the-fact queries from their readers. But their issues are quite similar to those of Snopes, a nugget of information has to be suspect in the first place, and a thorough fact-checking process can be time consuming and expensive.

Although my lawyer friends are not optimistic, I continue to think legal remedies should be pursued. December 21, 2020, provided one of my favorite moments in the mayhem-ridden November 3–January 20 window. That was the day that Dominion Voting Systems registered its intention to use legal challenges to pursue the right-wing journalists, members of Trump's legal team, and other parties who had circulated bogus conspiracy theories about their product and their company. Suddenly, many of the journalists and Trump lawyers ceased and desisted after Dominion

initiated its correspondence warning potential litigants to save their documents. The proliferation of news stories about Dominion's actions served
a rebuttal purpose as well. Some of the folks on the right who had been
told that the voting machine company was "foreign," and used Venezu-
elan software, learned that the company was founded and has always been
based in the United States. If we are serious about disincentivizing the
spread of patently false information, it makes sense to make sure defama-
tion, libel, and slander laws are updated to reflect that goal.

Over time, these steps might well minimize the negative impact of disinformation, at least among the less passionate voters within any particular group. When it comes to changing the minds of the more entrenched
ideologues, I am more jaded. Too many discussions about what to "do"
about widespread belief in conspiracy theories make the false assumption
that people do not want to act on inaccurate information. For individuals
such as those on the front line of storming the Capitol in 2021 or the
QAnon leaders, the conspiracy theories don't have to adhere to journalistic standards of authenticity, they just have to reinforce their worldview.
These and other conspiracy theories constitute sacred texts to them that
provide spiritual sustenance and empower them to proselytize. When they
post a picture of Obama and Fauci, they are saying "These guys are at fault
for and will profit from our COVID-19 woes," and they are hoping their
friends will share it with their friends and join the cause.

"Belief" is a key word in this instance because they believe in Obama's
evilness with the same fervor they attach to their religious faith. Indeed,
it is a component of their religious faith. They believe in Obama's guilt
just as they believe that their savior died on a cross. Many of the anti-
Obama/pro-Trump adherents align themselves with evangelical Christian
churches. They saw nothing incongruous about the extreme level of force
they used to enter the Capitol building and their desire to say a collective
prayer once they were inside. Maybe—and this is a big maybe—we should
let such individuals know that just as there are unscrupulous pastors motivated solely by the dollar, the world of conspiracy theories is populated
by folks such as the boss birthers (chapter 3) and the QAnon profiteers
who support themselves by monetizing the faith of others.

In the introduction, I make the case that the 2016 election of Donald J. Trump could have been foreseen had more political watchdogs,

journalists, and others been attentive to the arc of the anti-Obama lore. The plot points of the core Obama story that resonated with many Americans—his African/white heritage, his marriage to a striving black woman, his life of public service, his first-class education—repulsed others who rejected stories of African American mobility. These folks sought to undermine Obama's credibility with inclusive Americans by generating a long list of stories that negated every positive aspect of his profile.

Donald J. Trump recognized that this slice of the electorate could be a game changer, and that he could succeed where John McCain and Mitt Romney failed. The geographic distribution of these voters played in his favor, putting him in the White House, where he continued to rely on the dissemination of stories that were false at the surface level but true to the worldview of his supporters.

The end of Trump's 2017–21 term as president of the United States was marked by unprecedented civic volatility from the close of business on November 3 until Joe Biden was sworn in on January 20. During that window of time, Trump tweeted about Obama eleven times. Almost all were about the 2012–2020 elections. Trump stated again that Obama had spied on his 2016 campaign. He was convinced that Biden's 2016 vote total in some swing state, black-majority districts outperformed Obama's 2012 performance in the same districts. He interprets Biden's success as further evidence of a "rigged election." Two of the tweets perpetuate the conspiracy theory that voting machines were manipulated in 2012 to switch Romney votes to Obama ones. Donald J. Trump's final tweet about Obama before Twitter suspended his account was about a different kind of "election":

> Barack Obama was toppled from the top spot and President Trump claimed the title of the year's Most Admired Man. Trump number one, Obama number two and Joe Biden a very distant number three. That's also rather odd given the fact that on November 3 Biden allegedly racked up millions more votes than Trump, but can't get anywhere close to him in this poll. No incoming president has ever done as badly in this annual survey." @MarkSteynOnline @TuckerCarlson That's because he got millions of Fake Votes in the 2020 election which was RIGGED![6]

Putting aside Trump's by then familiar unsubstantiated accusations about Biden and the election, it is noteworthy both that Trump chose to gloat about "toppling" Obama in this poll and that, in fact, that's just what happened. The poll is an annual one conducted by Gallup, and Trump did top the list, indicating that 18 percent of those surveyed put him in the number one spot and that was the highest percentage of any of those in contention.

To those who would want to conclude that the 2020 presidential election reflected a shift away from support for Trump policies, this is a sobering outcome. President Trump may have lost the election but he did command over seventy million votes. The thick catalog of conspiracy theories and rumors that he and his compatriots mastered and disseminated found receptive audiences ready to believe and to act in service of the goal of discrediting and diminishing the accomplishments of Barack Obama, the accomplishments of black America. We should also remember that Joe Biden, Obama's vice president and Kamala Harris, a mixed-race vice president, triumphed at the polls in part because they could reinvigorate the stories of promise and opportunity. It is my hope that by knowing, understanding, and taking seriously the trash talk we can move forward in productive ways. As Barack Obama would say, "yes, we can."

Acknowledgments

A nether region of my brain started working on this book in the hours and days following Barack Obama's speech nominating John Kerry at the Democratic National Convention in 2004. A little more of my brain kicked in during Obama's first campaign and in his first administration. Closure came many years later as Joe Biden was sworn into office in 2021. Along the way I was able to take advantage of the expertise and friendship of many people.

My ramblings get to be a real book because of my agent, Carol Mann, and my editor at UC Press, Naomi Schneider, both accomplished women who have backed me at other key junctures of my career. The services of Lauren Hamlin and Aaron Shulman were quite helpful when I was trying to balance my administrative responsibilities at UCLA with the demands of finishing a book. Several capable research assistants including Betty Glick, Justis Guardia, Sara Kapadia, and Chinyere Nwonye found, fetched, and contextualized many elements of the book.

Although I could probably make the case that the entire membership of the American Folklore Society (AFS) offered guidance along the way, I will single out a few of the subcommunities from the folklore world who were persistent in their support. The Association of African American Folklorists, including Marilyn White (president for life), Todd Lawrence, Diana Baird N'Daiye, Wanda Addison, and several others steadfastly attended my research talks and read drafts. Perhaps because I plied them with Urban Legend wine, members of the International Society for the Study of Contemporary Legend (ISCLR) endured my "Obama Talks" for more than a decade. Bill Ellis, Diane Goldstein, Elissa

Henken, Jeanmarie Rouhier-Willoughby (and Wes), Gail Arlene De Vos (and Peter), Ian Brodie, Andrea Kitta, Yvonne Milspaw (and Doug), Libby Tucker (and Jeff), and so many others truly from all of the corners of the globe shared their perspectives and led me to valuable primary and secondary sources. Spirited conversations at AFS and the Western States Folklore Society (WSFS) with Simon Bronner, Jay Mechling, and Wolfgang Mieder, aka my "gentlemen," often took place over a meal and wine (Diet Coke for Simon) and their feedback always took me in productive directions. In the last tumultuous year, marked by a pandemic and an insurrection at the Capitol, Luisa Del Giudice seemed to know just when to invite me over to her luscious garden where we could have a pandemically safe discussion, and when I needed a translation of Italian news coverage of anti-Obama conspiracy theories, she came through for me within hours of the request.

Darnell Hunt and Herman Gray took the time to do some reading and offer constructive feedback at a critical moment in the process. The nuts and bolts of getting me into the presence of all of these colleagues were handled by Arlene Jones, Jody Conrad, Sharon Knox, Angelina Herron, Manuela Friedman, Lisa Audish, and Dean Krouch.

The in-laws and outlaws of my family have comforted me with many a meal and spirited conversation—numerous Turner and Smith branches, the Yennies, the Sykes, the whole Omaha contingent—reinforced my conviction that this was a project worth pursuing. *Trash Talk* is dedicated to several women friends who have graced my life for many years—Peggy Canale, Victoria Frisch, Rhonda Gomes, and Carolyn Whitehurst. It's amazing how much can be resolved in a walk along Long Beach.

Always in my corner, my husband, Kevin Smith, and our son, Daniel Turner Smith, are no doubt the happiest people to see this book complete. Although I do need to do some fieldwork on the next project, guys. . . .

Notes

INTRODUCTION

1. See https://www.urbandictionary.com/define.php?term=Moochelle.

2. Although not exhaustive, the bibliography identifies several folklorists whose critiques of the terms *urban legend, rumor"* and *contemporary legend*s have influenced my consideration of these texts. For example, Trevor Blank, "Examining the Transmission of Urban Legends: Making the Case for Folklore Fieldwork on the Internet," *Folklore Forum* 37, no. 1 (2007); Jan Harold Brunvand, *Encyclopedia of Urban Legends: Updated and Expanded Edition* (Santa Barbara, CA: ABC:CLIO,2012); Gary Alan Fine and Bill Ellis, *The Global Grapevine: Why Rumors of Terrorism, Immigration, and Trade Matter* (Oxford: Oxford University Press, 2010); Eda Kalmre, "Introduction: The Social and Political Dynamic of Conspiracy Theories, Rumours, Fake News and Belief Narratives," *Folklore: The Electronic Journal of Folklore* 69 (2017): 7–14; Elliott Oring, "Legendary and the Rhetoric of Truth," *Journal of American Folklore* 121, no. 480 (2008): 127–66.

3. Conspiracy theories have often been researched within the realms of the social sciences. The definitive source is Richard Hofstadter, "The Folklore of Populism," in *Conspiracy: The Fear of Subversion in American History*. ed. Richard O. Curry and Thomas M. Brown (New York: Holt, Rinehart & Winston, 1972), 101. For a good overview of folkloristic approaches see John Broder et al.,

Covid-19 Conspiracy Theories: QAnon, 5G, the New World Order and Other Viral Ideas (Jefferson, NC: McFarland, 2020), 15–17.

4. A special issue of the *Journal of American Folklore* in 2018 is very helpful for the variety of ways folklorists view this term. See in its entirety *Journal of American Folklore* 131 (2018).

5. Several folklorists have discussed the lore embedded in comments. See Robert Glenn Howard, "Vernacular Authority: Critically Engaging 'Tradition,'" in *Tradition in the 21st Century: Locating the Role of the Past in the Present*, ed. Trevor J. Blank and Robert Glenn Howard (Boulder, CO: Utah State University Press, 2013), 72–99; Andrea Kitta, *The Kiss of Death: Contagion, Contamination, and Folklore* (Louisville, CO: Utah State University Press, 2019), 13.

6. Patricia A. Turner, *I Heard It Through The Grapevine: Rumor in African American Culture* (Berkeley: University of California Press), 174.

7. Barack Obama, *The Audacity of Hope: Thoughts on Reclaiming the American Dream* (New York: Crown Publishers, 2006), 160.

8. "Crush on Obama," YouTube video, 3:19, The Key of Awesome, June 13, 2007 (accessed 02/10/21), https://www.youtube.com/watch?v=wKsoXHYICqU.

9. Gary Alan Fine and Patricia A. Turner, *Whispers on the Color Line: Rumor and Race in America* (Berkeley: University of California Press, 2001), 193.

10. Turner, *I Heard It Through the Grapevine*, 44.

11. Tim Madigan, *The Burning: The Tulsa Race Massacre of 1921* (New York: St. Martin's Press, 2003).

12. Fine and Turner, *Whispers on the Color Line*, 184.

13. All quotes in this paragraph from Barack Obama "Nomination Speech Democratic Convention," Boston, MA, July 27, 2004.

CHAPTER 1. FLAGGED DOWN

1. Barack Obama, *A Promised Land* (New York: Crown Publishers, 2020), 132.

2. Iconic, "9/11 George W. Bush visits Ground Zero," video, 1:33, YouTube, September 6, 2011, https://www.youtube.com/watch?v=SeVEUNI-Cuo.

3. teatempest, "Congress Sings God Bless America," video, 1:02 YouTube, January 20, 2013, https://www.youtube.com/watch?v=4o0FMTMeYmg.

4. Jay Newton Small, "Obama's Flag Pin Flip-Flop," *Time*, May 14, 2008, http://content.time.com/time/politics/article/0,8599,1779544,00.html.

5. Small, "Obama's Flag Pin Flip-Flop".

6. Veracifier, "Kingston Slams Obama for Flag Pin w/o Wearing One Himself," video, 1:39, YouTube, February 28, 2008, https://www.youtube.com/watch?v=G5LZI5odMbM.

7. Hobobob1o, "(4/10) 2008 PA ABC Democratic Debate," video, 9:59, YouTube, April 10, 2008, https://www.youtube.com/watch?v=3GPiHQh_Sts.

8. Small, "Obama's Flag Pin Flip-Flop."

9. David Mikkelson, "Obama Explains National Anthem Stance?," Snopes, February 15, 2008, http://snopes.com/politics/obama/stance.asp.

10. "United States Flag Code," The American Legion, Title 36, Subtitle I, Part A section 301 United States Code—National Anthem, https://www.legion.org/flag/code?web=1&wdLOR=c9F9B7312-F462-ED40-BD83-F60F7265ED57.

11. David Mikkelson, "Who Is Barack Obama?" Snopes, January 2007, (http://www.snopes.com/politics/obama/muslim.asp).

12. Gordon W. Allport and Leo Postman, *The Psychology of Rumor* (New York: Henry Holt, 1947), ix.

13. Patricia A. Turner, *I Heard It Through the Grapevine: Rumor in African American Culture* (Berkeley: University of California Press, 1993) 224.

14. Mikkelson, "Obama Explains National Anthem Stance" Snopes, February 2008, (https://www.snopes.com/fact-check/national-anthem-stance/).

15. Almost every folklorist who studies contemporary or urban legends develops a discrete list of attributes of the genre, a full citation of those that I have admired in the past thirty-plus years would contain at least a dozen references. Many of us are indebted to the work that was done by Jan Harold Brunvand, author of several books, but useful in this regard is Jan Harold Brunvand, *Encyclopedia of Urban Legends, Updated and Expanded Edition.* (Santa Barbara, CA: ABC: CLIO 2012).

16. Mikkelson, "Obama Explains National Anthem Stance" Snopes, February 2008, (https://www.snopes.com/fact-check/national-anthem-stance/).

17. Jerome R. Corsi, *The Obama Nation: Leftist Politics and the Cult of Personality* (New York: Threshold Editions, 2008) 255.

18. Obama, *A Promised Land*, 132.

19. C-SPAN, "President Barack Obama 2009 Inauguration and Address," video, 21:50, YouTube, January 20, 2009, https://www.youtube.com/watch?v=VjnygQo2aW4.

20. Personal Correspondence, Jay Mechling to Patricia A. Turner, February 26, 2016.

21. David Mikkelson, "Obama Refuses to Sign Eagle Scout Certificates" Snopes.com,. October 7 2010, https://www.snopes.com/fact-check/eagle-scouts/.

22. David Mikkelson, "Flag Pin Dismissal," Snopes, April 4, 2015, https://www.snopes.com/fact-check/pinning-the-blame/.

23. David Mikkelson, "Did President Obama Decline to Lay Wreaths at Arlington on Memorial Day?" Snopes, May 26, 2010 https://www.snopes.com/fact-check/potus-at-arlington-on-memorial-day/.

24. Jess Henig, "Mirror Image," FactCheck.org, January 11, 2010, https://www.factcheck.org/2010/01/mirror-image/.

25. Henig, "Mirror Image."

26. David Mikkelson, "Barack Obama Removes Flag From Air Force One" Snopes, Snopes Media Group, Inc, April 16, 2012, https://www.snopes.com/fact-check/an-american-tail/.

27. Spacewoman Spiff (@BellaPelosi), #YoujustpulledanObama If You Fly the Flags at Half mast for a crack-smoking drug addict (Whitney Houston) but not an American hero (Chris Kyle). Twitter, April 27, 2013 (accessed February 11, 2021), https://twitter.com/search?q=Whitney%20Houston%20Chris%20Kyle& src=typed_query.

28. Cindi R (@Cindie_J), So our president lowers the flag for Whitney Houston but not Nancy Reagan? Drug Overdose vs First Lady," Twitter, March 7, 2016 (accessed February 11, 2021), https://twitter.com/search?q=Nancy%20Reagan %20Whitney%20Houston&src=typed_query.

29. Dan Lamothe, "How 'American Sniper' Chris Kyle's Truthfulness Is in Question Again," *Washington Post*, May 25, 2016 (accessed February 11, 2021), https://www.washingtonpost.com/news/checkpoint/wp/2016/05/25/how -american-sniper-chris-kyles-truthfulness-is-in-question-once-again/.

30. Ruth Braunstein, *Prophets and Patriots, Faith in Democracy across the Political Divide* (Oakland: University of California Press, 2017) 3.

31. Sarah Palin, *Going Rogue: An American Life* (New York: Harper Collins, 2009).

CHAPTER 2. ARTICLES OF FAITH

1. Barack Obama, *The Audacity of Hope: Thoughts on Reclaiming the American Dream* (New York: Crown Publishers, 2006), 3.

2. Obama, *The Audacity of Hope*, 11.

3. Obama, *The Audacity of Hope*, 197.

4. Obama, *The Audacity of Hope*, 203.

5. Obama, *The Audacity of Hope*, 204–5.

6. Obama, *The Audacity of Hope*, 204.

7. Obama, *The Audacity of Hope*, 204.

8. Obama, *The Audacity of Hope*, 205.

9. Obama, *The Audacity of Hope*, 207–8.

10. Obama, *The Audacity of Hope*, 217.

11. Obama, *The Audacity of Hope*, 218.

12. Wolfgang Mieder, *Yes We Can: Barack Obama's Proverbial Rhetoric* (New York: Peter Lang, 2009), 21–22.

13. Obama, *The Audacity of Hope*, 224.

14. Obama, *The Audacity of Hope*, 225.

15. Obama, *The Audacity of Hope*, 226.

16. ABC Television Stations, "McCain Defends Obama as 'Decent Family Man' on Campaign Trail," video :38, YouTube, August 26, 2018, https://www.youtube .com/watch?v=cxQFb71nVFc.

17. ABC Television Stations, "McCain Defends Obama."

18. The Uptake, "McCain Responds to 'Arab' Epithet at Rally: Obama a decent family man." *HuffPost*, October 10, 2008, https://www.huffpost.com/entry/mccain-responds-to-arab-a_b_133820.

19. The Uptake, "McCain Responds to 'Arab' Epithet."

20. Patricia A. Turner, *I Heard It Through the Grapevine: Rumor in African-American Culture* (Berkeley: University of California Press, 1993), 224.

21. David Benjamin, "The Little Lie and How It Grew," Commondreams.org, October 16, 2008. https://www.commondreams.org/views/2008/10/16/little-lie-and-how-it-grew.

22. Benjamin, "The Little Lie."

23. David Mikkelson, "Did Barack Obama Admit to His 'Muslim Faith'? Snopes, October 23, 2008, https://www.snopes.com/fact-check/my-muslim-faith/.

24. The Uptake, "McCain Responds to 'Arab' Epithet."

25. Jennifer Steinhauer, "Confronting Ghosts of 2000 in South Carolina," *New York Times*, October, 19, 2007, https://www.nytimes.com/2007/10/19/us/politics/19mccain.html?_r=1&sq=john%20mccain%20oblack%20obaby&scp=1&pagewanted=all.

26. Rachel Sklar, "David Remnick on That New Yorker Cover: It's A Satire Meant to Target Distortions and Misconceptions and Prejudices about Obama," *HuffPost*, July 21, 2008, https://www.huffingtonpost.com/2008/07/13/david-remnick-on-emnew-yo_n_112456.html.

27. Paul Lewis, "*New Yorker*'s 'Terrorist' Obama Cover Under Fire," *The Guardian*, July 14, 2008, https://www.theguardian.com/world/deadlineusa/2008/jul/14/newyorkercover.

28. Quoted in Jess Henig, "Sliming Obama," Factcheck.org, Annenberg Public Policy Center, January 11, 2008. https://www.factcheck.org/2008/01/sliming-obama/.

29. David Mikkelson, "Who Is Barack Obama," Snopes, July 7, 2009, https://www.snopes.com/fact-check/who-is-barack-obama/.

30. Ian Haney Lopez, *Dog Whistle Politics: How Coded Racial Appeals Have Reinvented Racism and Wrecked the Middle Class* (Oxford: Oxford University Press, 2014), ix.

31. Barack Obama, *Dreams from My Father: A Story of Race and Inheritance* (New York: Three Rivers Press, 1995), 37.

32. John Vause, "CNN Debunks False Report about Obama," CNN, January 23, 2007, https://www.cnn.com/2007/POLITICS/01/22/obama.madrassa/.

33. David Mikkelson, "Barack Obama—Trinity United Church of Christ," Snopes, March 16, 2008, https://www.snopes.com/fact-check/holy-trinity/.

34. Mikkelson, "Barack Obama—Trinity United Church of Christ."

35. Michael Eric Dyson, *The Black Presidency: Barack Obama and the Politics of Race in America* (Boston: Mariner Books, 2016), 83.

36. "Section Two: Obama's Religious Beliefs," Pew Research Center October 28, 2008, https://www.pewresearch.org/politics/2008/10/21/section-2-candidate-traits/.

37. David Mikkelson, "Did President Obama Cancel the National Day of Prayer?" Snopes, December 14, 2009, https://www.snopes.com/fact-check/national-day-of-prayer/.

38. David Mikkelson, "Muslim Prayer Curtin in the White House," Snopes, June 8, 2010, https://www.snopes.com/fact-check/muslim-prayer-curtain-white-house/.

39. David Mikkelson, "Obama's Wedding Ring," Snopes.com, Snopes Media Group Inc., July 18, 2014, https://www.snopes.com/fact-check/lord-of-the-ring/.

40. Joseph Liu, "Little Voter Discomfort with Romney's Religion," Pew Research Center, July 26, 2012, https://www.pewforum.org/2012/07/26/2012-romney-mormonism-obamas-religion/ .

41. Liu, "Little Voter Discomfort."

42. David Mikkelson, "Ban on Military Proselytizing," Snopes, May 6, 2013, https://www.snopes.com/fact-check/ban-on-military-proselytizing/.

43. D'Angelo Gore, "Eight Years of Trolling Obama," FactCheck.org, Annenberg Center for Public Policy, June 19, 2017, https://www.factcheck.org/2017/01/eight-years-of-trolling-obama/.

44. Adam Taylor, "The 'Obama Is a Muslim' Conspiracy Theory Is Still Reverberating in the Middle East," *Washington Post*, January 20, 2016, https://www.washingtonpost.com/news/worldviews/wp/2016/01/21/the-obama-is-a-muslim-conspiracy-theory-is-still-reverberating-in-the-middle-east/.

45. "Trump Jokingly Reprimands Supporters in New Hampshire," *Don Lemon Tonight*, CNN, June 1, 2016. https://www.cnn.com/videos/politics/2016/01/06/donald-trump-new-hampshire-muslim-sot-lemon-ctn.cnn.

CHAPTER 3. BORN TO RUN

1. William Jelani Cobb, *The Substance of Hope: Barack Obama and the Paradox of Progress* (New York: Bloomsbury Publishing, 2020), 25.

2. Gary A. Fine and Patricia A. Turner, *Whispers on the Color Line: Rumor and Race in America* (Berkeley: University of California Press, 2001), 133–34.

3. Fine and Turner, *Whispers on the Color Line*, 135.

4. David Remnick, *The Bridge: The Life and Rise of Barack Obama* (New York: Alfred A. Knopf, 2010), 462.

5. Michelle Obama, *Becoming* (New York: Crown Publishing, 2018), 242.

6. Doug Gross, "Dictionary Word of the Year: 'Unfriend,'" CNN, November 17, 2009, https://www.cnn.com/2009/TECH/11/17/unfriend.word/index.html.

7. Amy Hollyfield, "Obama's Birth Certificate: Final Chapter," Politifact, June 27, 2008, https://www.politifact.com/truth-o-meter/article/2008/jun/27/obamas-birth-certificate-part-ii/.

8. David Mikkelson, "Who Is Barack Obama," Snopes, July 7, 2009, https://www.snopes.com/fact-check/who-is-barack-obama/.

9. See Jan Harold Brunvand, *The Choking Doberman: And Other "New" Urban Legends* (New York: W.W. Norton, 1984,) 169–86, for a full and lively account of the Proctor and Gamble cycle.

10. Tamotsu Shibutani, *Improvised News: A Sociological Study of Rumor* (Indianapolis: Bobbs-Merrill, 1966), 175.

11. See Andrew Marantz, "Trump and the Truth: The Viral Candidate," *New Yorker*, November 4, 2016, https://www.newyorker.com/news/news-desk/trump-and-the-truth-the-viral-candidate.

12. Wikipedia offers a very comprehensive list of the law suits filed regarding Barack Obama's eligibility for the presidency. See "Barack Obama presidential eligibility litigation," Wikipedia, https://en.wikipedia.org/wiki/php?title=BarackObamapresidentialeligibilitylitigation&oldid=1002653695 (accessed February 13, 2021).

13. Loren Collins, *Bullspotting: Finding Facts in the Age of Misinformation* (New York: Prometheus Books, 2012), 122.

14. Loren Collins, "The Secret Origins of Birtherism," *Bullspotting: Finding Facts in the Age of Misinformation* (blog), September 2016, http://www.bullspotting.com/articles/the-secret-origins-of-birtherism/.

15. Ben Smith, "Fighting Smears, Gaming Google," *Ben Smith Blog*, Politico, June 12, 2008, https://www.politico.com/blogs/ben-smith/2008/06/fighting-smears-gaming-google-009659.

16. Smith, "Fighting Smears."

17. Nancy L. Rosenblum and Russel Muirhead, *A Lot of People Are Saying: The New Conspiracism and the Assault on Democracy* (Princeton, NJ: Princeton University Press, 2019), 103.

18. Jerome Corsi, Hawaii's Statement on Obama Birth Record Breaks Law?," WND, WorldNetDaily, July 28, 2009, https://www.wnd.com/2009/07/105262/; Joseph Farah, "Obama's State Secret: His Birth Certificate!," WND, WorldNetDaily, November 21, 2008, https:// www.wnd.com/2008/11/81581/.

19. Orly Taitz, "Defend Our Freedoms Foundation," http://www.orlytaitzesq.com (accessed February 13, 2021).

20. Dan Nakaso, "Obama's Certificate of Birth OK, State Says," *Honolulu Advertiser*, November 1, 2008, http://the.honoluluadvertiser.com/article/2008/Nov/01/ln/hawaii811010345.html.

21. Joseph Farah, "Last Chance for Constitution?," WND, WorldNetDaily, November 30, 2008, https://www.wnd.com/2008/11/82370/.

22. Patrik Jonsson, "A Last Electoral Hurdle for Obama," *Christian Science Monitor*, November 26, 2008, https://www.csmonitor.com/USA/Politics/2008/1126/a-last-electoral-hurdle-for-obama.

23. WilliamDawesinDE, "Mike Castle on Barack H. Obama Birth certificate," WilliamDawesin DE, July 10, 2009, YouTube video, 2:55 https://www.youtube.com/watch?v=9V1nmn2zRMc.

24. Mark Memmott, "'Birther' Debate Never Ends," NPR, July 22, 2009, https://www.npr.org/sections/thetwo-way/2009/07/birther_debate_never_seems_to.html.

25. "Hawaii Confirms Obama's Birthplace, Again," CBS News, July 28, 2009, https://www.cbsnews.com/news/hawaii-confirms-obamas-birthplace-again/.

26. Andrew Marantz, *Anti-Social: On-Line Extremists, Techno-Utopians, and the Hijacking of the American Conversation* (New York: Viking, 2019), 184–85.

27. *Good Morning America*, "'GMA' Exclusive: Trump a Birther?," video 7:08, ABC News, March 17, 2011, https://abcnews.go.com/GMA/video/gma-exclusive-trump-birther-13155432.

28. "Donald Trump Says Obama Should Stop Playing Basketball and Lower Gas Prices," *Los Angeles Times*, April 27, 2011, https://latimesblogs.latimes.com/washington/2011/04/donald-trump.html.

29. Lynmarie Morales, "Obama's Birth Certificate Convinces Some but Not All, Skeptics," Gallup, May 13, 2011, https://news.gallup.com/poll/147530/obama-birth-certificate-convinces-not-skeptics.aspx.

30. "CNN: President Obama Zings Donald Trump, birthers at White House Correspondents' Dinner," CNN, May 2, 2011, YouTube video, 3:58, https://www.youtube.com/watch?v=zeGpLgob3DE.

31. Amy B. Wang, "Did the 2011 White House Correspondent's Dinner Spur Trump to Run for President?," *Chicago Tribune*, February 26, 2017, https://www.chicagotribune.com/nation-world/ct-white-house-correspondents-dinner-trump-20170226-story.html.

32. Bill Ellis, "Humor as an Integral Part of the Contemporary Legend Process," in *Rumor Mills: The Social Impact of Rumor and Legend*, ed. Gary Alan Fine, Veronique Campion-Vincent, and Chip Heath (New Brunswick, NJ: Transaction Publishers, 2005), 135.

33. Maricopa County, "Welcome to Maricopa County," accessed February 10, 2021. https://www.maricopa.gov/5289/Maricopa-County.

34. Joe Hagan, "The Long, Lawless Ride of Sheriff Joe Arpaio," *Rolling Stone*, August 2, 2012, https://www.rollingstone.com/culture/culture-news/the-long-lawless-ride-of-sheriff-joe-arpaio-231455/.

35. John M. Woodman, "Exposed: Sheriff Joe Arpaio Birther Scam: Here's Proof That Arpaio's Posse Fabricated Evidence and Lied to the Nation," *Investigating the Obama Birth Mysteries* (blog), July 24, 2012, http://www.obamabirthbook.com/http:/www.obamabirthbook.com/2012/07/exposed-sheriff-joe-arpaio-corsi

-birther-scam-heres-the-proof-that-arpaios-posse-fabricated-evidence-and-lied
-to-the-nation/.

36. Hagan, " The Long, Lawless Ride."

37. CBS News, "Sheriff Arpaio Profiting from Birther Battle?," CBS News July 18, 2012, YouTube video, 2:35 https://www.youtube.com/watch?v=Z43G
-Obm4uA.

38. CBS News, "Sheriff Arpaio Profiting from Birther Battle?"

39. FactCheck.org, "Donald Trump, Ted Cruz Think Hillary Clinton Is a Birther, but That's Not True," *HuffPost*, July 2, 2015, https://www.huffpost.com
/entry/hillary-clinton-birther_n_7715666.

40. FactCheck.org, "Donald Trump, Ted Cruz'"

41. John Nolte, "Bombshell: '*Washington Post*' Confirms Hillary Clinton Started the Birther Movement," Breitbart, September 26, 2015, https://www
.breitbart.com/politics/2015/09/26/washington-post-confirms-hillary-clinton
-started-the-birther-movement/.

42. Julia Glum, "Some Republicans Still Think Obama Was Born in Kenya as Trump Resurrects Birther Conspiracy Theory," *Newsweek*, December 11, 2017, https://www.newsweek.com/trump-birther-obama-poll-republicans-kenya-744195.

43. Michelle Obama, *Becoming*, 352–53.

CHAPTER 4. MICHELLE MATTERS

1. Barack Obama, *The Audacity of Hope: Thoughts on Reclaiming the American Dream* (New York: Crown Publishing, 2006), 328.

2. Patricia A. Turner, *Ceramic Uncles and Celluloid Mammies: Black Images and Their Influence on Culture* (New York: Anchor Books, 1994), 101.

3. Michelle Obama, *Becoming* (New York: Crown Publishers, 2018), 262.

4. Rebecca Sinderbrand, "Cindy McCain, Michelle Obama in Patriotism Flap," CNN Political Ticker, February 19, 2008 (accessed February 14, 2021), https://politicalticker.blogs.cnn.com/2008/02/19/cindy-mccain-michelle-obama
-in-patriotism-flap/comment-page-16/.

5. Bryan, "Michelle Obama Hasn't Been Proud of America in at Least 26 Years?," *Hot Air*, February 18, 2008 (accessed February 14, 2021), https://
hotair.com/archives/bryan/2008/02/18/michelle-obama-hasnt-been-proud-of
-america-in-at-least-26-years/.

6. Rich Galen, "I've Always Been Proud of America," *Townhall*, February 20, 2008 (accessed February 14, 2021), https://townhall.com/columnists/richgalen
/2008/02/20/ive-always-been-proud-of-america-n1103633.

7. Alexander Mooney, "Michelle Obama Takes Heat from Tennessee GOP," CNN Politics, May 16, 2008 (accessed February 14, 2021), http://www.cnn.com
/2008/POLITICS/05/15/michelle.tennessee/.

8. E. Thomas, "Michelle Obama 'Proud' Remarks," *Newsweek*, March 13, 2008, https://www.newsweek.com/michelle-obamas-proud-remarks-83559.

9. Michelle Obama, *Becoming* (New York: Crown Publishers, 2018) 260.

10. Stephen L. Carter, *Reflections of an Affirmative Action Baby* (New York: Basic Books, 1992).

11. Angie Drobnic Holan, "Her Senior Thesis Doesn't Say That," May 30, 2008 (accessed February 14, 2021), Politifact, https://www.politifact.com/factchecks /2008/may/30/chain-email/her-senior-thesis-doesnt-say-that/.

12. David Mikkelson, "Was Michelle Obama's Thesis Restricted until after the 2008 Election?" Snopes, n.d. (accessed February 14, 2020), https://www.snopes .com/fact-check/michelle-obamas-thesis/.

13. David Mikkelson, "Obama Explains National Anthem Stance?," Snopes, February 15, 2008 (accessed February 14, 2021), https://www.snopes.com/fact -check/national-anthem-stance/.

14. D'Angelo Gore, "Michelle Obama's Staff," FactCheck.org, August 5, 2009 (accessed February 14, 2021), https://www.factcheck.org/2009/08/michelle -obamas-staff/.

15. Gore, "Michelle Obama's Staff."

16. Paul L. Williams, "First Lady Requires More Than Twenty Attendants," *Canada Free Press*, July 7, 2009 (accessed February 14, 2021), https:// canadafreepress.com/article/first-lady-requires-more-than-twenty-attendants.

17. Gore, "Michelle Obama's Staff."

18. David Mikkelson, "Michelle Obama and Daughters at the 2012 London Olympics," Snopes, August 30, 2012 (accessed February 14, 2021), https://www .snopes.com/fact-check/olympic-meddle/.

19. "Michelle's Spain Vacation," *Fellowship of the Minds* (blog), July 27, 2010 (accessed May 15, 2015), http://fellowshipoftheminds.com/2010/07/27/michelles -spain-vacation-30-rooms-for-4-days/.

20. "Michelle's Spain Vacation."

21. Eun Kyung Kim, "Brits Portray Michelle Obama as Queen—of Fashion," *Today*, March 21, 2013 (accessed February 14, 2021), https://www.today.com /style/brits-portray-michelle-obama-queen-fashion-1C8994788 .

22. David Mikkelson, "Post Office to Sell Michelle Obama Stamps," Snopes, December 15, 2014 (accessed February 14, 2021), https://www.snopes.com/fact -check/queen-obama/.

23. Tom Mould, *Overthrowing the Queen: Telling Stories of Welfare in America* (Bloomington: Indiana University Press, 2020).

24. Gary Alan Fine and Patricia A. Turner, *Whispers on the Color Line: Rumor and Race in America* (Berkeley: University of California Press, 2001), 121.

25. Michelle Obama, *Becoming*, x.

26. Jerome R. Corsi, "Claim: Obama Hid 'Gay Life' to Become President," World Net Daily, September 11, 2012 (accessed February 14, 2021), https://www .wnd.com/2012/09/claim-obama-hid-gay-life-to-become-president/.

27. R. Rozzy, "#JoanRivers Says President Obama Is Gay and Michelle Is a Tranny!" (video), YouTube, July 5, 2014 (accessed February 15, 2021), https://www.youtube.com/watch?v=3mwJWH8mWhA.

28. Christian Toto, "Can Joan Rivers Survive Calling Obama Gay, First Lady 'Tranny'?" Breitbart, July 4, 2014 (accessed February 15, 2021), https://www.breitbart.com/entertainment/2014/07/04/can-joan-rivers-survive-obamas-insults/.

29. Toto, "Can Joan Rivers Survive?"

30. joemiller33, "i forgot her head-to-shoulder ratio is that of a man NOT a woman and he/she was Michael LaVaughn" (comment on Toto, "Can Joan Rivers Survive").

31. Knowsrightfromwrong, "Of course she wasn't kidding. Since bozo's turn for the worst, there's evidence surfacing that supports the facts (comment Toto, "Can Joan Rivers Survive").

32. K. Ramisetti, "Joan Rivers Calls President Obama Gay, Says Michelle Obama Is a 'Tranny,'" *New York Daily News*, https://www.nydailynews.com/entertainment/gossip/joan-rivers-calls-obama-gay-lady-tranny-article-1.1855378.

33. "Introducing Michael LaVaughn Robinson; The First Lady of the United States of America," *Outrageousminds* (blog), July 3, 2014 (accessed February 14, 2021), https://outrageousminds.wordpress.com/2014/07/04/introducing-michael-lavaughn-robinson-the-first-lady-of-the-united-states-of-america/ https://outrageousminds.wordpress.com/2014/07/04/introducing-michael-lavaughn-robinson-the-first-lady-of-the-united-states-of-america/.

34. "New Shocking Facts about Michelle Obama's Gender," *USAReally* (blog), September 7, 2018 (accessed February 14, 2021), https://usareally.com/1354-new-shocking-facts-about-michelle-obama-s-gender.

35. John Nolte, " RIP Joan Rivers: No One Will Ever Call Michelle Obama a 'Tranny' Again," Breitbart, September 5, 2014 (accessed February 15, 2021), https://www.breitbart.com/entertainment/2014/09/05/rip-joan-rivers-no-one-will-ever-call-michelle-obama-tanny-again/.

36. Mark, "Obama is bi he belonged to the gay club in Chicago and Michelle does look like a Tranny *shrug*" (comment on. Nolte, "RIP Joan Rivers").

37. Jay, "She was snuffed" (comment on thread "Joan Rivers' Autopsy Reveals Cause of Death"), *Today* (video), YouTube, October 17, 2014 (accessed February 15, 2021), https://www.youtube.com/watch?v=lzgl6MWNBXs.

38. B U, "Predictable complication," comment on "Joan Rivers' Autopsy Reveals Cause of Death," *Today*.

39. *The Ellen Degeneres Show*, "Ellen and Michelle Break It Down" (video), YouTube, March 13, 2015 (accessed February 15, 2021), https://www.youtube.com/watch?v=UZO5qoB5wfw.

40. Susan Miller, "Michelle Obama 'Ape' Post Puts Tiny Town at Center of Firestorm," *USA Today*, November 15, 2016 (accessed February 15, 2021), https://www

.usatoday.com/story/news/nation/2016/11/15/michelle-obama-post-puts-tiny
-town-center-firestorm/93917502/?fbclid=IwAR3RGKW0FKj3_qz83jrUA3V
-GtyOrebjXsZBeYefdkHgri59VOPJ27V2430.

41. Miller, "Michelle Obama 'Ape' Post."

CHAPTER 5. PANDEMIC LEVELS

1. Kamala Harris, speech, Wilmington, Delaware, Delaware Online, August 12, 2020, https://www.delawareonline.com/story/news/politics/elections/2020/11/07/kamala-harris-victory-speech-delaware-full-text/6210399002/.

2. Jack Goodman, "US Election 2020: Kamala Harris Targeted by False Conspiracy Theories," BBC News, August 19, 2020 (accessed February 15, 2021), https://www.bbc.com/news/53826816.

3. Michelle Obama, "Speech at the 2020 Democratic National Convention," Milwaukee, Wisconsin, August 17, 2020, YouTube (accessed February 16, 2021), https://www.youtube.com/watch?v=VZwfEWpG_wA&t=180s.

4. Justin Sink, "President Obama's Ebola Problem," *The Hill*, October 16, 2014 (accessed February 15, 2021), https://thehill.com/news/administration/220922-president-obamas-ebola-problem.

5. "Conspiracy Theories of HIV/AIDS," Editorial, *The Lancet* 365 (9458) (February 5, 2005): 448 (accessed February 15, 2021), https://www.thelancet.com/journals/lancet/article/PIIS0140-6736(05)17875-1/fulltext.

6. This inventory of conspiracy theory activators reflects my engagement with the scholarship of many researchers whose work focuses on disease and belief. A partial list includes: John Bodner, Wendy Welch, Ian Brodie, Anna Muldoon, Donald Leech and Ashely Marshall, *COVID-19 Conspiracy Theories: QAnon, 5G, the New World Order and Other Viral Ideas* (Jefferson, NC: McFarland, 2020). Mary Douglas, *Purity and Danger: An Analysis of Concepts of Pollution and Taboo* (London: Routledge, 2003); Alan Dundes, ed., *The Blood Libel Legend: A Casebook in Anti-Semitic Folklore* (Madison: University of Wisconsin Press, 1991); Paul Farmer, *Infections and Inequalities: The Modern Plagues* (Berkeley: University of California Press, 2001); Diane Goldstein, *Once upon a Virus: AIDS Legends and Vernacular Risk Perception* (Logan: Utah State University Press, 2004); Andrea Kitta, *The Kiss of Death: Contagion, Contamination, and Folklore* (Logan: Utah State University Press, 2019).

7. Peter Piot and Ruth Marshall, *No Time to Lose: A Life in Pursuit of Deadly Viruses* (New York: W.W. Norton, 2012), 6.

8. Arthur Ashe and Arnold Rampersad, *Days of Grace: A Memoir* (New York: Ballantine Books, 1993), 148.

9. Ashe and Rampersad,. 149.

10. "AIDS Mary" as these legends are often titled, has been extensively documented. Examples include, Jan Harold Brunvand, *Too Good to Be True* (New

York : W.W. Norton, 1999); Gary Alan Fine, "Welcome to the World of AIDS: Fantasies of Female Revenge," *Western Folklore* 46 (3) 192–97; Diane Goldstein, *Once upon a Virus: AIDS Legends and Vernacular Risk Perception* (Logan: Utah State University Press, 2004).

11. James H. Jones, *Bad Blood: The Tuskegee Syphilis Experiment—A Tragedy of Race and Medicine* (New York: Free Press, 1982).

12. Patricia A. Turner, *I Heard it Through the Grapevine: Rumor in African-American Culture* (Berkeley: University of California Press, 1993), 141.

13. Turner, 156.

14. Turner, 156.

15. Tara C. Smith, "How *The Hot Zone* Created the Worst Myths about Ebola," Gizmodo, October 22, 2014 (accessed February 15, 2021), https://io9.gizmodo.com/how-the-hot-zone-created-the-worst-myths-about-ebola-1649384576.

16. Richard Preston, *The Hot Zone: The Terrifying True Story of the Origins of the Ebola Virus* (New York: Anchor Books, 1995), 2122.

17. Smith, "How *The Hot Zone* Created the Worst Myths about Ebola."

18. Susan Page, "Fauci Says 'Inadequate' World Response Won't Control Ebola." *USA Today*, September 29, 2014 (accessed February 16, 2021), https://www.usatoday.com/story/news/politics/2014/09/29/capital-download-nih-anthony-fauci-on-ebola-threat/16423303/.

19. Donald J. Trump (@realDonaldTrump), "Ebola patient will be brought . . . ," Trump Twitter Archive V2, July 31, 2014 (accessed February 15, 2021), https://www.thetrumparchive.com/?searchbox=%22Ebola%22.

20. Donald J. Trump (@realDonaldTrump), "President Obama - close down the flights from Ebola infected areas right now, before it is too late!," Trump Twitter Archive V2, October 4, 2014 (accessed February 15, 2021), https://www.thetrumparchive.com/?searchbox=%22ebola%22.

21. Donald J. Trump (@realDonaldTrump), "Why are we sending thousands of ill-trained soldiers into Ebola infested areas of Africa! Bring the plague back to U.S.?," Trump Twitter Archive V2, September 19, 2014b (accessed February 15, 2021), https://www.thetrumparchive.com/?searchbox=%22ebola%22.

22. Donald J. Trump (@realDonaldTrump), "Obama just appointed an Ebola Czar with zero experience in the medical area and zero experience in infectious disease control," Trump Twitter Archive V2, October 17, 2014 (accessed February 15, 2021), https://www.thetrumparchive.com/?searchbox=%22ebola%22.

23. Donald J. Trump (@realDonaldTrump), "Do you notice that because of Ebola, ISIS etc., ObamaCare has gone to the back burner despite horrible results coming," Trump Twitter Archive, V2, October 11, 2014 (accessed February 15, 2021), https://www.thetrumparchive.com/?searchbox=%22ebola%22.

24. As of this writing, this post is no longer available through the normal search channels. Nolan Rathborn, "Did the U.S. Just Secretly Fly in an Ebola Patient?" Blog, top comment *Freedom's Outpost*, November 10, 2014, https://freedomoutpost.com.

25. As of this writing, this post is no longer available through normal search channels. Bourne ID, "We can't seal ourselves off. . ." Comment, Yahoo News, October 29, 2014, https://news.yahoo.com/?guccounter=1&guce_referrer=aHRoc HM6Ly93d3cuYmluuZy5jb2ov&guce_referrer_sig=AQAAAIAE5uIGxX8LFU ExcRcCVgQueToC4dtuXUhiMri7Kl2gEx1ztC4koFTtlJzcVR-LwNTW71GKdXL 7V4lGOBB2fmHveqRDPJBJiH-M5eEWbyDDODsvyC4b8IHSDjHnyErYvZ5R9 K8cM-q5QyrJInfhpPQc2JOw8gBjC-X96OK6SW3z.

26. Sundance, "The Campaign Message," The Conservative Tree House, October 3, 2014 (accessed February 15, 2021), https://theconservativetreehouse.com /2014/10/03/2014-the-campaign-message/.

27. Ted Barrett and Deirdre Walsh, "Ebola Becomes an Election Issue," CNN Politics. October 3, 2014 (accessed February 15, 2021), https://www.cnn.com /2014/10/03/politics/ebola-midterms/index.html.

28. Folk beliefs that rise to panic levels have long been of interest to folklorists and our colleagues. Of particular interest see: John Bodner, Wendy Welch, Ian Brodie, Anna Muldoon, Donald Leech, and Ashely Marshall, *COVID-19 Conspiracy Theories: QAnon, 5G, the New World Order and Other Viral Ideas* (Jefferson, NC: McFarland, 2020; Bill Ellis, *Raising the Devil: Satanism, New Religions, and the Media* (Lexington: University of Kentucky Press, 2000); Jeffrey S. Victor, *Satanic Panic: The Creation of a Contemporary Legend* (Chicago: Open Court Publishing, 1993).

29. *Saturday Night Live*, "Dr. Anthony Fauci Cold Open-SNL," video 3:12, YouTube, April 25, 2020 (accessed February 16, 2021), https://www.youtube.com /watch?v=uW56CLopkog.

30. Rudy W. Giuliani (@RudyGiuliani), "Why did the US (NIH) in 2017 give $3.7m to the Wuhan Lab in China? Such grants were prohibited in 2014. Did Pres. Obama grant an exception?," Twitter, April 26, 2020, (accessed February 6, 2021), https://twitter.com/rudygiuliani/status/1254513987196248065.

31. Elizabeth Vaughn, "Rudy Giuliani Slammed Dr. Fauci over His Agency's $3.7 Million Grant to the Wuhan Institute of Virology," Red State, April 26, 2020 (accessed February 16, 2021), https://redstate.com/elizabeth-vaughn/2020/04 /26/rudy-giuliani-slammed-dr-fauci-over-his-agencys-3-7-million-grant-to-the -wuhan-institute-of-virology-n135540.

32. Madison Dibble, "'Paid for the Damn Virus That's Killing Us': Giuliani Rips Fauci over Grants to Wuhan Laboratory," *Washington Examiner*, April 26, 2020 (accessed February 16, 2021), https://www.washingtonexaminer.com/news /paid-for-the-damn-virus-thats-killing-us-giuliani-rips-fauci-over-grants-to -wuhan-laboratory.

33. Jim Hoft, "Breaking: Dr. Fauci and Obama Admin Gave Wuhan Lab $3.7 Million after Its Top Dr. Shi Zhengli Had US Project Shut Down and She Was Sent Back to China," The Gateway Pundit, April 28, 2020 (accessed February 16, 2021), https://www.thegatewaypundit.com/2020/04/breaking-dr-fauci

-obama-admin-gave-wuhan-lab-3-7-million-top-dr-shi-zhengli-us-project-shut
-sent-back-china/.

34. "Exclusive: Robert F. Kennedy Jr. Drops Bombshells on Dr. Fauci for Medical Cover Ups and Fraud; Fauci 'Poisoned an Entire Generation of Americans,'" April 16, 2020 (accessed February 16, 2021), https://truepundit.com/exclusive -robert-f-kennedy-jr-drops-bombshells-on-dr-fauci-for-medical-cover-ups-and -fraud-fauci-poisoned-an-entire-generation-of-americans/.

35. Gary Alan Fine, "The Goliath Effect: Corporate Dominance and Mercantile Legends," *Journal of American Folklore* 98 (1985), 63–84.

36. Dan Evon, "Is This Obama, Fauci, and Gates at a Wuhan Lab in 2015?," Snopes, July 13, 2020 (accessed February 16, 2021), https://www.snopes.com/fact -check/obama-fauci-gates-wuhan-lab/.

37. CMU Ambassadors, "Many Twitter Accounts Spreading COVID-19 Falsehoods May Be Bots ," Carnegie Mellon University, July 2020, https://www.cmu .edu/ambassadors/july-2020/covid-falsehoods.html.

CHAPTER 6. OBAMA LEGENDS IN THE AGE OF TRUMP

1. Michelle Obama, "Speech at the 2016 Democratic National Convention" (Philadelphia, Pennsylvania, July 25, 2016).

2. See "newest first" in comments section of Michelle Obama, "Speech at the 2020 Democratic Convention," YouTube, August 17, 2020 (accessed February 16, 2021), https://www.youtube.com/watch?v=VZwfEWpG_wA&t=180s.

3. Francesca Bacardi, "Malia and Sasha Obama Look Stunning at First State Dinner," *E Online*, March 11, 2016, https://www.eonline.com/news/747977/malia -and-sasha-obama-look-stunning-at-first-state-dinner; Olivia Bahou, "Malia and Sasha Obama Look All Grown Up at Their First State Dinner," *InStyle*, March 11, 2016, https://www.instyle.com/news/malia-sasha-obama-first-state-dinner.

4. g (@gillian_criddle), "I could pay off my college . . ." Twitter March 13, 2016 (accessed February 16, 2021), https://twitter.com/gillian_criddle/status/709088 722130591744.

5. Jim Hoft, "Sasha and Malia Wore $20,000 Dresses to State Dinner Paid for by US Taxpayers," The Gateway Pundit, March 15, 2016, https://www.thegateway pundit.com/2016/03/sasha-and-malia-wore-20000-dresses-to-state-dinner -paid-for-by-us-taxpayers/.

6. Hoft.

7. Hoft.

8. Hoft.

9. Dan Evon, "Sasha and Malia Obama's Dresses Cost Taxpayers $20,000 Each?" Snopes, March 16, 2016 (accessed February 16, 2021), https://www.snopes .com/fact-check/sasha-malia-obama-dress/.

10. TrumpAmerican (@TrumpAmerican), "LET THEM EAT CAKE!" Twitter, March 12, 2016 (accessed February 16, 2021), https://twitter.com/trumpamerican/status/708781410631331841.

11. H. Tankovska, "Twitter: Number of Monthly Active Users 2010–2019," Statista, January 27, 2021 (accessed February 16, 2021), https://www.statista.com/statistics/282087/number-of-monthly-active-twitter-users/.

12. Dan Evon, "False: Obama Signs Executive Order Allowing Military to Fight US Citizens," Snopes (accessed February 1, 2021), https://www.snopes.com/fact-check/obama-executive-order-military-citizens/.

13. Hillary Clinton, *What Happened* (New York: Simon & Schuster, 2017), 316.

14. For fascinating analyses of Pizzagate distribution, see Timothy R. Tangherlini, "Toward a Generative Model of Legend: Pizzas, Bridges, Vaccines, and Witches," *Humanities* 7, no. 1 (2018): 1–19; Timothy R. Tangherlini, Shadi Shahsavari, Behnam Shahbazi, Ehsan Ebrahimzadeh, and Vwani Roychowdhury, "An Automated Pipeline for the Discovery of Conspiracy and Conspiracy Theory Narrative Frameworks: Bridgegate, Pizzagate and Storytelling on the Web," *PLoS ONE* 15, no. 6 (August 2020): e0233879.https//doi.org/10.1371/journal.pone.0233879.

15. Donald J. Trump (@real DonaldTrump), "We've all wondered. . . .". October 16, 2016 (accessed February 16, 2021), https://www.thetrumparchive.com/?searchbox=%22how+Hillary+avoided+prosecution%22.

16. Andrew Kaczynski, "Michael Flynn Quietly Deletes Fake News Tweet about Hillary Clinton's Involvement in Sex Crimes," CNN Politics, December 14, 2016, https://www.cnn.com/2016/12/14/politics/kfile-flynn-deleted-tweets/index.html.

17. John Bodner et al., *COVID-19 Conspiracy Theories: QAnon, 5G, the New World Order and Other Viral Ideas* (Jefferson, NC: McFarland, 2020), 190.

18. Amanda Robb, "Anatomy of a Fake News Scandal," *Rolling Stone*, November 16, 2017, https://www.rollingstone.com/feature/anatomy-of-a-fake-news-scandal-125877/.

19. "Pizzeria owner targeted by fake news stories speaks out, YouTube Intellihub, December 15, 2016 (accessed February 16, 2021), https://www.youtube.com/watch?v=YXApkzwKIh8.

20. Peter Gelzinis, "Gelzinis: After Pizzagate Fiasco, Mike Flynn Should Take a Hike," *Boston Herald*,. December 8, 2016, https://www.bostonherald.com/2016/12/08/gelzinis-after-pizzagate-fiasco-mike-flynn-should-take-a-hike/.

21. Clinton, *What Happened*, 318.

22. This exchange was removed at some point between December 4, 2020, and February 16, 2021, but am doing some data mining to try to find it.

23. LibertymanMAGA (@LibertymanNick), "Unfortunately Obama will live in DC . . ." Twitter, January 16, 2017, https://twitter.com/LibertymanNick/status/821171285418012672.

24. Mike Rothschild, "2017's Biggest Conspiracy Theories," Snopes, December 29, 2017 (accessed February 16, 2021), https://www.snopes.com/news/2017/12/29/2017s-biggest-conspiracy-theories/.

25. Angie Drobnic Holan, "2017 Lie of the Year: Russian Election Interference Is a 'Made-up Story,'" Politifact, December 12, 2017, https://www.politifact.com/article/2017/dec/12/2017-lie-year-russian-election-interference-made-s/.

26. Jerome Corsi, *Coup d'Etat: Exposing the Deep State and the Plan to Reelect President Trump* (New York: Post Hill Press, 2020), 22–23.

27. Sean Hannity, *Live Free or Die: America (and the World) on the Brink* (New York: Threshold Editions, 2020).

28. Joel B. Pollak, "Mark Levin to GOP: Investigate Obama's 'Silent Coup' vs. Trump," Breitbart, March 3, 2017, https://www.breitbart.com/politics/2017/03/03/mark-levin-obama-used-police-state-tactics-undermine-trump/.

29. Donald J. Trump (@RealDonaldTrump), "Terrible! Just Found Out . . ." Twitter, March 4, 2017 (accessed February 16, 2021), https://www.thetrumparchive.com/?searchbox=%22This+is+McCarthyism%22.

30. Jessica Lee, "Did Obama Get Caught 'Spying' on Trump's 2016 Campaign?" Snopes, September 29, 2020, https://www.snopes.com/fact-check/obama-spying-trump-campaign/.

31. Whitney Phillips and Ryan M. Milner, "The Vernacular Vortex: Analyzing the Endless Churn of Donald Trump's Twitter Orbit," in *Folklore and Social Media*, ed. Andrew Peck and Trevor J. Blank (Logan: Utah State University Press, 2020), 67.

32. Ian Schwartz, "Obama on Flynn: No Precedent for Someone "Getting Off Scot-Free" for Perjury," RealClear Politics, May 9, 2020 (accessed February 17, 2021), https://www.realclearpolitics.com/video/2020/05/09/obama_on_flynn_no_precedent_for_someone_getting_off_scot-free_for_perjury.html#!

33. Donald J. Trump (@realDonaldTrump), "#ObamaGate Wow look what's trending on Twitter. I'll bet these guys aren't laughing today, Twitter, May 10, 2019, https://www.thetrumparchive.com/?searchbox=%22obamagate%22.

34. Roger Sollenberger, "Mike Flynn Swears Allegiance to QAnon in Fourth of July Video," *Salon*, July 6, 2002 (accessed February 17, 2021), https://www.salon.com/2020/07/06/mike-flynn-swears-allegiance-to-qanon-in-fourth-of-july-video/.

35. Rob Arthur, "We Analyzed More Than 1 Million Comments on 4chan. Hate Speech There Has Spiked by 40% Since 2015," *Vice*, July 10, 2019, https://www.vice.com/en/article/d3nbzy/we-analyzed-more-than-1-million-comments-on-4chan-hate-speech-there-has-spiked-by-40-since-2015.

36. John Bodner et al., *COVID-19 Conspiracy Theories: QAnon, 5G, the New World Order and Other Viral Ideas* (Jefferson, NC: McFarland, 2020), 184.

37. Oprah Winfrey (@Oprah), "Just got a phone call that my name is trending. And being trolled for some awful FAKE thing. It's NOT TRUE. Haven't been

raided, or arrested. Just sanitizing and self distancing with the rest of the world. Stay safe everybody [praying hands emoji]," Twitter, March 17, 2020, https://twitter.com/Oprah/status/1240150930840051712.

38. Ben Smith, "The 'Red Slime' Lawsuit That Could Sink the Right Wing Media," *New York Times*, December 12, 2020 (accessed February 17, 2021), https://www.nytimes.com/2020/12/20/business/media/smartmatic-lawsuit-fox-news-newsmax-oan.html.

39. Cesare Sacchetti, "Italygate, Part II: Obama and Renzi Accused of Being the Masterminds of the US Electoral Fraud," *La Cruna dell'ag* (blog), January 7, 2021 (accessed February 17, 2021), https://lacrunadellago.net/2021/01/07/italygate-part-ii-obama-and-renzi-accused-of-being-the-masterminds-of-the-us-electoral-fraud/?lang=en.

40. Sarah Ho (@sarahho12881425) "You seen the story coming out of Italy...," Twitter, January 8, 2021 (accessed February 17, 2021), https://twitter.com/sarahh012881425/status/1347702192397037569.

41. Nations in Action (accessed December 14, 2021), https://nationsinaction.org.

42. Camille Caldera, "Fact Check: Claims of Electoral Fraud in Rome, Dubbed 'ItalyGate,' Are Baseless," *USA Today*, January 8, 2021, https://www.usatoday.com/story/news/factcheck/2021/01/08/fact-check-italygate-claims-electoral-fraud-rome-baseless/6567335002/.

EPILOGUE

1. "Purported to Be the Dylann Roof 'Manifesto,'" http://media.thestate.com/static/roofmanifesto.pdf.

2. Michael Eric Dyson, *The Black Presidency: Barack Obama and the Politics of Race in America* (Boston: Mariner Books, 2016), 256.

3. Nicholas DiFonzo and Prashant Bordia, *Rumor Psychology: Social and Organizational Approaches* (Washington, DC: American Psychological Association, 2007).

4. Ian Tucker, "Yael Eisenstat: Facebook Is Ripe for Manipulation and Viral Misinformation," *The Guardian*, July 26, 2020, https://www.theguardian.com/technology/2020/jul/26/yael-eisenstat-facebook-is-ripe-for-manipulation-and-viral-misinformation.

5. Dan Evon, "Is This Obama, Fauci, and Gates at a Wuhan Lab in 2015?," Snopes, July 13, 2020 (accessed January 19, 2021), https://www.snopes.com/fact-check/obama-fauci-gates-wuhan-lab/.

6. Donald J. Trump (@realDonaldTrump), "Barack Obama was toppled from the top spot," Twitter, December 30, 2020, https://www.thetrumparchive.com/?searchbox=%22Obama%22.

Bibliography

ABC Television Stations. "McCain Defends Obama as 'Decent Family Man' on Campaign Trail." Video :38. YouTube, August 26, 2018. https://www.youtube.com/watch?v=cxQFb7inVFc.

Allport, Gordon W., and Postman, Leo. *A Psychology of Rumor*. New York: Henry Holt, 1947.

Arthur, Rob. "We Analyzed More Than 1 Million Comments on 4chan. Hate Speech There Has Spiked by 40% Since 2015." *Vice*, July 10, 2019. https://www.vice.com/en/article/d3nbzy/we-analyzed-more-than-1-million-comments-on-4chan-hate-speech-there-has-spiked-by-40-since-2015.

Ashe, Arthur, and Rampersad, Arnold. *Days of Grace: A Memoir*. New York:Ballantine Books, 1993.

Associated Press. "Dominion Worker Sues Trump Campaign and Conservative Media." Politico, December 22, 2020. https://www.politico.com/news/2020/12/22/dominion-worker-lawsuit-trump-campaign-450212.

Bacardi, Francesca. "Malia and Sasha Obama Look Stunning at First State Dinner." E Online, March 11, 2016. https://www.eonline.com/news/747977/malia-and-sasha-obama-look-stunning-at-first-state-dinner.

Bahou, Olivia "Malia and Sasha Obama Look All Grown Up at Their First State Dinner." InStyle, March 11, 2016. https://www.instyle.com/news/malia-sasha-obama-first-state-dinner.

Baldwin, Chuck. "Who Killed Joan Rivers?" Chuck Baldwin Live, September 11, 2014. Accessed February 15, 2021. http://chuckbaldwinlive.com/Articles/tabid/109/ID/1234/Who-Killed-Joan-Rivers.aspx.

"Barack Obama presidential eligibility litigation." Wikipedia, https://en.wikipedia
.org/wiki/php?title=BarackObamapresidentialeligibilitylitigation&oldid=
1002653695 (accessed February 13, 2021).

Barr, Andy. "Whispers Persist Despite Election." Politico, December 7, 2008.
https://www.politico.com/story/2008/12/whispers-persist-despite-election
-016257.

Barrett, Ted, and Walsh, Deirdre. Ebola Becomes an Election Issue. CNN
Politics. October 3, 2014. Accessed February 15, 2021. https://www.cnn.com
/2014/10/03/politics/ebola-midterms/index.html.

Benjamin, Daniel, and Steven Simon. "Why Steve Bannon Wants You to Believe
in the Deep State." Politico, March 21, 2017. https://www.politico.com
/magazine/story/2017/03/steve-bannon-deep-state-214935.

Benjamin, David. "The Little Lie and How It Grew." Commondreams.org,
October 16, 2008. https://www.commondreams.org/views/2008/10/16/little
-lie-and-how-it-grew.

Blank, Trevor. Examining the Transmission of Urban Legends: Making the
Case for Folklore Fieldwork on the Internet. Folklore Forum 37, no. 1 (2007).

Bodner, John, Wendy Welch, Ian Brodie, Anna Muldoon, Donald Leech, and
Ashley Marshall. COVID-19 Conspiracy Theories: QAnon, 5G, the New World
Order and Other Viral Ideas. Jefferson, NC: McFarland, 2020.

Boehlert, Eric. "Where's the Media's Ebola Mea Culpa?" Media Matters for
America, May 14, 2015. Accessed February 16, 2021. https://www.media
matters.org/rush-limbaugh/wheres-medias-ebola-mea-culpa.

Bourne ID, "We can't seal ourselves off" Comment, Yahoo News, October 29,
2014.

Braunstein, Ruth. Prophets and Patriots: Faith in Democracy across the
Political Divide. Oakland: University of California Press, 2017.

Browning, Bil. Evangelicals Are Praying That God "Exposes" Michelle Obama
as Transgender. LGBTQ Nation, January 10, 2020. Accessed February 15,
2021. https://www.lgbtqnation.com/2020/01/evangelicals-praying-god
-exposes-michelle-obama-transgender/?fbclid=IwAR0SVdV8dCILHrI
8d8sE4FIOJPVpIzDKZhJg50-kSYgFD63MiMgU9W_Oks4#.XiSRjnh-HtF
.facebook.

Brunvand, Jan Harold. The Choking Doberman: And Other "New" Urban
Legends. New York: W.W. Norton, 1984.

———. Encyclopedia of Urban Legends: Updated and Expanded Edition. Santa
Barbara, CA: ABC:CLIO, 2012.

———. Too Good To Be True. New York: W.W. Norton, 1999.

Bruce, Alexandra. "Report: Obama and Renzi Orchestrated the Theft of US
Elections." Forbidden Knowledge TV. Bruce Content, January 6, 2021.
https://forbiddenknowledgetv.net/report-obama-and-renzi-orhcestrated-the
-theft-of-us-elections/.

Bryan. Michelle Obama Hasn't Been Proud of America in at Least 26 Years? *Hot Air*, February 15, 2021. Accessed February 15, 2021. https://hotair.com /archives/bryan/2008/02/18/michelle-obama-hasnt-been-proud-of-america -in-at-least-26-years/.

B U. "Predictable complication." comment on Joan Rivers' Autopsy Reveals Cause of Death." *Today*. YouTube, October 17, 2014. Accessed February 15, 2021). https://www.youtube.com/watch?v=lzgl6MWNBXs.

Cadden, Mary, and Schnaars, Christopher. "Michelle Obama's 'Becoming' Is *USA Today*'s No. 1 Book of 2018. See the Others in Top 100." *USA Today*, January 5, 2019. https://www.usatoday.com/story/life/books/2019/01/05/usa -todays-top-100-best-sellers-becoming-no-1-2018/2473481002/.

Caldera, Camille. "Fact Check: Claims of Electoral Fraud in Rome, Dubbed 'ItalyGate,' Are Baseless." *USA Today*, January 8, 2021. https://www.usatoday .com/story/news/factcheck/2021/01/08/fact-check-italygate-claims-electoral -fraud-rome-baseless/6567335002/.

Carter, Stephen L. *Reflections of an Affirmative Action Baby*. New York: Basic Books, 1992.

CBS News, "Sheriff Arpaio Profiting from Birther Battle?" July 18, 2012. Video, 2:35. https://www.youtube.com/watch?v=Z43G-Obm4uA.

Cindi R (@Cindie_J) So our president lowers the flag for Whitney Houston but not Nancy Reagan? Drug Overdose vs First Lady." Twitter, March 7, 2016. Accessed 02/11/21. https://twitter.com/search?q=Nancy%20Reagan%20 Whitney%20Houston&src=typed_query.

Clinton, Hillary Rodham. *What Happened*. New York: Simon & Schuster, 2017.

CMU Ambassadors. "Many Twitter Accounts Spreading COVID-19 Falsehoods May Be Bots." Carneigie Mellon University, July 2020, https://www.cmu.edu /ambassadors/july-2020/covid-falsehoods.html.

Cobb, William Jelani. *The Substance of Hope: Barack Obama and the Paradox of Progress*. London: Bloomsbury Publishing, 2020.

Collins, Ben, Zadrozny, Brandy, and Timm, Jane C. "In Call to Georgia's Secretary of State, Trump Pushed QAnon and 4chan-Created Conspiracy Theories." Microsoft News, January 4, 2021. https://www.msn.com/en-us/news/politics /in-call-to-georgias-secretary-of-state-trump-pushed-qanon-and-4chan -created-conspiracy-theories/ar-BB1csMko?li=BBnb7Kz.

Collins, Loren. *Bullspotting: Finding Facts in the Age of Misinformation*. New York: Prometheus Books, 2012.

———. The Secret Origins of Birtherism." *Bullspotting: Finding Facts in the Age of Misinformation* (blog), September 2016. http://www.bullspotting.com /articles/the-secret-origins-of-birtherism/.

"Conspiracy Theories of HIV/AIDS." Editorial, *The Lancet*, February 5, 2005. Accessed February 15, 2021. https://www.thelancet.com/journals/lancet /article/PIIS0140-6736(05)17875-1/fulltext.

Corsi, Jerome R. "Claim: Obama Hid 'Gay Life' to Become President."World Net Daily, .September 11, 2012. Accessed February 15, 2021. https://www.wnd .com/2012/09/claim-obama-hid-gay-life-to-become-president/.

———. "Hawaii's Statement on Obama Birth Record Breaks Law?" WND, WorldNetDaily, July 28, 2009. https://www.wnd.com/2009/07/105262/.

———. The Obama Nation: Leftist Politics and the Cult of Personality. New York: Threshold Editions, 2008.

———. Unfit for Command: Swift Boat Veterans Speak Out Against John Kerry. Washington, DC: Regnery, 2004.

C-SPAN. "President Barack Obama 2009 Inauguration and Address." Video, 21:50 YouTube, January 20, 2009. https://www.youtube.com/watch?v= VjnygQo2aW4.

Cuccinello, Hayley C. "Trump Bump: How Sean Hannity Earned $36 Million This Year." Forbes. July 16, 2018. https://www.forbes.com/sites /hayleycuccinello/2018/07/16/sean-hannity-celebrity-100/?sh=5a5af40b2d93.

Devaney, Jason. "White House: 'Deep State' Real, Attacks Trump." Newsmax, March 21, 2017. https://www.newsmax.com/Politics/White-House-deep -state-resist-Democrats/2017/03/21/id/780036/.

Dibble, Madison. " 'Paid for the Damn Virus That's Killing Us': Giuliani Rips Fauci over Grants to Wuhan laboratory." Washington Examiner, April 26, 2020. Accessed February 16, 2021. https://www.washingtonexaminer.com /news/paid-for-the-damn-virus-thats-killing-us-giuliani-rips-fauci-over -grants-to-wuhan-laboratory.

Diserio, Rebecca. "Busted! Trump Finds Obama's Sick Secret Hiding in His Washington, DC Office." Mad World News. Mad World News, March 13, 2017. https://madworldnews.com/trump-obama-secret-dc-office/.

———. "Melania Gets Rid Of 'Sick Secret' Michelle Left in Place at White House—You'll Love This." Mad World News. Mad World News, October 20, 2017. https://madworldnews.com/melania-rid-michelle-white-house/.

Douglas, Mary. Purity and Danger: An Analysis of Concepts of Pollution and Taboo. London: Routledge, 2003.

"Donald Trump Says Obama Should Stop Playing Basketball and Lower Gas Prices." Los Angeles Times, April 27, 2011. https://latimesblogs.latimes.com /washington/2011/04/donald-trump.html.

Dubay, Eric. "Michelle Is a man, Barack Obama Is Gay!" The Atlantean Con-spiracy. September 10, 2014. Accessed February 15, 2021). http://www .atlanteanconspiracy.com/2014/09/michelle-obama-is-man.html.

Dundes, Alan, ed. The Blood Libel Legend: A Casebook in Anti-Semitic Folklore. Madison: University of Wisconsin Press, 1991.

Dyson, Michael Eric. The Black Presidency: Barack Obama and the Politics of Race in America. Boston: Mariner Books, 2016.

Edelman, Adam. "Trump Claims that Mueller's Team Will Be 'Meddling' in Midterm Elections." NBC News, May 29, 2018. https://www.nbcnews.com

/politics/donald-trump/trump-claims-mueller-s-team-will-be-meddling
-midterm-elections-n878126.

Editorial Board. "Barack Obama on Michael Flynn." *Wall Street Journal*,
May 10, 2020. https://www.wsj.com/articles/barack-obama-on-michael
-flynn-11589148648.

Ellis, Bill. *Raising the Devil: Satanism, New Religions, and the Media.* Lexington: University of Kentucky Press, 2000.

Evon, Dan. "False: Obama Signs Executive Order Allowing Military to Fight US
Citizens." Snopes. Accessed February 1, 2021. https://www.snopes.com/fact
-check/obama-executive-order-military-citizens/.

———. "Is This Obama, Fauci, and Gates at a Wuhan Lab in 2015?" Snopes,
July 13, 2020. Accessed February 16, 2021. https://www.snopes.com/fact
-check/obama-fauci-gates-wuhan-lab/.

———. "Sasha and Malia Obama's Dresses Cost Taxpayers $20,000 Each?"
Snopes, March 16, 2016. Accessed February 16, 2021. https://www.snopes
.com/fact-check/sasha-malia-obama-dress/.

"Exclusive: Robert F. Kennedy Jr. Drops Bombshells on Dr. Fauci for Medical
Cover Ups and Fraud; Fauci 'Poisoned an Entire Generation of Americans.'"
True Pundit, April 16, 2020. Accessed February 16, 2021. https://truepundit
.com/exclusive-robert-f-kennedy-jr-drops-bombshells-on-dr-fauci-for
-medical-cover-ups-and-fraud-fauci-poisoned-an-entire-generation-of
-americans/.

Factcheck.org. "Donald Trump, Ted Cruz Think Hillary Clinton Is a Birther, but
That's Not True." *HuffPost*, July 2, 2015. https://www.huffpost.com/entry
/hillary-clinton-birther_n_7715666.

Farah, Joseph. "Last Chance for Constitution?" WND, WorldNetDaily, November 30, 2008. https://www.wnd.com/2008/11/82370/.

———. "Michelle O's Inexplicable, Vile Bitterness." WND. WorldNetDaily,
June 5, 2016. https://www.wnd.com/2016/06/michelle-os-inexplicable-vile
-bitterness/.

———. "Obama's State Secret: His Birth Certificate!" WND, WorldNetDaily,
November 21, 2008. https://www.wnd.com/2008/11/81581/.

Farmer, Paul. *Infections and Inequalities: The Modern Plagues.* Berkeley:
University of California Press, 2001.

Fine, Gary Alan. "The Goliath Effect: Corporate Dominance and Mercantile
Legends." *Journal of American Folklore* 98 (1985): 63–84.

———. "Welcome to the World of AIDS: Fantasies of Female Revenge." *Western
Folklore* 46 (3): 192–97.

Fine, Gary Alan, Campion-Vincent, Veronique, and Heath, Chip. editors,
Rumor Mills: The Social Impact of Rumor and Legend. New Brunswick, NJ:
Transaction Publishers, 2005.

Fine, Gary Alan, and Ellis, Bill. *The Global Grapevine: Why Rumors of Terrorism, Immigration, and Trade Matter.* Oxford: Oxford University Press, 2010.

Fine, Gary Alan, and Turner, Patricia A. *Whispers on the Color Line: Rumor and Race in America*. Berkeley: University of California Press, 2001.

Florko, N. "Public Trust in CDC, Fauci, and Other Top Health Officials Is Evaporating, Poll Finds." Stat, September 1, 2020. https://www.statnews.com /2020/09/10/trust-cdc-fauci-evaporating/.

Fox News. "Pizzeria Owner Targeted by Fake News Stories Speaks Out." Fox News, December 15, 2016. Video, 8:52. https://www.youtube.com/watch?v =YXApkzwKIh8.

g (@gillian_criddle). "I could pay off my college. . . ." Twitter, March 13, 2016. Accessed February 16, 2021. https://twitter.com/gillian_criddle/status/7090 88722130591744.

Galen, Rich. "I've Always Been Proud of America." *Townhall*, February 20, 2008. Accessed February 15, 2021. https://townhall.com/columnists/rich galen/2008/02/20/ive-always-been-proud-of-america-n1103633.

Gelzinis, Peter. "Gelzinis: After Pizzagate Fiasco, Mike Flynn Should Take a Hike." *Boston Herald*, December 8, 2016. https://www.bostonherald.com /2016/12/08/gelzinis-after-pizzagate-fiasco-mike-flynn-should-take-a-hike/.

Giuliani, Rudy W. (@RudyGiuliani). Why did the US (NIH) in 2017 give $3.7m to the Wuhan Lab in China? Such grants were prohibited in 2014. Did Pres. Obama grant an exception? Twitter, April 26, 2020. Accessed February 16, 2021. https://twitter.com/rudygiuliani/status/1254513987196248065.

Glum, Julia. "Some Republicans Still Think Obama Was Born in Kenya as Trump Resurrects Birther Conspiracy Theory." *Newsweek*, December 11, 2017. https://www.newsweek.com/trump-birther-obama-poll-republicans -kenya-744195.

Good Morning America. "'*GMA*' Exclusive: Trump a Birther?" Video, 7:08. ABC News, March 17, 2011. https://abcnews.go.com/GMA/video/gma-exclusive -trump-birther-13155432.

Goldstein, Diane. *Once upon a Virus: AIDS Legends and Vernacular Risk Perception*. Logan: Utah State University Press, 2004.

Goodman, Jack. "US Election 2020: Kamala Harris Targeted by False Conspiracy Theories." BBC News, August 19, 2020. Accessed February 15, 2021. https://www.bbc.com/news/53826816.

Gore, D'Angelo. "Eight Years of Trolling Obama." FactCheck.org, June 19, 2017. https://www.factcheck.org/2017/01/eight-years-of-trolling-obama/.

———. "Michelle Obama's Staff." FactCheck.org, August 5, 2009. Accessed February 15, 2021. https://www.factcheck.org/2009/08/michelle-obamas-staff/.

Gross, Doug. "Dictionary Word of the Year: 'Unfriend.'" CNN, November 17, 2009. https://www.cnn.com/2009/TECH/11/17/unfriend.word/index.html.

Hagan, Joe. "The Long, Lawless Ride of Sheriff Joe Arpaio." *Rolling Stone*, August 2, 2012. https://www.rollingstone.com/culture/culture-news/the -long-lawless-ride-of-sheriff-joe-arpaio-231455/.

Hananoki, Eric. "CNBC Pushes Hoax Obama Birther Quote During Trump Interview." Media Matters for America, May 29, 2012. https://www.media matters.org/donald-trump/cnbc-pushes-hoax-obama-birther-quote-during -trump-interview?redirect_source=%2Fblog%2F2012%2F05%2F29%2Fcnbc -pushes-hoax-obama-birther-quote-during-tru%2F186702.

Hannity, Sean. *Live Free or Die: America (and the World) on the Brink*. New York: Threshold Editions, 2020.

Harris, Kamala. Speech. Wilmington, DE, Delaware Online, August 12, 2020, https://www.delawareonline.com/story/news/politics/elections/2020/11/07 /kamala-harris-victory-speech-delaware-full-text/6210399002/.

"Hawaii Confirms Obama's Birthplace, Again." CBS News, July 28, 2009, https:// www.cbsnews.com/news/hawaii-confirms-obamas-birthplace-again/.

Henig, Jess. "Mirror Image." FactCheck.org, January 11, 2010. https://www .factcheck.org/2010/01/mirror-image/.

———. "Sliming Obama." FactCheck.org, January 11, 2008. https://www.factcheck .org/2008/01/sliming-obama/.

Ho, Sarah (@sarahho12881425). "You seen the story coming out of Italy . . ." Twitter, January 8, 2021. Accessed February 17, 2021. https://twitter.com /sarahho12881425/status/1347702192397037569.

Hobobob10. "(4/10) 2008 PA ABC Democratic Debate." Video, 9:59. YouTube, April 10, 2008. https://www.youtube.com/watch?v=3GPiHQh_Sts.

Hofstadter, Richard. "The Folklore of Populism." In *Conspiracy: The Fear of Subversion in American History*. New York: Holt, Rinehart and Winston, 1972.

Hoft, Jim. "Breaking: Dr. Fauci and Obama Admin Gave Wuhan Lab $3.7 Million after Its Top Dr. Shi Zhengli Had US Project Shut Down and She Was Sent Back to China." The Gateway Pundit, April 28, 2020. Accessed February 16, 2021. https://www.thegatewaypundit.com/2020/04/breaking-dr -fauci-obama-admin-gave-wuhan-lab-3-7-million-top-dr-shi-zhengli-us -project-shut-sent-back-china/.

———. "By Not Investigating Historic and Massive Election Fraud, Are Deep State DOJ and FBI Attempting to Invalidate Election Fraud Suits?" The Gateway Pundit, December 9, 2020. https://www.thegatewaypundit.com /2020/12/not-investigating-historic-massive-election-fraud-deep-state-doj -fbi-attempting-invalidate-election-fraud-suits/.

———. "Sasha and Malia Wore $20,000 Dresses to State Dinner Paid for by US Taxpayers." The Gateway Pundit, March 15, 2016. https://www.thegateway pundit.com/2016/03/sasha-and-malia-wore-20000-dresses-to-state-dinner -paid-for-by-us-taxpayers/.

Hollyfield, Amy. "Obama's Birth Certificate: Final Chapter." Politifact, June 27, 2008. https://www.politifact.com/truth-o-meter/article/2008/jun/27/obamas -birth-certificate-part-ii/.

Holan, Angie Drobnic. "Her Senior Thesis Doesn't Say That." Politifact, May 30, 2008. Accessed February 15, 2021. https://www.politifact.com/factchecks /2008/may/30/chain-email/her-senior-thesis-doesnt-say-that/.

———. "2017 Lie of the Year: Russian Election Interference Is a 'Made-up Story.'" Politifact, December 12, 2017. https://www.politifact.com/article/2017/dec/12 /2017-lie-year-russian-election-interference-made-s/.

Howard, Robert Glen. "Vernacular Authority: Critically Engaging "Tradition"" in *Tradition in the 21st Century: Locating the Role of the Past in the Present*, edited by Trevor J. Blank and Robert Glen Howard, 72–99. Logan: University of Utah Press, 2013.

Iconic. "9/11 George W. Bush visits Ground Zero." Video, 1:33. YouTube, September 6, 2011. https://www.youtube.com/watch?v=SeVEUNI-Cuo.

Jay. "She was snuffed." Comment on thread *Today*. "Joan Rivers' autopsy reveals cause of death." YouTube. October 17, 2014. Accessed February 15, 2021. https://www.youtube.com/watch?v=lzgl6MWNBXs.

joemiller33. "i forgot her head-to-shoulder ratio is that of a man NOT a woman and he/she was Michael LaVaughn." (Comment on Toto, "Can Joan Rivers Survive"). Breitbart, July 4, 2014. Accessed February 15, 2021. https://www.breitbart.com /entertainment/2014/07/04/can-joan-rivers-survive-obamas-insults/.

Jones, James H. *Bad Blood: The Tuskegee Syphilis Experiment—A Tragedy of Race and Medicine*. New York: Free Press, 1982.

Jonsson, Patrik. "A Last Electoral Hurdle for Obama." *Christian Science Monitor*, November 26, 2008. https://www.csmonitor.com/USA/Politics /2008/1126/a-last-electoral-hurdle-for-obama.

Kaczynski, Andrew. "Michael Flynn Quietly Deletes Fake News Tweet about Hillary Clinton's Involvement in Sex Crimes." CNN Politics, December 14, 2016. https://www.cnn.com/2016/12/14/politics/kfile-flynn-deleted-tweets /index.html.

Kalmre, Eda. "Introduction: The Social and Political Dynamic of Conspiracy Theories, Rumours, Fake News and Belief Narratives." *Folklore: The Electronic Journal of Folklore* 69: 7–14.

Kang, Cecilia, and Sheera Frenkel. "'PizzaGate' Conspiracy Theory Thrives Anew in the TikTok Era." *New York Times*, June 14, 2020. https://www.nytimes.com /2020/06/27/technology/pizzagate-justin-bieber-qanon-tiktok.html.

Kim, Eun Kyung. "Brits Portray Michelle Obama as Queen—of Fashion." *Today*, March 21, 2013. Accessed February 15, 2021. https://www.today.com/style /brits-portray-michelle-obama-queen-fashion-1C8994788.

Kitta, Andrea. *The Kiss of Death: Contagion, Contamination, and Folklore*. Louisville, CO: Utah State University Press, 2019.

Klayman, Larry. "Obama, BLM Inspired Dallas Massacre." WND. WorldNetDaily, July 8, 2016. https://www.wnd.com/2016/07/obama-blm-inspired -dallas-massacre/.

Knowsrightfromwrong. "Of course she wasn't kidding. Since bozo's turn for the worst, there's evidence surfacing that supports the facts that." (Comment on Toto,. "Can Joan Rivers Survive). Breitbart, July 14, 2014. Accessed February 15, 2021. https://www.breitbart.com/entertainment/2014/07/04/can-joan -rivers-survive-obamas-insults/.

Lacey, Marc. "Despite Setbacks, Arizona Sheriff Won't Yield the Spotlight." *New York Times*, April 14, 2011. https://www.nytimes.com/2011/04/15/us/15arpaio .html.

Lamothe, Dan. "How 'American Sniper' Chris Kyle's Truthfulness Is in Question Again." *Washington Post*, May 25, 2016. Accessed February 11, 2021. https:// www.washingtonpost.com/news/checkpoint/wp/2016/05/25/how-american -sniper-chris-kyles-truthfulness-is-in-question-once-again/.

Larkin, M. AIDS Conspiracy Theories Common among Black Americans. *The Lancet Infectious Diseases*, 5, no. 3): 134–35. https://doi.org/10.1016/S1473 -3099(05)01293-4.

Lee, Jessica. "Did Obama Get Caught 'Spying' on Trump's 2016 Campaign?" Snopes, September 29, 2020. https://www.snopes.com/fact-check/obama -spying-trump-campaign/.

Lewis, Paul. "*New Yorker*'s 'Terrorist' Obama Cover Under Fire." *The Guardian*, July 14, 2008. https://www.theguardian.com/world/deadlineusa/2008/jul/14 /newyorkercover.

LibertymanMAGA (@LibertymanNick). "Unfortunately Obama will live in DC. . . ." Twitter, January 16, 2017, https://twitter.com/LibertymanNick /status/821171285418012672.

Liu, Joseph. "Little Voter Discomfort with Romney's Religion." Pew Research Center, July 26, 2012. https://www.pewforum.org/2012/07/26/2012-romney -mormonism-obamas-religion/.

Lopez, Ian Haney. *Dog Whistle Politics: How Coded Racial Appeals Have Reinvented Racism and Wrecked the Middle Class.* Oxford: Oxford University Press, 2014.

Madigan, Tim. *The Burning: The Tulsa Race Massacre of 1921.* New York: St. Martin's Press, 2003.

Mark. "Obama is bi he belonged to the gay club in Chicago and Michelle does look like a Tranny shrug*." (Comment on Nolte, "RIP Joan Rivers" Breitbart, September 5, 2014. Accessed February 15, 2021. https://www.breitbart.com /entertainment/2014/09/05/rip-joan-rivers-no-one-will-ever-call-michelle -obama-tanny-again/#comment-1575457765.

Marantz, Andrew. *Anti-Social: Online Extremists, Techno-Utopians, and the Highjacking of the American Conversation.* New York: Viking, 2019.

———. "Trump and the Truth: The Viral Candidate." *New Yorker*, November 4, 2016, https://www.newyorker.com/news/news-desk/trump-and-the-truth -the-viral-candidate.

Maricopa County. "Welcome to Maricopa County." Accessed February 10, 2021.
    https://www.maricopa.gov/5289/Maricopa-County.

Mazza, Ed. "Trump's Old Tweets about Hillary Clinton's Email Look Really Bad
    for Ivanka Trump." *Huffpost*, November 11, 2018. https://www.huffpost.com
    /entry/donald-trump-ivanka-hillary-clinton-email_n_5bf39915e4b0d9e72
    83c7a63.

McGahan, Jason. "Inside QAnon, the Conspiracy Cult That's Devouring
    America." *Los Angeles Magazine*, August 17, 2020. https://www.lamag.com
    /citythinkblog/qanon-gop/.

"Megyn Kelly Fails to Ask Even One Legitimate Question to James Alefantis
    over 'Pizzagate' Conspiracy." Intellihub, December 16, 2016. Accessed
    February 16, 2021. https://www.intellihub.com/megyn-kelly-fails-to-ask-one
    -legitimate-question-alefantis-pizzagate/.

Memmott, Mark. "'Birther' Debate Never Ends." NPR, July 22, 2009. https://
    www.npr.org/sections/thetwo-way/2009/07/birther_debate_never_seems
    _to.html.

"Michelle's Spain Vacation." *Fellowship of the Minds* (blog), July 27, 2010.
    Accessed May 15, 2015. http://fellowshipoftheminds.com/2010/07/27/michelles
    -spain-vacation-30-rooms-for-4-days/.

Mieder, Wolfgang. *Yes We Can: Barack Obama's Proverbial Rhetoric*. New York:
    Peter Lang, 2009.

Mikkelson, David. "Ban on Military Proselytizing." Snopes, May 6, 2013. https://
    www.snopes.com/fact-check/ban-on-military-proselytizing/.

———. "Barack Obama Removes Flag from Air Force One?" Snopes, April 16,
    2012. https://www.snopes.com/fact-check/an-american-tail/.

———. "Barack Obama—Trinity United Church of Christ." Snopes, March 16,
    2008. https://www.snopes.com/fact-check/holy-trinity/.

———. "Did Barack Obama Admit to His 'Muslim Faith'?" Snopes, October 23,
    2008. https://www.snopes.com/fact-check/my-muslim-faith/.

———. Did President Obama Cancel the National Day of Prayer? Snopes,
    December 14, 2009, https://www.snopes.com/fact-check/national-day-of
    -prayer/.

———. "Did President Obama Decline to Lay Wreaths at Arlington on Memorial
    Day?" Snopes, May 26, 2010, https://www.snopes.com/fact-check/potus-at
    -arlington-on-memorial-day/.

———. "Flag Pin Dismissal." Snopes, April 4, 2015, https://www.snopes.com/fact
    -check/pinning-the-blame/.

———. "Is Barack Obama a Natural-Born Citizen of the U.S.?" Snopes.com.
    Snopes Media Group Inc., October 17, 2008. https://www.snopes.com/fact
    -check/native-son/.

———. "Michelle Obama and Daughters at the 2012 London Olympics." Snopes,
    August 30, 2012. Accessed February 15, 2021. https://www.snopes.com/fact
    -check/olympic-meddle/.

————. "Muslim Prayer Curtin in the White House." Snopes, June 8, 2010. https://www.snopes.com/fact-check/muslim-prayer-curtain-white-house/.

————. "Obama Explains National Anthem Stance?" Snopes, February 15, 2021. Accessed February 15, 2021. https://www.snopes.com/fact-check/national -anthem-stance/.

————. "Obama Refuses to Sign Eagle Scout Certificates" Snopes.com, October 7 2010, https://www.snopes.com/fact-check/eagle-scouts/.

————. "Obama's Wedding Ring." Snopes, July 18, 2014. https://www.snopes.com /fact-check/lord-of-the-ring/.

————. "Post Office to Sell Michelle Obama Stamps." Snopes, December 15, 2014. Accessed February 15, 2021. https://www.snopes.com/fact-check/queen-obama/.

————. "Section Two: Obama's Religious Beliefs." Pew Research Center. October 21, 2008. https://www.pewresearch.org/politics/2008/10/21/section-2 -candidate-traits/.

————. "Was Michelle Obama's Thesis Restricted until After the 2008 Election?" Snopes, n.d. Accessed February 15, 2021. https://www.snopes.com/fact-check /michelle-obamas-thesis/.

————. "Who Is Barack Obama?" Snopes, July 7, 2009. https://www.snopes.com /fact-check/who-is-barack-obama/.

Miller, S. "Michelle Obama 'Ape' Post Puts Tiny Town at Center of Firestorm." *USA Today*, November 15, 2016. Accessed February 15, 2021. https://www .usatoday.com/story/news/nation/2016/11/15/michelle-obama-post-puts-tiny -town-center-firestorm/93917502/?fbclid=IwAR3RGKWoFKj3_qz83jrUA3V -GtyOrebjXsZBeYefdkHgri59VOPJ27V2430.

Mooney, Alexander. "Michelle Obama Takes Heat from Tennessee GOP." CNN Politics, May 16, 2008. Accessed February 15, 2021. http://www.cnn.com /2008/POLITICS/05/15/michelle.tennessee/.

Mora, Edwin. "NYT: Obama Admin Kept Alleged Trump-Russia Intel at Low Classification for Easier Sharing." Breitbart, March 2, 2017. https://www .breitbart.com/politics/2017/03/02/report-obama-admin-disseminate-trump -russia-info/.

Morales, Lymari. "Obama's Birth Certificate Convinces Some, but Not All, Skeptics." Gallup, May 13, 2011. https://news.gallup.com/poll/147530/obama -birth-certificate-convinces-not-skeptics.aspx.

Mould, Tom. *Overthrowing the Queen: Telling Stories of Welfare in America*. Bloomington: Indiana University Press, 2020.

Nakaso, Dan. "Obama's Certificate of Birth OK, State Says." *Honolulu Advertiser*, November 1, 2008. http://the.honoluluadvertiser.com/article/2008/Nov /01/ln/hawaii811010345.html.

Nations in Action. Accessed February 1, 2021. https://nationsinaction.org.

"New Shocking Facts about Michelle Obama's Gender." *USAReally*, blog, September 7, 2018. Accessed February 14, 2021. https://usareally.com/1354 -new-shocking-facts-about-michelle-obama-s-gender.

Nolte, John. "Bombshell: *'Washington Post'* Confirms Hillary Clinton Started the Birther Movement." Breitbart, September 26, 2015. https://www.breitbart.com /politics/2015/09/26/washington-post-confirms-hillary-clinton-started-the -birther-movement/.

———. "RIP Joan Rivers: No One Will Ever Call Michelle Obama a 'Tranny' Again." Breitbart, September 5, 2014. Accessed February 15, 2021. https:// www.breitbart.com/entertainment/2014/09/05/rip-joan-rivers-no-one-will -ever-call-michelle-obama-tanny-again/.

nom de paix. "If Obama bin HUSSEIN al Barack was born in Kenya, how can he run for president in the US? Isn't that why Arnold whats-his-name can't run?" Yahoo! Answers, 2011.

Obama, Barack. *The Audacity of Hope: Thoughts on Reclaiming the American Dream*. New York: Crown Publishing, 2006.

———. *Dreams from My Father: A Story of Race and Inheritance*. New York: Three Rivers Press, 1995.

———. "Nomination Speech, Democratic National Convention." Boston, MA, July 24, 2004.

———. *A Promised Land*. New York: Crown Publishers, 2020.

Obama, Michelle. *Becoming*. New York: Crown Publishing, 2018.

———. "Speech at the 2016 Democratic National Convention." Philadelphia, Pennsylvania, July 25, 2016.

———. "Speech at the 2020 Democratic Convention." YouTube video August 17, 2020, (Accessed February 16, 2021), (https://www.youtube.com/watch?v= VZwfEWpG_wA&t=180s.

O'Neill, Marnie. "'They Have Poisoned Me, They Have Smeared Me . . . Tried to Kill Me.'" NewsComAu. Nationwide News Pty Limited, March 16, 2017. https://www.news.com.au/technology/online/hacking/extrump-adviser -roger-stone-claims-he-is-target-of-deep-state-assassination-plot/news -story/26d93745652971129d90b6592e0a1830.

Oring, Elliott. "Legendary and the Rhetoric of Truth. *Journal of American Folklore* 121, no. 480 (2008): 127–66.

Ortiz-Ospina, E. *The Rise of Social Media*. Our World in Data, 2019, September 18. https://ourworldindata.org/rise-of-social-media#:~:text=The%20 percentage%20of%20US%20adults,to%20around%2030%%20in%202018.

Outrageousminds. "Introducing Michelle LaVaughn Robinson; the First Lady of the United States of America. *Outrageous Minds: Alternative News Lunatic Fringe Esoteric* (blog), July 4, 2014. Accessed February 15, 2021. https://outrageousminds.wordpress.com/2014/07/04/introducing-michael -lavaughn-robinson-the-first-lady-of-the-united-states-of-america/.

Page, Susan. "Fauci Says 'Inadequate' World Response Won't Control Ebola." *USA Today*. September 29, 2014. Accessed February 16, 2021. https://www

.usatoday.com/story/news/politics/2014/09/29/capital-download-nih
-anthony-fauci-on-ebola-threat/16423303/.

Palin, Sarah. *Going Rogue: An American Life*. New York: Harper Collins, 2009.

Parker, Ashley, and Steve Eder. "Inside the Six Weeks Donald Trump Was a
Nonstop 'Birther.'" *New York Times*, July 2, 2016. https://www.nytimes.com
/2016/07/03/us/politics/donald-trump-birther-obama.html?ref=politics.

Pascaline, Mary. "5 Times Republicans Called Michelle Obama a Primate."
Yahoo News, November, 15, 2016. Accessed February 15, 2021. https://news
.yahoo.com/5-times-republicans-called-michelle-102442092.html.

Peltz, Madeline. "Right-Wing Media Latch on to 'Shadow Government' Conspiracy to Absolve Trump from Russia Controversy." Media Matters for
America, March 3, 2017. https://www.mediamatters.org/sean-hannity/right
-wing-media-latch-shadow-government-conspiracy-absolve-trump-russia
-controversy.

Phillips, Whitney, and Milner, Ryan M., "The Vernacular Vortex: Analyzing the
Endless Churn of Donald Trump's Twitter Orbit. " In *Folklore and Social
Media*, edited by Andrew Peck and Trevor J. Blank. Logan: Utah State
University Press, 2020.

Piot, Peter, and Marshall, Ruth, *No Time to Lose: A Life in Pursuit of Deadly
Viruses*. New York: W.W. Norton, 2012.

Pollack, Joel B. "Mark Levin to GOP: Investigate Obama's 'Silent Coup' vs.
Trump." Breitbart, March 3, 2017. https://www.breitbart.com/politics/2017
/03/03/mark-levin-obama-used-police-state-tactics-undermine-trump/.

Poor, Jeff. "Newt: Obama Legacy 'Is Going to Disappear Within a Year.'"
Breitbart, December 21, 2016. https://www.breitbart.com/clips/2016/12/21
/newt-obama-legacy-going-disappear-within-year/.

Preston, Richard. *The Hot Zone: The Terrifying True Story of the Origins of the
Ebola Virus*. New York: Anchor Books, 1995.

Ramisetti, Kirthana. "Joan Rivers Calls President Obama Gay, Says Michelle
Obama Is a 'Tranny.'" *New York Daily News*, July 4, 2014. Accessed February 15, 2021. https://www.nydailynews.com/entertainment/gossip/joan
-rivers-calls-obama-gay-lady-tranny-article-1.1855378.

Rathborn, Nolan. "Did the U.S. Just Secretly Fly in an Ebola Patient?" Blog, top
comment *Freedom's Outpost*, November 10, 2014, https://freedomoutpost.com.

Remnick, David. *The Bridge: The Life and Rise of Barack Obama*. New York:
Alfred A. Knopf, 2010.

Robb, Amanda. "Anatomy of a Fake News Scandal." Rolling Stone, November 16, 2017. https://www.rollingstone.com/feature/anatomy-of-a-fake-news
-scandal-125877/.

Roberts, Roxanne. "I Sat Next to Donald Trump at the Infamous 2011 White
House Correspondents' Dinner." *Washington Post*, April 28, 2016. https://

www.washingtonpost.com/lifestyle/style/i-sat-next-to-donald-trump-at-the
-infamous-2011-white-house-correspondents-dinner/2016/04/27/5cf46b74
-obea-11e6-8ab8-9ad050f76d7d_story.html.

Roig-Franzia, Manuel. "Inside the Spectacular Fall of WorldNetDaily, the
Granddaddy of Right-Wing Conspiracy Sites." *Seattle Times*, April 2, 2019.
https://www.seattletimes.com/nation-world/nation/inside-the-spectacular
-fall-of-worldnetdaily-the-granddaddy-of-right-wing-conspiracy-sites/.

Rondeau, Sharon. "Category: Obama Certificate." The Post & Email, November 17, 2020. https://www.thepostemail.com/category/obama-birth
-certificate/.

Rosenblum, Nancy L., and Russel Muirhead. *A Lot of People Are Saying: The
New Conspiracism and the Assault on Democracy*. Princeton, NJ: Princeton
University Press, 2019.

Rothschild, Mike. "2017's Biggest Conspiracy Theories." Snopes, December 29,
2017. https://www.snopes.com/news/2017/12/29/2017s-biggest-conspiracy
-theories/.

Rozzy R. "#JoanRivers Says President Obama Is Gay and Michelle Is a Tranny!"
[Video]. YouTube, July 5, 2014. Accessed February 15, 2021. https://www
.youtube.com/watch?v=3mwJWH8mWhA.

Sacchetti, Cesare. "Italygate, Part II: Obama and Renzi Accused of Being the
Mmasterminds of the US Electoral Fraud." *La Cruna dell'ag* (blog), January 7, 2021. Accessed February 17, 2021. https://lacrunadellago.net/2021/01
/07/italygate-part-ii-obama-and-renzi-accused-of-being-the-masterminds
-of-the-us-electoral-fraud/?lang=en.

Sadeghi, McKenzie. "Fact Check: Ellen, Oprah, Many Others Are Not Under
House Arrest for Child Sex Trafficking." *USA Today*, June 18, 2020. https://
www.usatoday.com/story/news/factcheck/2020/06/18/fact-check-ellen
-degeneres-oprah-winfrey-others-not-house-arrest/5333585002/.

Saturday Night Live. "Dr. Anthony Fauci Cold Open-SNL." Video, 3:12.
YouTube, April 25, 2020. https://www.youtube.com/watch?v=uW56CLopkog.

Schwartz, Ian. "Obama on Flynn: No Precedent for Someone "Getting Off
Scot-Free" for Perjury." RealClear Politics, May 9, 2020. Accessed February 17, 2021. https://www.realclearpolitics.com/video/2020/05/09/obama_on
_flynn_no_precedent_for_someone_getting_off_scot-free_for_perjury
.html#!

Shibutani, Tamotsu. *Improvised News: A Sociological Study of Rumor*. Indianapolis: Bobbs-Merrill, 1966.

Silverstein, Jason. (2020, May 21). "Bots Are Spreading COVID-19 Misinformation." MSN, May 21, 2020. accessed February 16, 2021. https://www.msn
.com/en-us/news/us/bots-are-spreading-covid-19-misinformation/ar
-BB14qCHz.

Sinderbrand, Rebecca. "Cindy McCain, Michelle Obama in Patriotism Flap."
CNN Political Ticker, February 19, 2008. Accessed February 15, 2021. https://

politicalticker.blogs.cnn.com/2008/02/19/cindy-mccain-michelle-obama-in
-patriotism-flap/comment-page-16/.

Sink, Justin. "President Obama's Ebola Problem." *The Hill*, October 16, 2014. Accessed February 15, 2021. https://thehill.com/news/administration /220922-president-obamas-ebola-problem.

Sklar, Rachel. "David Remnick on That *New Yorker* Cover: It's a Satire Meant to Target Distortions and Misconceptions and Prejudices about Obama." *HuffPost*, July 21, 2008. https://www.huffingtonpost.com/2008/07/13/david -remnick-on-emnew-yo_n_112456.html.

Small, Jay Newton. "Obama's Flag Pin Flip-Flop." *Time*, May 14, 2008. http:// content.time.com/time/politics/article/0,8599,1779544,00.html.

Smith, Ben. "Fighting Smears, Gaming Google." *Ben Smith Blog*. Politico, June 12, 2008. https://www.politico.com/blogs/ben-smith/2008/06/fighting -smears-gaming-google-009659.

———. "The 'Red Slime' Lawsuit That Could Sink the Right Wing Media." *New York Times*, December 12, 2020. Accessed February 17, 2021. https://www .nytimes.com/2020/12/20/business/media/smartmatic-lawsuit-fox-news -newsmax-oan.html.

Smith, Tara C. "How *The Hot Zone* Created the Worst Myths about Ebola." Gizmodo, October 22, 2014. Accessed February 15, 2021. https://io9 .gizmodo.com/how-the-hot-zone-created-the-worst-myths-about-ebola -1649384576.

Sollenberger, Roger. "Mike Flynn Swears Allegiance to QAnon in Fourth of July Video." *Salon*, July 6, 2002. Accessed February 17, 2021). https://www.salon .com/2020/07/06/mike-flynn-swears-allegiance-to-qanon-in-fourth-of-july -video/.

Sommer, Will. "Meet 'The Storm,' the Conspiracy Theory Taking over the pro-Trump Internet." Medium, January 12, 2018. https://medium.com/ @willsommer/meet-the-storm-the-conspiracy-theory-taking-over-the-pro -trump-internet-3ec94bf7d8a3.

Spacewoman Spiff (@BellaPelosi). #YoujustpulledanObama If You Fly the Flags at Half mast for a crack-smoking drug addict (Whitney Houston) but not an American hero (Chris Kyle). Twitter, April 27, 2013. Accessed February 11, 2021. https://twitter.com/search?q=Whitney%20Houston%20Chris%20Kyle &src=typed_query.

Steinhauer, Jennifer. "Confronting Ghosts of 2000 in South Carolina." *New York Times*, October, 19, 2007. https://www.nytimes.com/2007/10/19/us/politics /19mccain.html?_r=1&sq=john%20mccain%20black%20baby&scp=1& pagewanted=all.

Sumner, Mark. "Where Were You When Q Arrested Barack Obama and Hillary Clinton at George Bush's Funeral?" Daily Kos, December 6, 2018. https:// www.dailykos.com/stories/2018/12/6/1817486/-Where-were-you-when-Q -arrested-Barack-Obama-and-Hillary-Clinton-at-George-Bush-s-funeral.

Sundance. "2014 The Campaign Message." The Conservative Tree House, October 3, 2014, (Accessed February 16, 2021), https://theconservativetree house.com/2014/10/03/2014-the-campaign-message/.

Tangherlini, Timothy R. "Toward a Generative Model of Legend: Pizzas, Bridges, Vaccines, and Witches." *Humanities* 7, no. 1 (2018): 1–19

Tangherlini, Timothy R., Shadi Shahsavari, Behnam Shahbazi, Ehsan Ebrahim-zadeh, and Vwani Roychowdhury, "An Automated Pipeline for the Discovery of Conspiracy and Conspiracy Theory Narrative Frameworks: Bridgegate, Pizzagate and Storytelling on the Web." *PLoS ONE* 15, no. 6 (August 2020): e0233879.https//doi.org/10.1371/journal.pone.0233879.

Tankovska, H. "Twitter: Number of Monthly Active Users 2010–2019." Statista, January 27, 2021. Accessed February 16, 2021. https://www.statista.com /statistics/282087/number-of-monthly-active-twitter-users/.

Tashman, Brian. "Alex Jones: 'Hillary Clinton Has Personally Murdered and Chopped Up and Raped' Children." Right Wing Watch. People for the American Way, December 8, 2016. https://www.rightwingwatch.org/post /alex-jones-hillary-clinton-has-personally-murdered-and-chopped-up-and -raped-children/.

Taylor, Adam. "The 'Obama Is a Muslim' Conspiracy Theory Is Still Reverberat-ing in the Middle East." *Washington Post*, January 20, 2016. https://www .washingtonpost.com/news/worldviews/wp/2016/01/21/the-obama-is-a -muslim-conspiracy-theory-is-still-reverberating-in-the-middle-east/.

teatempest. "Congress Sings God Bless America." Video, 1:02. YouTube, Janu-ary 20, 2013. https://www.youtube.com/watch?v=400FMTMeYmg.

Thomas, E. "Michelle Obama 'Proud' Remarks." *Newsweek*, March 13, 2008. https://www.newsweek.com/michelle-obamas-proud-remarks-83559.

Toto, Christian. "Can Joan Rivers Survive Calling Obama Gay, First Lady 'Tranny'?" Breitbart, July 4, 2014. Accessed February 15, 2021. https://www .breitbart.com/entertainment/2014/07/04/can-joan-rivers-survive-obamas -insults/.

Trump, Donald J. (@realDonaldTrump). "Do you notice that because of Ebola, ISIS etc., ObamaCare has gone to the back burner despite horrible results coming." Trump Twitter Archive V2. October 11, 2014. Accessed February 16, 2021. https://www.thetrumparchive.com/?searchbox=%22ebola%22.

———. (@realDonaldTrump). "Ebola patient will be brought . . . ." Trump Twitter Archive, vol. 2, July 31, 2014. Accessed February 15, 2021. https://www.the trumparchive.com/?searchbox=%22Ebola%22.

———. (@TrumpAmerican). "LET THEM EAT CAKE!" Twitter, March 12, 2016. Accessed February 16, 2021. https://twitter.com/trumpamerican/status /708781410631331841.

———. (@realDonaldTrump). "Obama just appointed an Ebola Czar with zero experience in the medical area and zero experience in infectious disease control." Trump Twitter Archive, vol. 2, October 17, 2014. Accessed February 16, 2021. https://www.thetrumparchive.com/?searchbox=%22ebola%22.

———. (@realDonaldTrump)."#ObamaGate Wow look what's trending on Twitter. I'll bet these guys aren't laughing today. Twitter, May 10, 2019. https://www.thetrumparchive.com/?searchbox=%22obamagate%22.

———. (@realDonaldTrump). "President Obama—close down the flights from Ebola infected areas right now, before it is too late!" Trump Twitter Archive, vol. 2, October 4, 2014. Accessed February 15, 2021. https://www.thetrumparchive.com/?searchbox=%22ebola%22.

———. (@RealDonaldTrump). "Terrible! Just Found Out . . ." Twitter, March 4, 2017. Accessed February 16, 2021. https://www.thetrumparchive.com/?searchbox=%22This+is+McCarthyism%22.

———. (@real DonaldTrump). "We've all wondered . . ." October 16, 2016. Accessed February 16, 2021. https://www.thetrumparchive.com/?searchbox=%22how+Hillary+avoided+prosecution%22.

———. (@realDonaldTrump). "Why are we sending thousands of ill-trained soldiers into Ebola infested areas of Africa! Bring the plague back to U.S.?" Trump Twitter Archive, vol. 2, September 19, 2014. Accessed February 16, 2021. https://www.thetrumparchive.com/?searchbox=%22ebola%22.

"Trump Jokingly Reprimands Supporters in New Hampshire." *Don Lemon Tonight*, CNN, June 1, 2016. https://www.cnn.com/videos/politics/2016/01/06/donald-trump-new-hampshire-muslim-sot-lemon-ctn.cnn.

Turner, Patricia A. *Ceramic Uncles and Celluloid Mammies: Black Images and Their Influence on Culture.* New York: Anchor Books, 1994.

———. *I Heard It Through The Grapevine: Rumor in African-American Culture.* Berkeley: University of California Press, 1993.

"United States Flag Code." The American Legion, Title 36, Subtitle I, Part A section 301 United States Code—National Anthem, https://www.legion.org/flag/code?web=1&wdLOR=c9F9B7312-F462-ED40-BD83-F60F7265ED57.

The Uptake. "McCain Responds to 'Arab' Epithet at Rally: Obama a Decent Family Man." *HuffPost*, October 10, 2008, https://www.huffpost.com/entry/mccain-responds-to-arab-a_b_133820.

Vaughn, Elizabeth. "Rudy Giuliani Slammed Dr. Fauci over His Agency's $3.7 Million Grant to the Wuhan Institute of Virology." Red State, April 26, 2020. Accessed February 16, 2021). https://redstate.com/elizabeth-vaughn/2020/04/26/rudy-giuliani-slammed-dr-fauci-over-his-agencys-3-7-million-grant-to-the-wuhan-institute-of-virology-n135540.

Vause, John. "CNN Debunks False Report about Obama." CNN, January 23, 2007. https://www.cnn.com/2007/POLITICS/01/22/obama.madrassa/.

Veracifier. "Kingston Slams Obama for Flag Pin w/o Wearing One Himself." Video, 1:39. YouTube, February 28, 2008, https://www.youtube.com/watch?v=G5LZI50dMbM.

Victor, Jeffrey S. *Satanic Panic: The Creation of a Contemporary Legend*. Chicago: Open Court Publishing, 1993.

Walker, Clarence E., and Smithers, Gregory. *The Preacher and The Politician: Jeremiah Wright, Barack Obama, and Race in America*. Charlottesville: University of Virginia Press, 2009.

Wang, Amy B. "Did the 2011 White House Correspondents' Dinner Spur Trump to Run for President?" *Chicago Tribune*, February 26, 2017. https://www.chicagotribune.com/nation-world/ct-white-house-correspondents-dinner-trump-20170226-story.html.

WilliamDawesinDE. "Mike Castle on Barack H. Obama Birthcertificate." Video, 2:55. YouTube, July 10, 2009. https://www.youtube.com/watch?v=9V1nmn2zRMc.

Williams, Paul L. "First Lady Requires More Than Twenty Attendants." *Canada Free Press*. July 7, 2009. Accessed February 15, 2021. https://canadafreepress.com/article/first-lady-requires-more-than-twenty-attendants.

WND Staff. "Obama Birth-Certificate Doubts Head to Capitol." WND. WorldNetDaily.com, Inc., June 3, 2013. https://www.wnd.com/2013/06/obama-birth-certificate-doubts-head-to-capitol/.

Winfrey, Oprah (@Oprah)."Just got a phone call that my name is trending. And being trolled for some awful FAKE thing. It's NOT TRUE. Haven't been raided, or arrested. Just sanitizing and self distancing with the rest of the world. Stay safe everybody [praying hands emoji]." Twitter, March 17, 2020. https://twitter.com/Oprah/status/1240150930840051712.

Wochit Entertainment. " Michelle Obama Dances with Ellen DeGeneres to "Uptown Funk."Video. YouTube, March 14, 2015. Accessed February 15, 2021. https://www.youtube.com/watch?v=SpJMR4sGigk.

Woodman, John M. "Exposed: Sheriff Joe Arpaio Birther Scam: Here's Proof That Arpaio's Posse Fabricated Evidence and Lied to the Nation." *Investigating the Obama Birth Mysteries* (blog), July 24, 2012. http://www.obamabirthbook.com/http:/www.obamabirthbook.com/2012/07/exposed-sheriff-joe-arpaio-corsi-birther-scam-heres-the-proof-that-arpaios-posse-fabricated-evidence-and-lied-to-the-nation/.

Zadrozny, Brandy, and Ben Collins. "How Three Conspiracy Theorists Took 'Q' and Sparked Qanon." NBC News, August 14, 2018. https://www.nbcnews.com/tech/tech-news/how-three-conspiracy-theorists-took-q-sparked-qanon-n900531.

Index

Founded in 1893,
UNIVERSITY OF CALIFORNIA PRESS
publishes bold, progressive books and journals
on topics in the arts, humanities, social sciences,
and natural sciences—with a focus on social
justice issues—that inspire thought and action
among readers worldwide.

The UC PRESS FOUNDATION
raises funds to uphold the press's vital role
as an independent, nonprofit publisher, and
receives philanthropic support from a wide
range of individuals and institutions—and from
committed readers like you. To learn more, visit
ucpress.edu/supportus.